THE DUAL SOUL CONNECTION

The Alien Agenda for Human Advancement

The Dual Soul Connection
The Alien Agenda for Human Advancement

UFOCUS NZ
PO Box 624
7th Avenue
Tauranga 3140
New Zealand

First edition 2014
Second edition 2016

Printed by CreateSpace

ISBN: 978-0-473-29564-6

Artists:
Cover illustration by Dane Madgwick
Illustrations by Thomas Hansen and Dane Madgwick

Photographer:
Dean Preston, Life by Lens

www.communicatorlink.com

www.ufocusnz.org.nz

THE DUAL SOUL CONNECTION

The Alien Agenda for Human Advancement

SUZY HANSEN

With

DR. RUDY SCHILD

Emeritus Astrophysicist
Harvard/Smithsonian Centre for Astrophysics
Commentary and Scientific Epilogue

Skylight Books

Acknowledgements

I extend my heartfelt thanks to

My husband and family,

and

Dr. Rudy Schild.

My special thanks to

the late Graeme Opie, Angela Opie, Bryan Dickeson,
Wally & Jill Ingram, Wendy Burnham, Peter O'Brien,
John Cordy, Michael Wyatt,
Daisy Kirkby, Brenda Wilson, Flor Amanowicz, William Johnson,
Beverlea Parsons, Jill Marshall, Robin and Paul Mason,
Mary Rodwell, Mariana Flynn, Suzanne Singleton,
Margaux Green, Helen Towgood, Jenny Argante,
Dean Preston, Norman Bilbrough,
the late Harvey Cooke, and the late Dr. David Higgins, GP.

And to the many other people who have assisted me along the way –
I offer my sincere thanks.

Foreword

Beyond the Shock and Awe: the other Side of Disclosure

For the last twenty years, UFO investigators have been obsessed with two major concerns:

1. Disclosure – what do the United States and other authorities know about the UFO phenomenon, when did they know it, and why do they NOT want the rest of the world to know about UFOs?
2. Contact with extraterrestrials – why are they interested in interfacing with humanity?

While these two considerations appear to be very different, investigators are now starting to appreciate that they may actually show some similarities.

Since the 1950s there have been numerous attempts to address the Disclosure issue, with constant petitions to the United States Congress, public appeals and representations made to political institutions, and so on. During that time, the United States authorities have always chosen to ignore and downgrade the subject, so there is no reason to assume American institutions will "disclose" anything soon. Have all of our Disclosure campaigns been a complete waste of time and resources?

However, we must also remember that the UFO phenomenon is not restricted to the United States, so Disclosure could well come from somewhere else.

The second, the "contact question", has also been a difficult issue to resolve. There appears to be a process of "graded contact" for less-technological cultures such as ours. Perhaps when aliens encounter a less-sophisticated society, then it might help to open up further contact with them by first creating and promoting an awareness of other worlds, other realities besides their own. Establishing star-sects or sky-oriented religions would help, and these could be "tweaked" by the superior culture during subsequent visits to the planet as part of an overall "contact strategy". There will always come a point when the "lesser" culture must first acknowledge, then interact back to the overseeing culture, and we may now be approaching that point.

Alien contact and interaction experiences are the most confronting, most enigmatic aspect of the UFO phenomenon, attracting publicity, both good and bad. As someone providing support for abductees and experiencers in New Zealand and Australia, I spend forty to seventy per cent of my time with abductees "talking them down from the ceiling" because of the trauma some experience. The sheer alien-ness of such contacts is difficult to reconcile with normal human existence, and the social isolation often encountered by these people when they speak about their experiences to friends and family, can be profound. Once initial contact is established, further contact seems inevitable. Difficulties can increase if the abductee/experiencer confides in people who have not had an alien experience and who can reasonably expect not to have one.

Contact experiences, by their very nature, are wide-ranging, complex, and often not well-remembered. At present, both pure conscious memories of experiences, and those retrieved from hypnotic regressions remain at the very centre of the contact phenomenon. After several decades we can start to sense something of the aliens, behind the often fractured and disjointed memories retained by those experiencing contact. So far we can sense an over arching neutrality, a detachment from "Them". If ongoing contact is to be established, more complexity and subtlety must develop. It is the potential for real discussion, real Disclosure from the aliens themselves that excites us.

When you compare the sensory experiences reported by abductees/experiencers – the lighting, colours, sounds and sensations, there is a commonality that is almost boring in its similarity. Works of fantasy or fiction would be much more varied, more idiosyncratic, but the common elements in alien contacts are muted and consistent in their range. This consistency suggests that we may have a way of "witnessing" alien activities to develop a better picture of them.

Also, while some of these common elements seem exotic, even magical or humorous to us, their occurrence across the contact experience is persistent. This suggests there are elements of alien science and technology which are only slightly beyond our own, that we could observe and possibly develop – exotic technologies and applications that we would find useful.

After several decades of "alien abductions" and shock and awe, we have a more recent group that has emerged, a new wave of experiencers who are prepared to pursue the possibility of alien contact further. This shift has arisen because our attitudes towards alien contact have also evolved. Experiencers offer us an important opportunity to monitor alien interactions from a "human" perspective that we have only just begun to explore. From the quieter moments in such accounts we find that whenever an experiencer asks an intelligent question, they tend to get an intelligent reply. Once we get past the shock and awe, we can get to know them better. Species-to-species dialogue, or communication, now seems possible.

Suzy Hansen belongs to this new wave and she has consistently reported her experiences through public speaking with a high degree of candour and detail. Communication is not just about words. How things are communicated is also very important. Emotional nuances, their range and value are useful for this. Experiencers like Suzy are creating this important conversation, those nuances that convey a very real sense of having "been there", bridging the gap between alien and human worlds.

Suzy provides great recall, and is sufficiently grounded, mature and composed to provide excellent information in a level-headed and measured way. Alien contact is a process which requires a commitment, focus and effort. She has always maintained the integrity of the contact phenomenon as something deserving proper, in-depth consideration. Suzy "gets" both her own point of view and that of the people around her. She also has the presence of mind to ask her extraterrestrial contacts the kinds of questions we would all like to ask an alien, and to remember the answers clearly and unambiguously. You actually become part of a two-way "conversation", a developing complexity, a dialogue, empathy between alien and human. She and a few experiencers like her are developing this important conversation.

I have known Suzy Hansen as a friend and colleague for sixteen years, but only recently have I had the very real pleasure of working with her as a hypnotherapist, and it has been something of a revelation. Her "voice" is truly remarkable and we need more people like her to facilitate greater contact and Disclosure, from the "other side".

Therefore, I am delighted to welcome you to Suzy's story.

Bryan Dickeson
UFO and Contact Researcher and Hypnotherapist
New Zealand and Australia

Introduction

Uncovering a Co-reality

My memories of other-worldly communications with souls and spirits began in childhood, but it was not until early adulthood that I pieced together enough information to convince myself I was also experiencing contact with other entities, known to most of us as extraterrestrials, aliens, off-world intelligences, or non-human entities. These vivid memories were persistent, like some "background life" taking place alongside my everyday human existence, and it was ever-present. What did it mean? Was there a purpose? Did other people experience this too? I wondered often about how I should examine these memories.

Throughout the late 1970s to the 1990s the use of regressive hypnosis was a hotly debated topic in the UFO field, a new investigative procedure to use with those experiencing alien contact. Over this time throughout my late twenties to early forties, the extent of my conscious memories of contacts with non-human entities progressively increased, with details of environments, technology, activities, and species on their craft. There was much discussion in the global UFO community about the importance of "pure" memories, and having examined both sides of the hypnosis debate, I was determined to keep mine that way and not undertake regressive hypnosis at all. I decided these memories, albeit with some gaps in them, would suffice.

As a result, for over twenty years I took an investigative approach to examining my memories for possible explanations, searched for corroborative, anecdotal, or scientific data and evidence, and noted similarities discovered through research and meeting other experiencers. Despite increasing encouragement by some colleagues to undertake hypnosis to further explore these memories, I resisted this. I developed a strong commitment to the contact phenomenon and to sharing only my consciously recalled experiences thus far through public speaking.

However this was all about to change when I awoke one morning in 2005 with the intense desire to seek regressive hypnosis on some of the more scantly recalled contact experiences. What a turn-around! It was as if I had somehow been briefed on what I must do and within five days I had flown to another country and was about to open a door into a co-reality, from which there would be no turning back.

The idea of writing a book about my encounters, which I had thought about for some years, was about to become a daunting and challenging reality.

Periodically between 2005 and 2012, I worked with three regression therapists, confirming that the general nature of the experiences and the way in which I expressed them, did not alter between therapists. I have always been absolutely clear about my consciously recalled memories (many of my accounts are recorded on conference speech DVDs), and those retrieved through hypnosis, however a combination of the two kinds of memories eventually formed the book's framework. As before, I took an investigative approach to the regression material, seeking corroborative data and input from the scientific community.

It is important to note that the majority of the experiences described in this book are based on my conscious memories of the contacts, and related UFO sightings and periods of missing time, some of which I further explored through regression. However unrecalled events also emerged, engendering a whole new perspective for me on the contacts taking place. These experiences are pieces of my own personal puzzle, but when combined with the "puzzles" of other experiencers, and the many which have yet to surface, the evidence for human contact with off-world intelligences, I believe, will be undeniable and overwhelming.

Back in 2005, I viewed a video speech by Dr. Rudolph (Rudy) Schild, Harvard-Smithsonian astrophysicist. I felt compelled to contact Rudy, but this was at first unsuccessful. In 2011, I sent Rudy some information and initial chapters and he offered to contribute to the book with footnotes, commentary and a scientific epilogue, for which I am sincerely grateful. We both believe it is important to bridge the gap between science and experiencers' material, and Rudy is to be commended for his open-minded commitment to such a partnership of discussion and examination.

I would also like to acknowledge my peers – fellow humans worldwide who have experienced contact with extraterrestrials of various species. Three main groups have emerged over several decades: 1) contactees, who encountered mainly peaceful human-like aliens around the 1960s, 2) abductees, who reported more negative and traumatic encounters with aliens in the 1970s/80s onwards, and,

3) experiencers, whose contacts with aliens within a similar time-period, are largely transformative and positive.

Relationships between these groups have sometimes been strained and marred by misunderstandings and even antagonism. My perspective is that these divisions must dissolve, as we need to pull together and assist and support each other through the revelations and probable turmoil of coming years, concerning exposure of the reality of the extraterrestrial presence. Our common ground is that we are all what I refer to as "communicators", regardless of our current groupings or labels.

There are multiple issues of importance facing mankind at this time in our planetary evolution, some which may affect our civilisation in positive ways, while others could equally destroy it. Advances in technology are on the brink of irrevocably altering the way we lead our lives, ultimately transforming our medical technology and regimes, transport, industry, the environment, space exploration and communication systems.

Through my contact with alien species and visits onboard their craft, I have been privileged to witness and use their advanced "conscious" and 3-dimensional technology. At first this seemed the stuff of dreams, and in fact I believed for some time that these memories of other-worldly environments *were* in fact dreams. However over time, I have noticed technology emerging in our own world that is strikingly similar to, but less sophisticated than that which I have observed on craft. On a number of occasions I have been taken with groups of humans to underground and undersea bases, where aliens and humans work alongside each other, so I have every reason to believe that at least some of our current more advanced technology has originated from these alien species.

Although wondrous technology is beginning to change our lives, it is our collective realisation that we are not alone in the universe and we have cosmic neighbours that will be the turning point for humanity, the greatest revelation. This more than anything will challenge us to reassess who we are and where we have come from, and it will define our course into the future.

However change does not take place without upheaval, and I believe a massive shift in consciousness, a planetary spiritual transformation, must occur before we can all relate to other inhabitants of our galaxy, because all of our lives will be irrevocably changed by their presence.

A major part of this global examination-of-self must include a deeper understanding of the soul and consciousness – how we arrive and depart from our lives and what happens in-between.

It is through my relationships with alien species that I have come to understand the deeper soul connections we have with each other, and with them. I discovered not only a parallel life or co-reality, but a dual soul status – the reality that I entered this life with a soul formed of two distinct soul identities: "alien" and "human". I outline the steps involved in preparing for this life, through a soul enhancement and education process that constitutes the dual soul. All of this took place under the guidance of alien species and a universal governing body of wise souls, associated with our planet.

This dual soul connection is a major revelation in understanding of the nature of life and humanity, and is the key point of this book.

Thousands of humans are involved in a joint soul-alien venture to uplift and upgrade humanity through this unique combination of intelligences.

The dual soul connection is closely aligned with the "Three Waves", a programme the aliens first told me about when I was eight years old, involving volunteer souls progressively called to lead lives on our planet to assist mankind at this time of spiritual transition.

The accounts I have selected to present in this book are each a complete story in themselves, but collectively they outline my lifetime of communication with an alien species called the "Greys", and their associated species. Through their complex, multi-layered education programmes designed to advance humankind, I gained knowledge of their culture, genetics, technology and modes of telepathy.

The dual soul connection and the implementation of the positive agenda it represents is an integral part of our civilisation's movement towards higher awareness and evolution, eventually taking our place in a cosmic community.

Suzanne Hansen

Director UFOCUS NZ Research Network
Co-ordinator Communicatorlink.com

Contents

PART ONE

Beginnings

"Your work is to discover your world
and then with all your heart, give yourself to it."

Buddha

Chapter 1

The Wake-up Call

Hawkes Bay, 1975

At the age of twenty, I experienced an event that was utterly incomprehensible. I was afraid to reveal the details of this experience to anyone for fear of ridicule and disbelief, as it was beyond the boundaries of what most people would consider "normal". No matter what facade I carefully constructed around it in order to cope with it, I knew for sure the experience was real, that it *had* happened, and I knew with unnerving certainty it could happen again.

On a sunny autumn day, my flat-mate and I travelled out of town into the countryside to visit friends. We both enjoyed country life and looked forward to helping out on our friends' sheep farms, which were both in the same area. "Pete" (not his real name) dropped me at my friend's farm mid-morning and arranged to pick me up at 4.30 pm.

Later that day as I waited for him to arrive, I suddenly experienced a strong premonition. An anxious sensation whirled around in my stomach, a familiar feeling of knowing that something was about to happen, a forewarning or gut feeling we all experience at one time or another. I tried to put the feeling to one side, but it hung around regardless.

Pete eventually arrived and told me he intended to travel home on a country back-road, Highway 50, instead of the usual main road State Highway 2, which passed through several small townships on the way north towards the town of Hastings. He enjoyed giving his old sports car a burn-out every so often and there was less likelihood of seeing traffic police on the back-road. However on hearing this, my stomach did a complete flip and there was that strange feeling again, with all senses wired up and on red alert. Anyway, we set off and I began to relax as we swapped stories about how we had spent the day. We intended to be home at our flat in time for dinner and the 6.30 pm news on television (as it was in those days in New Zealand).

State Highway 50 was a lonely road passing through rolling countryside where farmhouses were few and far between. This was sheep station country with vast emerald green paddocks sparsely dotted with sheep, and the mountains forming a rugged backdrop. We travelled in silence, watching the golden sunlight on the farmland and the changing pastel colours of the late afternoon sky at that time of the day when distant trees become stark silhouettes on the hilltops.

At some point we reached the brow of a hill and below in the valley, a long stretch (straight) of road ran parallel to a line of hills for some distance. It was then we noticed two bright white lights, large and stationary, side-by-side in the sky some distance ahead of us and off to the left above the hills.

"Helicopter," said Pete.

"It's not moving," I replied.

"Hovering," he said.

"Landing lights?" I thought perhaps they were the lights of a top-dresser (agricultural aircraft) heading directly towards us, flying to a farm airstrip for the night.

"Helicopter," Pete insisted.

But the lights remained in the same position.

By now we were descending towards the straight and that anxious feeling returned as we watched the lights. I looked briefly at Pete and saw a mixture of interest and uncertainty on his face, which I attributed to him wanting to be right about it being a helicopter rather than a light aircraft. He liked to be right!

Abruptly, the lights switched off, or disappeared and reappeared together instantaneously above the hills directly to our left and parallel with our car. We were dumbfounded with shock and surprise and for a split second there was a confused and disbelieving silence between us. Time skipped a beat, and then we both burst into exclamations.

"It's not a helicopter! They can't do that!" I said.

"Of course it's a bloody helicopter! What else could it be?"

We were at the beginning of the long straight now and Pete instinctively eased off on the accelerator and changed down into second gear. The two lights hung motionless and exceedingly bright in the sky, close over an adjacent hill – too close for comfort as far as I was concerned. Only a few seconds had elapsed since we first saw them and for a few seconds more, nothing else untoward happened. I felt a flood of relief and Pete's emphatic words, *it's a bloody helicopter,* had a reassuring ring about them. In those suspended seconds in time, my rational mind was already telling me everything was okay, trying to fit a bizarre occurrence into a familiar box to appease my senses and emotions. *It must be a fast-moving helicopter.*

But this was not to be. With alarming speed, the lights again switched off and reappeared instantaneously back along the line of hills ahead of us, near where we had first sighted them. Now fear and panic really gripped us both and we were barely crawling along in second gear, eyes fastened on the lights.

Pete murmured, "What the hell is that?" Uncertainty tinged his voice now.

"Well it's not a helicopter and I'm scared!"

"Shut up!"

The lights pulsed several times in quick succession, before expanding and brightening, as if merging into one larger light. Pete halted the car completely. In retrospect that seems like a strange thing for him to have done as I'm sure most people would have rammed their foot to the floor and got out of there as fast as they could. I wouldn't say our curiosity got the better of us, but we were as if transfixed by this spectacle, waiting to see what would happen next.

The light(s) switched off again. We frantically swivelled our heads around, scanning the sky, expecting to see them reappear somewhere else. I wound my window right down for a better look. Nothing.

"I think it's gone. What do you think it was?" I asked.

"How the hell would I know? Let's get out of here. This is really weird!"

Pete accelerated off and in his haste to get away, crunched the gears and swore loudly, thrashing into third gear. Cool mind-clearing air rushed in the open window. Perhaps Pete was right, or maybe the lowering sun had distorted the appearance of an aircraft's landing lights as it turned away from us, seeming to reappear elsewhere as it changed direction. The incident had given us a fright but at least we were moving again, lost in our own thoughts. Normality returned.

Now the initial shock had dissipated, I wondered about the possibility of the lights being a UFO. My family and I had seen a glowing orange cigar-shaped light hovering over the Bombay Hills, south of Auckland, when I was a child in the 1960s, so my mind was open to the idea that as-yet unidentified flying objects can appear in our skies. Not so for Pete, a devout sceptic and persistent debunker of anything unusual. I didn't dare express such thoughts to him and anyway, it was gone now.

But within seconds, Pete's voice broke the secure silence.

"Oh god!" he said quietly.

"What! What's the matter?"

Pete's eyes were fixed on the rear vision mirror! All the colour had drained from his face and his mouth was a thin purple line.

"It's coming up behind us!" he shouted.

I stuck my head out the window, struggling to hold onto my long hair flailing in the wind. For some reason I had to see it myself, even though terrible fear was mixed with an equally terrible sense of awe and curiosity! An enormous sphere of brilliant white light, as wide as the road, was racing up behind our car about thirty metres or so above the ground. It was too bright to look at directly and my eyes squinted and watered in a struggle to see anything at all.

Pete was absolutely yelling now, "Quick, get your head in the bloody window! Hey! Hell! What's going on?"

The car's motor died.

It was upon us now. I could hear Pete shouting and swearing, and someone screaming, a piercing high-pitched shrill descending to a guttural choking sound as breath ran out (I later realised it was me). Dazzling white light radiated around us as if we had been swallowed up by it. Surely this thing would pass over us and carry on down the road! In the midst of the hell and confusion, my brain registered the fact that Pete had suddenly lapsed into silence and it seemed to take ages to turn my head in his direction. I could only just see him, sitting motionless as if asleep, with his arms flopped at his sides.

An intense buzzing, a rasping electronic sound reverberated through my entire body and my ears hurt as if a forceful suction was being applied to my ear canals. The car vibrated violently, followed by a feeling of compression and then smoothness, as if the car had actually left the road and become airborne, and I could liken it to the feeling you get in the pit of your stomach as an aircraft rises from the tarmac. Using every remaining bit of energy and determination I tried to shut the window, and the last image I recall seeing through narrowed eyelids was my arm moving as if in slow motion towards the window winder.

The intensity of the light was excruciating and the continuous buzzing noise had increased in both pitch and rate of vibration until it was almost unbearable. Everything surrounding me became so blindingly white that I can only assume my body and mind must have shut down and at that point, I too must have lost consciousness.

A sharp cracking sound in my eardrums woke me from what I thought was a deep sleep, into pitch black surroundings. I felt vague and confused, uncertain where I was. There was a soothing rocking sensation, like flotation and forward movement, a whooshing sound of rushing air and my hair was blowing all around my face. Someone moved near me and a loud familiar voice jolted me abruptly into a strange reality.

"What the hell's going on?"

I bounced and lurched forward on the seatbelt as the car hit the ground with a terrific thud. The motor revved into life and lights came on in front of me, snapping me instantly into full awareness and I cried out, gripping the seatbelt to steady myself. Pete was swearing and fighting to regain control of the car as the bridge at the far end of the straight loomed up in front of us. Roaring and ringing sounds blared in my ears, and I was unbearably thirsty, my mouth devoid of moisture. Memory of some lights in the sky sprang into my mind, along with confusion and panic about something.

"Where's the light, Pete?" I asked tentatively.

"What light?"

"You know ... we saw some lights." I scanned the sky, now transformed from my memory of late afternoon sunlight to complete darkness. A rising sense of panic gripped me as vague memories began to filter back of the lights.

"Shut the bloody window! It's freezing," Pete roared.

"It's dark! Something's happened! Remember the lights? It must have been a UFO!"

"It was a helicopter!" he snapped.

For several minutes we continued a disjointed conversation, me trying to jog his memory as more of my own flooded in. Pete became increasingly annoyed and distressed by the minute and it seemed he had little awareness of details, or was concealing his fear and confusion with outright anger.

"Shut up about the bloody lights, do you hear me? I don't want to know about them!"

Why was he doing this, denying what we had seen and experienced? Pete was driving way too fast and I decided it was better to drop the subject, both of us lapsing into strained silence for the rest of the journey home.

But my mind chattered on in the silence trying to make sense of the situation. I could remember the golden sunshine and seeing lights in the sky behaving strangely. Was it a helicopter? We had watched them and then driven off, I think. How did it get dark so quickly? How did we get to the far end of the straight?

Clear and definitive explanations evaded me and I was on edge and shaky. One minute I felt cold and the next, the palms of my hands and my armpits were sweating – and that raging thirst! Pete's mood was dark and tense, and we eventually we arrived home, gathered our gear from the car with a few terse words and went inside.

Our flat-mates were surprised and curious, "You're late! It's after eight o'clock. Your tea's in the oven but it's probably ruined now."

It should have been around 6.30 pm! Pete and I glanced at each other in confusion and disbelief and I looked at the television where the evening news should have been on, but a later programme was screening instead. I tried to question Pete again but he became confrontational and in front of our flat-mates, denied seeing anything other than a helicopter. His hands and voice shook and he abruptly disappeared into his room and didn't come out again. I downed a couple of glasses of water and retreated to my room as well.

One of the girls followed to talk with me, wanting to know what had happened, and it was only then the shocking reality hit home to me that I couldn't answer any of her questions. I could only tell her a vague story about lights in the sky, maybe a UFO, and what must have sounded like an unbelievable incident. How do we describe unfathomable events to others?

The next morning I attempted to replay the journey in my mind like a roll of film, but try as I may, I couldn't fill in the gap created by the appearance of those lights. For years, I relived the event over and over trying to come up with a logical explanation, but the result was always the same: sheer frustration and anxiety that I could not assemble the pieces of the puzzle. An approximate ninety minute slice of my life was missing or somehow blanked from my recall.

Eventually I realised the mere memory of the incident elicited physical symptoms: clammy palms, racing heart, and dry mouth. Emotionally, I felt jittery and anxious, and eventually tired and angry. What few memories I had retained repeatedly immobilised me in every way.

Over the weeks, an uncharacteristic change took place in Pete as our once good-natured flat-mate became morose and unapproachable. He continued to refuse to discuss the event with me or anyone else however, after some persistence on my part he admitted the incident was too bizarre for him to comprehend and he preferred not to be reminded of it. That was how Pete coped, by shutting it out, but clearly he still had private thoughts and fears that were taking a toll on him. Some months later he moved out of the flat and we lost contact.

For me, the incident on that remote highway became a wake-up call. Over the ensuing years, in my search for logical answers, I began to re-examine other strange incidents that had occurred throughout my life since early childhood.

Some years later, I read about alleged close encounters with UFOs and extraterrestrials, and those now highly relevant words "missing time" sprang out at me from the pages. I also read about "screen memories", where a person may sincerely believe they have seen a known object, such as a helicopter, only to discover through flash-backs or regressive hypnosis that it was in fact, something different. These distressing flash-backs are also common to those who suffer post-traumatic stress from a profoundly life-changing event.

Fast-forward twenty five years. Along with the UFO sighting I witnessed in childhood with my family, this 1975 encounter led to my lifelong interest in UFOs and in the year 2000, I founded a nationwide UFO sighting investigation and research group, UFO Focus New Zealand Research Network (UFOCUS NZ).

In 2005, I placed a description of the incident on our website. Before long I received an email from a New Zealand scientist, stating his belief that the sphere of light that had descended over our car would undoubtedly have been ball lightning, aligned with his theory that most UFO sightings can be simply explained by this phenomenon. I replied, pointing out pertinent specifics and factors that would discount the theory of ball lightning being the cause of the incident. Ball lightning, although sometimes attracted to metal objects, is generally small and drifts slowly. The light that engulfed our car was fast-moving and as wide as the road, travelling in a purposeful manner in a clear sunny sky, but our next recollection after the encounter was of darkness. I received no response.

Further communication from this scientist, perhaps showing a willingness to interview me about the experience in detail, may have provided him with an opportunity to assimilate new information or change his perspectives. Most significantly, the fact both Pete and I became either unconscious or incapacitated (Pete was no longer in control of the car) meant that after stalling, our vehicle should have remained at the beginning of the straight, but it did not. Of equal importance is the immediate physical and psychological impact the incident had on us both, and on our relationship and our world view.

Logical examination of the circumstances surrounding this experience convinced me the spherical light was a UFO (unidentified flying object), certainly not a helicopter or any natural or meteorological phenomenon. In fact, in the same sense as a term used by the late Dr J. Allen Hynek, US astrophysicist and UFO researcher, Pete and I went through a classic "escalation of hypotheses". We first took a simple guess as to what we were observing, but as we struggled to find the right category to put the event in, we upgraded this guess several times, seeking natural or logical explanations first before considering any explanation beyond that. Pete guessed it was a helicopter, then I guessed a top-dresser aircraft, but it was not until the light(s) disappeared instantaneously for the third time, that I upgraded my hypothesis to "possible UFO". I had tried, but failed to rationalise what I was seeing in terms of a familiar object with a logical explanation.

Something profound was set in motion by this incident on a lonely country highway, which I struggled to make sense of. An influence emerged in my day-to-day life, powerful and persistent. Sometimes I felt drawn towards certain places or topics at what would turn out to be a significant or opportune time. People crossed my path with timely advice and support, or challenged my thinking and perspectives.

The influence was ever-present and I somehow knew, and at that time feared, that further experiences awaited me.

Chapter 2

Night-times Elsewhere

Seeing, is believing

I was born and grew up in small-town rural New Zealand. From an early age I followed in my mother's family's footsteps of having intuitive abilities or extrasensory perceptions. My grandmother spoke of seeing balls of light in her room which "spoke" to her, bringing her comfort during long years of disability due to rheumatoid arthritis. My mother is an intuitive artist, and several of my great-aunts were involved in early spiritualist and healing groups in New Zealand. Such topics were normal conversation in my maternal family.

One Sunday afternoon when I was four years old we visited my grandmother for afternoon tea, and three great-aunts were there as well. Not being involved in the adult chatter, I decided to go up the long hallway to play with my grandmother's wind chimes, hanging just within tinkling-reach inside her front door. Upon entering the hall and closing the dining room door, I was terrified to see a man creeping down the hall towards me and cried out in fear. This prompted a stampede of great-aunts from the dining room to see what was happening and I pointed at the figure just as it faded from my perception.

It was evident even to a child that nobody else had seen the man, but I noticed meaningful looks passing between them, along with hushed phrases ... *she's like us*; *she's seen a spirit.* Seeing and communicating with people and animals who appeared and disappeared randomly had become a natural part of my life, and now I had a name for the figures I could see – spirits.

My early connection with the spirit world brought a dichotomy of spirit encounters in childhood, with what I distinguished as either good or bad spirits. I learnt at a young age that a person's nature does not suddenly change after death, becoming angelic; it is a continuum – for a while at least. In the same way that we learn to identify a variety of signals and messages from body language and facial expressions, which help us to form a perception of a person's nature, mood or intentions, I learnt to perceive the benevolent or malevolent intentions or natures of spirits by their energetic emanations. Perhaps this is the spiritual gift referred to in *The Holy Bible* as "discernment of spirits" (1 Corinthians 12:10). Some spirits had an air of beneficence, while others emanated a pervasive energy of malevolence. Looking back, I believe these incidents were a training ground for situations I would have to deal with, and work I would be drawn towards, in the future.

Growing up

In 1950s and 60s New Zealand, any family difficulties were rarely discussed in public and people went to great lengths to disguise or conceal what went on behind closed doors. My family was not financially well-off, although there was always sufficient food on the table as my father was a market gardener (vegetable farmer).

I had little in the way of toys, sports equipment and books, which was not so bad really because it prompted me to create my own entertainment with household objects, or build toys with bits and pieces found in the outside shed or at the beach. Creativity and enthusiasm knew no bounds, and I recall painting my old bike with my father's precious bright red tractor paint which I had found in the tool-shed, and leaving the lid off afterwards resulting in a tin of spoiled paint, for which I was soundly smacked.

But overall, I had a relatively normal childhood doing all the usual things New Zealand children did in the great outdoors – playing with friends and pets, riding bikes at breakneck speed, helping Mum pick plums and make jam, and swimming at the beach.

Having been academically inclined from the time I started school, the lack of educational books in our household was disheartening until I discovered the wonderful home library owned by our elderly neighbour, a retired school teacher. This treasure trove of literature became a central part of my education in childhood, and my reading skills, which were reputedly advanced for my age, allowed me to study a wide range of topics, visiting places in the world or in history and mythology that my schoolmates had not yet heard of. Black-and-white television arrived in New Zealand in the 1960s and I was allowed to run up the road to a friend's place a couple of afternoons a week to watch Disney cartoons on their precious "box", until such time as our family could afford one of our own.

However, looking back, we can probably all pinpoint times, events or circumstances in childhood which may have been turning points or catalysts in some way in our development – changing our perspectives, forcing us to grow up, opening up a new chapter in our lives, or deeply affecting our emotions in some way.

A number of such events occurred in my 0-18 years.

A family UFO sighting, mid-1960s

One such event happened on a Friday night at around 8.30 pm, irrevocably enhancing my youthful concept of the great unknown.

My father had gone outside to lock the garage, but soon came rushing back indoors shouting at us all to get out onto the terrace at the front of the house. We raced out the front door wondering what was going on and he pointed out an unusually bright light in the north-eastern sky. Over the following hour and a half, we observed a glowing orange cigar-shaped light stationary over the Bombay Hills, south of Auckland, some twenty or more kilometres away from our position. It was enthralling to watch this brilliant bar of orange light and my father fetched his ancient ship's telescope, nicknamed *Captain Bligh,* and we could see the light flare or pulse periodically. My mother rang the neighbours, who soon appeared on their terrace to watch too and speculative conversations were carried out back and forth over the low boundary hedge. Each bright pulse of the light was greeted with loud exclamations and conjecture, until the light finally moved off southward. It was the most exciting event of my life so far and I couldn't get to sleep that night thinking about it, staring into the darkness wide-eyed with pure wonder and awe.

The speculation continued and gained momentum when my mother discovered the event reported in the newspaper, and we learnt the light was seen by hundreds of people that Friday evening as it moved south over the Franklin and Waikato districts of the North Island. My parents agreed the light could not have been caused by any natural phenomenon or aircraft and guessed it must have come from "outer space" – a UFO. This declaration had a powerful effect on me and my mind examined the notion that if this was the case, there must have been someone flying it! Looking back, I believe my psyche was altered in an instant by this possibility and I viewed the night sky through a new light of discovery and potential, with a fascination that has never diminished.

The night visitors

In childhood, I sometimes woke at night to see three small figures beside my bed, like glowing silhouettes. I would wake suddenly, completely, as if someone had called to me, and there they would be. Although the figures never made a sound verbally or audibly, their calm and loving thoughts reached into my mind and it seemed perfectly natural to think back to them in response, as if it had always been this way. There existed a sense of mutual trust and familiarity.

The procedure was always the same: the trio would express their pleasure in seeing me again, one of them would convey, "We're going now", and I knew they were about to take me somewhere with them. But just as I sat up in bed to push back the blankets, everything would become blank and I remembered nothing more until I found myself saying goodbye to them. They would thank me, telling me they were pleased with me. One would instruct me to turn over, face the wall and go to sleep, which I obeyed instantly thus being unaware of the manner in which they entered and departed from my room.

The next day I often felt my mind had been stuffed with information, but just out of recall's reach. Small associated and perplexing details did not go unnoticed by me and on one occasion after seeing these figures during the night, I woke in the morning to find myself on top of the sheets and blanket but under the quilt, without a pillow and at the wrong end of the bed. I never felt the urge to reach out and touch these luminous figures with their curiously large heads, and no distinct facial features or outline of clothing. Although they were short and child-like in body, I did not relate to them as if they were other children, but rather I felt I was communicating with wise intelligences I had grown familiar with from an early age.

I did not discuss these occasions with anyone except my mother, but even so, the significant fact the visitors were short in stature with overly large heads was a secret I kept, as if I had been instructed not to divulge this pertinent detail to anyone, and instead, I spoke of kind "people" talking to me at night. My mother came from a Christian family background, but one that also accepted the existence of a spirit

The Night Visitors

The author aged eight and twenty years, when significant incidents occurred.

realm thus she considered they were either guardian angels, or alternatively, the benevolent and protective spirits of family members who had passed on from this life. I knew categorically these figures were not spirits, but just exactly what the visitors were or where they came from, I did not know or even consider further as a child.

Powerful mind-memories

I also experienced some reoccurring dreams in childhood. Although I use the word "dreams" loosely to describe them, they felt more like distinct memories of reality to me, experiences in another place. I would dream I was with a group of three pale indistinct figures (there is that trio again) standing in a white-walled room. A member of this group would tell me I was learning to help other people and it was a great responsibility, not to be taken lightly.

In the dream, they would ask me to envisage a scene, the details of which immediately dropped into my mind and the circumstances caused me to concentrate with extreme focus. These situations or settings were different in each of the dreams I recalled, but shared similar aims and outcomes. They always involved either helping a group of people affected by a condition, problem, or series of events, or, they involved observing a tragic situation with accompanying guidance from the group on how I should deal with it – unusually in-depth detail for such a young child.

During one such dream, I found myself in the familiar white room with the indistinct trio. Having conversed with them non-verbally, a setting emerged in my mind and I envisaged myself floating in the ocean, although I was still aware of the trio guiding and instructing me. In this mind-scenario there were other people floating near me in the sea, and I felt real fear as I observed a shark swimming towards us. The trio encouraged me to chase the shark away using the power of my mind to influence it, and keen to cooperate and please them, I concentrated hard on this task until I mentally saw the shark turn and swim off into the distance. The envisaged scene immediately disappeared from my mind, leaving me standing with the group of three in the white room again. One of them expressed pleasure and praise that I was attaining these mind skills, echoing the words of the night visitors, but strangely, perhaps because these figures appeared in dream-like memories rather than physically in my bedroom, I never associated them with the glowing nocturnal visitors.

On another occasion I found myself in the familiar white dream-room, where the figures told me they wished to show me the tragedies of armed conflict between humans. Suddenly everything went black, with a feeling of pressure as if some part of me was literally being pulled out of my body. Instantaneously, I found myself without a body, but still cognisant and flying through the air in daylight above a foreign landscape where two groups were engaged in armed conflict. I felt a great sense of freedom, but deep sadness as I swooped down through bullets and gunfire, smoke and explosions of earth, where men lay dead or injured, while others tried to escape the crossfire. All the while a member of the trio accompanied me, guiding my raw emotions through an exposure of how man treats his fellow man and the results of warfare, greed and power-mongering. All of this I understood on some level, albeit at a young age.

In adulthood, when thinking about these memories, I recalled the sensation of pressure, of something being pulled from my body, along with the recognition my mind was active and yet free of a physical form. I wondered if this and other similar memories indicated astral travelling, rather than dreams, and if so, who were the three familiar figures that always participated, guiding me? Eventually I began to forge more links, and I considered the "dreams" with the trio could be related to the appearance of the three nocturnal visitors by my bed in childhood, and our trips elsewhere.

In the 1990s, I considered other possible explanations after reading a book by Princeton University historian, author and abduction researcher, Dr. David Jacobs PhD, entitled *Secret Life: Firsthand Accounts of UFO Abductions.* In light of my early memories, I now wondered if I had been taken onboard extraterrestrial craft in childhood, where entities used mind control techniques to train my thought processes and teach me how to use the power of the mind. Had they projected specific realistic scenes or enactments into my mind to train me in these skills, or perhaps to study my reactions and emotions in response to varied situations? Certainly most of my "dream memories" revolved around urgent or stressful situations, analytical problem-solving, and evoked strong emotions.

And if I was being visited by extraterrestrials in childhood, did they prevent or shield me from seeing (or recalling) their actual facial features and bodily forms so as not to frighten me? Had I left my body during sleep and astral travelled on occasions with them? This might explain my "war-zone" dream memory and others like it.

The possibility of some kind of ongoing education or training in an otherworldly place had emerged from early childhood, and it eventually became clear to me later in life that the glowing figures which had appeared by my bed, and the trio of indistinct figures recalled in dreams, were likely one and the same.

Insights and extra-sensory perceptions

During my eighth year, the night visitations increased and I believe this contributed to the rapid upswing in psychic awareness I experienced that year. Paranormal experiences occurred frequently, animal telepathy, precognition, spirit contact and the like, to the extent I felt as if I did not quite fit anywhere. I learnt the hard way that I perceived many things differently from my schoolmates, with spontaneous outbursts about what I could see or sense invariably resulting in derision and ostracism. Nevertheless, I saw vibrant colours surge around people's bodies, spirits appeared and spoke to me, and I sometimes felt I knew what people were thinking, which was often different from what they actually said. I soon learnt it was best not to talk about these experiences – and it was lonely.

It is widely accepted nowadays that spirituality and religion are not necessarily the same, and certainly this was my experience as a child. Our family attended church on Sundays because it was the thing-to-do in the 1950s and 60s, but from an early age I had an innate aversion to the pomp and ceremony of the church we attended, which seemed unrelated to the world I was growing up in and the circumstances of my life. Attending Sunday school and Bible study soon convinced me that obvious scare tactic techniques were being applied to young minds by some well-meaning individuals. Sometimes God was exalted for his loving compassion, while at other times presented as a vengeful God and I could not reconcile the two – the latter behaviour sounding too human in nature. I already understood we do not necessarily have to worship in this way to know goodness and truth and I found true expressions of God, a supreme power of goodness, in everyday things instead. Nature, the companionship of animals, a vivid sunset, trees in the wind, kind words, the bright emanation from a benevolent spirit, and the night visitors were happy representations of God to me, and were all I needed to feed my soul. I grew up independent, not wishing to belong to any group that might restrict my right to free and intelligent thought.

Throughout childhood and my teenage years I developed empathy with animals and drew strength from my love of nature, but it was through my contact with the spirit realms I realised that in both life, and after death, our consciousness and existence is ongoing in one form or another.

Throughout my years at High School I focused on academic achievement and musical pursuits. The intuitive abilities that had been prominent in earlier childhood receded into the background somewhat, perhaps as I concentrated all my energy and mind-power on passing exams.

After leaving High School and completing three years tertiary education at Teacher's College, I qualified as a registered New Zealand primary school teacher in 1975 and began my professional career. That same year, at the age of twenty, the experience described in Chapter 1 became a catalyst for change and investigation.

I would eventually re-examine many of the experiences of my life so far, in the unanticipated context of contact with extraterrestrials.

Chapter 3

Companion Species

Some readers may wonder why I have chosen to include a chapter on animals in this book, but what better way to demonstrate consciousness than to recount some animal stories involving telepathy and the power of intent.

I believe consciousness is universal and influences all life forms, in all realms, realities or dimensions, and therefore, universal souls may inhabit not just humans, but any number of sentient life-forms, including animals. Taking this one step further, I would say that many creatures and life-forms are able to convey that sentience and consciousness through energy, thought or telepathy within their own species, or to other receptive states of awareness or minds.

Inter-species communication was normal to me as a child. I sensed or telepathically heard thought-forms and emotions from animals in the same way I sometimes perceived what a person was thinking or feeling, without any verbal or physical cues or indication from them. I sometimes spoke to our cocker spaniel dog with my mind when I went to bed at night, and I recognised the instant she had registered my thoughts, and responded with an exchange of energy and thought-forms that is beyond description in words. Even plants exuded identifiable signals and I could sometimes sense when a plant was struggling or flourishing, regardless of how it actually looked. Recent research indicates that plants communicate with each other and can even differentiate between beneficial and harmful human intentions.

I shared a close affinity with my pets, usually knowing when they were in pain or upset. Domesticated animals in particular can be perceptive to human sorrows and tragedies, or human joy and delight, in the same way our families and friends might express empathy with us in times of need, or happiness at our successes. If we are open to such communication, animal intelligence and sentiency can transcend the intellectual boundaries we have imposed that separate human from creature. I have been privileged to share my life with several such animal friends.

Animal compassion

On the day I was diagnosed with a serious illness in 1989, I sat on our garden path in the sun feeling stunned and empty. My elderly black Labrador dog, Siva, was nowhere to be seen at the time and I assumed she was in her kennel. She suffered from arthritis and could no longer make it up the steep flight of steps onto the section of garden where I was seated however, after several minutes I noticed her peering up at me from the garden wall. Deep in my own thoughts, I ignored her until I realised she was painstakingly climbing the stairs towards me, something she had not done for a couple of years. She walked straight over to where I was seated, licked my neck and lay the side of her face against my chest. I folded my arms around her neck and we stayed in this position for several minutes. Siva never moved or left me until I felt composed again and then she padded indoors with me, becoming my shadow for several hours, keeping me company until my family came home. I cannot believe this was coincidence or that she was acting out of instinct, seeking food or attention. I believe she had sensed my sad thoughts and emotions, sought me out and responded to my needs with intelligent intent, compassion and love.

Throughout adulthood, my ability to communicate with animals became more intense and I had some unforgettable ordeals relating to animal cruelty, finding all manner of creatures that "spoke" to me, needing help, love, or veterinary care. One incident in particular illustrated to me the reality that like us, animals have the ability to communicate via consciousness with receptive humans, and have spirits that survive physical death. Sadly, this account also illustrates the tragic plight of domestic animals that are neglected by their owners.

Agani

I was driving home through the countryside after a visit to the supermarket, feeling relaxed and not thinking about anything in particular. Slowly, I became aware of a voice calling somewhere in the back of my mind, a thin, reedy sound with a sad and desperate note to it – a heart-rending call, repeated over and over at intervals. Someone or something needed help, and I tried to ascertain who or what it was, but without success. There was no accompanying message and I felt emotionally unsettled by it.

A random thought occurred to me, suddenly and urgently in fact, that I had forgotten to buy some lemons! In an instant another thought followed, that I could make a quick detour off the main road and pick some lemons at an acquaintance's place (who I will call "A"). I'd heard she was away on holiday, but I knew she would not mind me helping myself to lemons. The moment I made this decision, I noticed the caller's voice fell silent.

As I entered the driveway and parked, I could only recall an old gnarly lemon tree around the back of the house, and curiously, the certain knowledge there was a new lemon tree behind shrubs near the driveway had vanished from my mind at that point.

I hurried around the back of the house when I was startled by the sound of a chain rattling, and swinging around I was confronted by a tragic sight that will stick in my mind for the rest of my days.

A's husband's elderly Afghan hound "Agani" (not his real name), was crouched on the dirt beside a chicken coop, which evidently was his home, a heavy chain attached to his collar. But wasn't the family away on holiday? Who was looking after the dog? I was appalled at what I saw. Agani's eyes were weeping pus and it was obvious he was in poor condition, ill and in pain, but the worst image was the look in his eyes, a haunting pleading look of helplessness and despair. I knew I had found the caller.

After filling his water bowl and reassuring him I would return very soon, I drove home as fast as I could. I made a phone call to one of A's relatives and found he was in charge of feeding the dog, but it seemed urgent veterinary attention and exercise were not part of the care. An hour or so later I called at his house and challenged him concerning the dog's state of health, giving him the ultimatum of taking the dog to the vet, or I would. An argument ensued during which he threw a heavy set of keys at me, but I managed to obtain A's holiday contact details. The relative was adamant there was nothing wrong with the dog and accused me of being emotional and over-reacting. His conversation became increasingly confrontational and fearing he would remove the dog from the property, I drove back there with my children and took Agani home with us for the night.

The next day I was able to get an emergency appointment at a local veterinary clinic. Several staff members were close to tears when they saw the dog's dreadful condition, and the vet stated it was one of the worst cases of animal neglect he had seen in all his years of practice, and he was keen to prosecute the owner.

The dog's skin was crusted with infected sores and pus wept from his eyes and ears. Much of his face was hairless and clearly itchy, caused by a mite infestation. His body hair, which should have been long and luxurious, was dirty and matted into tight knots and pulling cruelly on his skin. Agani had not been groomed for months, probably much longer, and the numerous clumps housed dirt and fleas. He was underweight, suffering from arthritis, and unused to walking freely.

Beyond Agani's poor physical condition, one can only wonder what terrible emotional and psychological torment he had endured on the end of that chain, frequently ignored and alone, without love and companionship, ill, and without dignity and hope.

The vet outlined the length of time and the expense involved in bringing Agani back to health, and given his age and severely neglected condition, he recommended the kindest course of action would be euthanasia. The alternative was to have the owner relinquish ownership and to find a foster home for Agani with people willing to pay the veterinary fees. The vet requested I contact the owners to ascertain whether they were willing to pay for the dog's care, or authorise his euthanasia. They opted for the latter.

I watched Agani that evening as he played with my sons, now with a light in his eye and a spring in his step from the attention and change of scenery. I made up my mind to try to find a new owner for him rather than have him put down.

However, this was not to be, and I believe spiritual forces already had the situation in hand and just needed me to accept it. That night I dreamt Agani stood before me, but now in perfect health, his hair flowing and glossy. He looked into my eyes, and I perceived a simple message – *I want to go.* It was emphatic and final and I believed his soul had spoken to me. The next morning I knew what had to be done, and so a small group of compassionate animal lovers at the vet clinic surrounded Agani in his final moments.

We drove back out into the country to bury Agani under the trees near his chicken coop kennel. On the way, I became aware of his spirit standing up on the back seat with his head hanging over my shoulder and as I turned, he raised his regal head, becoming alert as if he had seen something of interest. With a graceful leap, his spirit departed through the side of the car and for a few seconds, I saw him running alongside us before he faded from vision. Once again he was youthful, magnificent, and free at last.

An eel in distress

Compelling evidence has been compiled recently by international researchers, supporting the existence of consciousness even in the group of vertebrates including fish, eels and octopi.

Another incident certainly corroborated this research.

I was driving to another city for the day, a journey during which I would pass through a picturesque gorge with a small settlement. As I approached the gorge I began to feel decidedly agitated, coupled with a deep sense of despondency, and I recognised these feelings were not my own.

I was swamped by an overwhelming desire to turn into the parking area of the settlement's café because I sensed this overlay of emotions originated from there, and suspected it was from an animal. I entered the café and wandered around, half expecting to see a dog or cat in poor health, but there were none to be seen and so I decided to take a break from driving and ordered a coffee.

But the inflow of unsettling emotions continued, and eventually I was drawn to a small rectangular fish tank I found on a table in full sunlight. I was shocked to see a freshwater eel some forty five centimetres long in a fish tank only around thirty centimetres in length. The tank was devoid of plants or rocks, or anywhere for the eel to hide as is their habit – just water and a bit of gravel. The eel could not move around much and its body was constantly in a wavy shape in order to fit in the undersized tank. It was clearly distressed and the sad emotions were amplified as I leaned over the tank and looked into its murky eyes.

I approached the café owner to politely express my concerns about the eel's well-being, however this was met with an attitude of defensiveness and derision at the suggestion eels could feel emotions of discomfort and helplessness. Later that evening, I left a message on the local SPCA answer-phone requesting that someone visit the premises for an inspection. An officer returned my call the next day, explaining that fish were not under their jurisdiction, only birds and animals, however she was concerned enough to agree to speak to the café owner in the hope that her status as an SPCA officer might carry some weight.

Several days later she rang back to report the owner was willing to improve conditions, with an assurance the eel would be set free in the river when it grew bigger. I called in at the café again some weeks later and found the eel was now in a large aquatic tank in a dark shady corner, complete with plants, a pipe to hide in, gravel and rocks, aquatic toys and a model of a sunken shipwreck! It had apparently now become an attraction for children, and there was a sign next to the tank assuring customers the eel was well cared for (now). Both the eel and I were happy.

As yet, we do not collectively understand the complex emotional and energetic emanations that comprise communications from the Animal and Plant Kingdoms. I believe that in the future, a greater understanding of these concepts could lead to an increased frequency of harmony on our planet, and advances in our knowledge of plant consciousness and energy may lead to breakthroughs in healing. There is spiritual, emotional and even physiological relevance in maintaining a close relationship with animals (and birds and other creatures) in our lives, through both caring for our domestic animals and ensuring suitable habitat for wild animals.

Recent research by psychologists and criminologists indicates that if a person is cruel to an animal they are more likely to commit assault on humans, and cruelty to animals by children is now seen as an indicator of possible assault incidents on humans later in adulthood. The research indicates that children who grow up with animals as part of their family circle or community, and who are taught to love and care for those animals by responsibly meeting their needs, are more likely to be loving and caring parents who extend that nurturing to neighbours, friends, and community.

In July 2012, the question of animal consciousness was discussed in detail by a group of scientists gathered at the University of Cambridge for the first annual Francis Crick Memorial Conference. The result of this meeting was the *Cambridge Declaration on Consciousness*. It concluded that nonhuman animals have the neuroanatomical, neurochemical, and neurophysiological substrates of conscious states, along with the capacity to exhibit intentional behaviours.

We are not the most advanced sentient species on the planet after all. Evidence indicates that humans are not unique in possessing the neurological substrates that generate consciousness, and nonhuman animals, including all mammals and birds, and many other creatures, including octopi, also possess these neurological substrates. Animals across many different species have complex intelligence, methods of interaction and problem-solving, feel empathy for their species companions, or are self-aware. An increasing body of scientific evidence is showing that animals are conscious in the same way we are, and it is no longer something we can ignore. This knowledge requires a re-examination of our perspectives, and in particular, our attitudes towards animal cruelty and inhumane treatment.

My love of animals is an integral part of who I am. Over the years, I have realised that my relationship with both animals and spirits is simply a form of communication with other universal non-human intelligences. This understanding is inextricably interwoven with my extraterrestrial contact experiences, and thus must be a part of this book.

Many other abductees and experiencers report having heightened awareness of other species, and soul interactions with animals and creatures. Perhaps we are tapping into an important energetic component of life on this planet, as yet unrecognised by the majority – a universal form of communication linking sentient life.

Chapter 4

Spirit

Worldwide research into human contact with extraterrestrials indicates that paranormal factors are commonly reported in association with UFO encounters and contact experiences. Some experiencers report having an expanded intuitive awareness from early childhood, while others report these abilities developed after specific encounters in later life. Many also have the ability to see and converse with spirits.

Often spirits have appeared to me quite randomly and inconsequentially, as if they just happened to be passing and I just happened to look up and see them. I recall sitting up in bed one evening having a cup of tea, when I looked up and saw the figure of a woman wearing an elegant dress from another era, appear through one wall of the room. Suddenly realising she was in the privacy of my bedroom and that I could see her, she looked at me in surprise and I heard her voice (the ability to hear/perceive a spirit voice is called "clairaudience") as she apologised, before disappearing through an adjacent wall. From such experiences, I realised that other realms of existence are operating all around us, parallel, coexisting.

At the age of twenty (the same year as the encounter described in Chapter 1), I experienced a life-influencing prophetic dream in which I was walking through a beautiful garden with "someone". Their features remained indistinct and difficult to see apart from the swirl of a garment. This benevolent being or spirit, revealed in detail the many tragic and difficult times that lay ahead in my life, and I felt immense sorrow alternating with a range of other emotions associated with each incident that was outlined. Just as the anguish became almost too much to bear and I felt no desire to continue living this life, the being accompanying me began to outline small improvements and changes in the circumstances of my life in the future. Painfully slowly, my life would eventually improve until finally, a significant event would occur in my later years, creating much joy.

I was staying at my mother's place at the time, and I was woken by the sound of her walking down the driveway with her dog. At that moment I had clear recollection of the details of the dream and immediately attempted to call out to her, but I was shocked to find my voice would not work! I simply could not articulate words and no sound came out of my mouth. During those few split seconds, all the finer details of the dream drained from my mind, leaving only the framework described above – and then my voice came back. Perhaps I was not meant to consciously recall specific details, knowledge which may have altered my life, veering me away from destiny.

My life has indeed followed the framework outlined by the kindly companion in the dream-garden. At times when life was hard, I recalled the final positive outcome of a difficult future that was laid out before me, and I have picked myself up again and kept going. Some may call this faith. My mother told a family friend about my experience, who in turn told a local church vicar, and he considered it a religious revelation or vision. I simply called it spirit at work. Many people experience similar.

There was never any question in my mind that life continues after the demise of the physical body. I have seen my father, sister, grandparents, and other family members, friends and acquaintances who are deceased, but who have appeared to me in spirit form to offer advice, warnings, moral support and humour.

When in my mid-thirties, I joined a Spiritual Society. We had moved to town after nine years of living in a remote area and I felt the need to seek out the company of like-minded people. In the years to follow I facilitated groups in healing, meditation and psychic development. I have never charged a fee for the particular intuitive work I do, but on one occasion a person offered me monetary compensation. He was a very proud old man who was embarrassed when I declined, and so to avoid offence to his pride I accepted $10 to cover petrol costs. I then drove into town to carry out a few errands and on returning to my car, I found a parking ticket under my windscreen wiper blades for the sum of $10. In one hand and out the other – and I doubt it was coincidence.

At times, there are specific messages or reasons accompanying the appearance of a spirit, forewarning of a situation, alerting us to impending danger so we may become an instrument for the spirit realms. This was the case on one occasion when I was on my way to an exercise class.

The Bridge Incident

Summer rain had poured down for a couple of hours and the country highway was slippery and awash with puddles. It was a Thursday, late afternoon, with heavy traffic heading into the city, moving at a steady pace but with drivers paying little heed to the worsening conditions.

A young woman was riding a motor scooter in front of me, struggling with the downpour, soaked to the skin and inadequately dressed in shorts and sandals. A couple of car loads of young guys had passed us, weaving in and out of traffic and leaving everyone in a shower of muddy water. The girl on the scooter was travelling slowly and so when the opportunity arose, I too decided to pass her.

As I indicated and began to pull out, I experienced clairaudience and heard a distinct (spirit) woman's voice say urgently and loudly, "Don't pass her, protect her!"

I immediately pulled back in behind the scooter and maintained a close distance from it, thus preventing another car from pulling in between us, and I paced the scooter as we proceeded more speedily down a hill towards a river. Within seconds, the cars up ahead came to an abrupt halt as a result of a vehicle breaking down at the far end of the bridge, causing the girl braked hard just as she hit a puddle, flipping the scooter, which dragged her along the road with it. I was virtually standing on my brake pedal in an attempt to stop, and all I could see was her body lying in a heap directly in my path. When my car finally stopped I ran around the front of it to find her lying in a foetal position right up against the front bumper, with her hands over her head, sobbing. If I had not prevented other cars from pulling in between us, protecting her as the spirit woman had asked me to, I believe she would likely have been hit, and seriously injured or killed by another vehicle.

Miraculously, she had no broken bones, but deep gashes, and as both her parents worked at the hospital she asked me to drive her there. After the young woman was taken to the emergency ward, her mother, a nurse, accompanied me back to my car and asked about the accident. Under these circumstances, I would not normally have divulged the fact that a spirit contact was associated with the incident, however for some reason I felt compelled to mention this. I described the distinct tone of the spirit voice, a deep, husky, older woman's voice. The nurse's face paled and she said her own mother, who had died several years earlier, had a raspy voice just like that, a smoker's voice. She thanked me for mentioning this, as she had often worried about whether her mother was "still around" and if she was okay. She now felt comforted by the thought it may have been her mother's spirit who spoke to me, and that she was safe and watching over her family. Somewhat shaken, I headed off to my exercise session where I found the venue was closed, and it was only then I remembered this week's session had been cancelled as the instructor was on holiday. Was it merely coincidence I forgot this fact and ended up on the road behind the girl, at just the right moment? Or did this spirit foresee the situation looming and needed a receptive person to hear their plea to protect the girl?

Like many people, I have seen the spirit form of people sometimes days, weeks, and even centuries (judging by their attire) after their death, indicating their soul has not yet returned to the "source". It is my understanding that the soul is capable of consciously (intelligently) manipulating and transforming energy to manifest in a visible spirit form. This is also evident when people have an out-of-body experience or astral travel, sometimes as a ball of light, but at other times manifesting in spirit form. I recall an occasion when I visited an elderly friend in hospital, who was in a coma. That night I woke just on midnight to see her standing beside my bed, talking to me fondly and thanking me for visiting. She passed away in the early hours of the morning, but her spirit had manifested to say goodbye to me before her passing, despite her physical body being in an unconscious state.

In more recent years, public awareness of the realms of spirit has rapidly increased and from the evidence presented in books such as, *Proof of Heaven,* by neurosurgeon Dr. Eben Alexander (US), it is clear more professionals in the fields of medicine and psychology are exploring and validating such topics as near-death-experiences and out-of-body-experiences. A paradigm shift in our awareness of soul and spirit is taking place leading us towards greater understanding of consciousness, and who and what we really are.

The ability to communicate with spirits has enriched my life beyond measure, but at times I have also seen balls of light, vibrantly coloured, and often communicating with me. These balls of light seemed imbued with intelligence and eventually I would discover their origin and identity, and their purpose in my life – the intimate soul connection.

Chapter 5

Illuminating Experiences

"What's going on in the sky around Gisborne?
Why have there been so many UFO sightings here in the past month – the heaviest spate recorded in New Zealand?"
Gisborne Herald, Sat. Dec 17, 1977

In 1977, my partner and I moved to the remote East Coast region, north of the city of Gisborne, North Island. I had already quizzed my partner (who I will call "Dave") about his views on the notion of UFOs and although his stance seemed neutral, I did not elaborate on my earlier frightening experience in Hawkes Bay for fear of disbelief. We settled into life in a coastal community, at first completely unaware we were now situated slap-bang in the middle of a UFO flap.

A "UFO flap" is terminology denoting a time period with a significant rise in the number of UFO sightings (global, national, or regional), often sharing similar descriptions or characteristics and concentrated in a particular area. 1977 heralded a time of intense UFO sightings around the city of Gisborne, throughout the remote rural areas of the East Coast region, and in particular, in the infamous and somewhat spooky Waimata Valley north of Gisborne. These events became known as the Gisborne UFO flap (and similar UFO flaps were occurring worldwide at the time).

It was characterised by hundreds of reported sightings of UFOs and unconventional lights. Daytime sightings of matt-black or silver metallic UFOs, and glowing orange cylindrical flying objects occurred. Blazing white light illuminated entire valleys or hillsides. A thirteen metre wide circle of scorched soil and shrubbery was discovered on a farm in the Waimata Valley. Disc-shaped objects with rotating bands of coloured lights were seen, and highly reflective objects emitting beams of blue light. Anomalous blue-green crystalline material associated with these UFOs, sometimes called "angel's hair", fell upon properties and vehicles, quickly dissolving.

Witnesses reported clusters of lights merging into a single larger light, or alternatively large lights splitting into a number of smaller lights.

The local *Gisborne Herald* newspaper published regular UFO sighting reports over many months, and then periodically for several years. A UFO investigation group sprang to life in Gisborne with the provocative motto, "Ridicule without investigation is the crown of ignorance upon the head of a fool". The most intense period of sightings occurred during 1977-79, and after that reports began to drop off into the early 1980s, but still continue spasmodically today.

The remoteness and sparse population of the area surrounding Gisborne meant many sightings witnessed in rural areas were never reported. Even so, over two hundred people reported sightings to the police, the media, and the Gisborne UFO investigation group – ordinary people ranging from fishermen to shepherds on remote sheep stations, from businessmen to housewives. Over the years, I have interviewed many witnesses to the Gisborne UFO sightings. Ongoing communications I have received up to the present day contain vivid descriptions revealing the range of human emotions and attitudes the events elicited in ordinary people's lives, both short and long term.

Notably, from these Gisborne events emerged the first publicly reported accounts of alleged "missing time" and "alien abduction" experiences in New Zealand, describing encounters with short pale entities with large heads and dark eyes. The circumstances of these encounters were generally recalled as frightening.

However at the time, having just moved to this remote area, we heard only scant mention of these events unfolding further south. But we were soon to have a riveting experience of our own.

The Tokomaru Bay illuminated valley

East Coast Highway 35, north of Gisborne, North Island, New Zealand, March 1978

Dave and I had driven to the city of Gisborne for the day, shopping for supplies, where we enjoyed an evening meal with friends and left at around 10.30 pm on our 2 ½ -3 hour journey home up the East Coast. The car was laden with groceries and other goods so it was a slow trip in our small vehicle.

At the summit of the hills near Tokomaru Bay there is an isolated section of highway, and from this panoramic vantage point you can look out over hills and valleys towards the coast, and inland to remote mountainous areas. We reached this spot at around 11.30 pm.

As we proceeded over the brow of the hill we were startled by an unexpected sight: a massive glow of intensely bright white light suddenly emanated up into the air from the floor of a valley less than a kilometre away from us, as if someone had flicked on a switch. The car stalled. We were stunned and my heart was pounding. What the hell was that?

The magnitude of this light was entirely different from anything we had ever seen and it lit the valley like daylight, with every tree on the hillsides transformed to silvery-white. It permeated everything so completely that there appeared to be no shadows, and yet great detail was still distinguishable. Momentarily numb with disbelief, we both stared at this strange intense light.

We soon snapped out of our initial shock and began to panic like hell, voices raised, trying to work out what it could be, but the high-strangeness of the situation rapidly turned our confusion to fear, and with no obvious explanation for this spectacle, we finally resorted to nervous whispers. Oddly, we did not even think to try to start the car and instead, looked back along the road hoping some late-night traffic would come along and provide security in numbers. But none did.

Dave tried to reassure me (and perhaps himself too) that the light was probably a spotlight used by hunters out possum shooting. Well, I have lived in the countryside most of my life but I have never seen a hunter's spotlight so powerful and widespread that it could illuminate an entire valley and surrounding hillsides in every direction, including a hundred metres or so into the air in a dome-like shape.

While we sat there staring and whispering, I noticed my arms and legs were feeling numb and tingly, like when you get pins-and-needles, and my body felt unusually heavy. The atmosphere in the car changed with a feeling of pressure, my thoughts became vague and confused and our surroundings looked indistinct. Within seconds I became aware of a deep buzzing sound and at the same time, I felt dizzy and faint. When I attempted to ask Dave if he felt the same the buzzing rapidly increased in pitch and intensity, until I found myself unable to move my limbs or speak. At this point I had enough wits left to register a momentary streak of pure terror at this loss of control and then, nothing. I cannot remember finishing what I was trying to say to him.

My next recollection was of us both sitting still in the car, the valley now in darkness. I felt drained and stared out the front window of the car, I don't know for how long, but Dave remained unresponsive, his head rested against the door jamb.

Finally I said to him, "The light's gone."

He didn't move or reply so I asked, "Shall we go now?"

He mumbled, "Okay", started the car, and we set off on the remainder of the journey, travelling in silence.

The next day we felt unusually tired and attributed it to the fact we'd had a late night. I experienced sensitive hearing for several days and unexpected sounds startled me – my heart raced, my armpits prickled in a cold sweat, and my mouth dried up. For a week or so I behaved like a frightened rabbit, but apart from feeling tired, Dave did not suffer these effects.

I recalled the blazing light in the valley and attempted to quiz Dave about what he thought it could have been, but he became apprehensive, not wishing to discuss it. This attitude left me feeling alone in my need for a logical explanation, and as I had done after the Hawkes Bay incident three years earlier, I replayed the event in my mind like a roll of film for years afterwards. I could recall the moment when we were panicking as the light illuminated the valley in front of us, but in the next moment of recollection the light had somehow gone. There was something missing, incongruous, indicated by the disjointed flow of events, and oddly, I could not recall putting away several boxes of groceries when we arrived home.

Our minimal conversation following the incident seemed understated for two people who had just witnessed such a sight and yet following this, we travelled the rest of the way home in silence – no discussion or investigation, no peering down the valley as we passed, no scanning of the sky. This was in vivid contrast to the pandemonium that first broke loose in the car.

I recalled the buzzing sound and from that time on, I became jittery if I heard a noise that even vaguely resembled it, and the once-familiar sound of a chainsaw took on a whole new nerve-wracking persona. Unfortunately, spontaneous fear of the unknown can override logical thinking and induce irrational reactions at times, and our emotions and powers of discernment become scattered and unreliable at that very moment.

Dave and I enjoyed putting out a long fishing set-line and pulling it in late at night by torchlight, but I was now apprehensive about being out after dark on a lonely coastal beach. Car lights shining on our house at night caused me to peer fearfully through chinks in the curtains, even though my rational mind told me it was only local farmers on their way home from the pub after a hard day's work. It became important to me to search for plausible, logical explanations for the light and the accompanying buzzing sound. But the question lingered: why was this scenario being repeated in my life?

We were not alone.

In April, I held a casual conversation with a local woman, "Mrs. V". She described a recent occasion when she got up in the middle of the night to go to the bathroom and looking out her living room windows, she saw moonlight on the hills behind the house – unusually bright white light, illuminating and defining every tree and rocky outcrop. On returning to the bedroom she woke her husband as she wanted him to see this amazing moonlit sight, but he stated categorically there was no moon that night. Mrs. V returned to the living room, noticing immediately that now it was dark outside and there was indeed no moon to be seen. She double-checked, looking for a source of the light before returning to bed bewildered.

I listened in silence to her account, working hard at maintaining an expressionless face but inside, my stomach churned. There were those familiar reactions again: pounding heart, prickling armpits, a cold clammy sweat. I should have been reassured hearing Mrs. V. describe something similar to what Dave and I had experienced, but instead, I felt only dread and fear of what it all meant, wondering if our safety was at risk. I could not bring myself to relate our own experience to Mrs. V. for fear of disbelief and ridicule. This may seem strange considering she had witnessed something similar herself, but it is common behaviour for a person who is struggling with the irrationality of a situation and their fear of being labelled as barmy if they divulge it. (Even today, despite the fact we are active UFO researchers and sighting investigators and our UFOCUS NZ website displays UFO sighting reports, some people still express fear of being disbelieved when relating their experiences to UFOCUS NZ staff.)

Corroborative evidence of this encounter in the hills near Tokomaru Bay has continued to turn up over the years. In 2002, I came across a *Gisborne Herald* newspaper clipping from January 26, 1978, entitled, "Valley was lit up by beam from object". It described how two Waimata Valley farming couples and their children watched a bright egg-shaped object light an entire valley for over an hour.

But for me, an experience even more personal and petrifying was yet to come.

The "sheep truck" incident
East Coast, North Island, New Zealand, 1978

Our house was situated on a seaside road leading to the village, with several fields between our property and the settlement, and hills lay beyond to the east and south. Following a normal evening at home, Dave and I went to bed and fell asleep.

At some time during the night, I suddenly awoke, and when I say "suddenly", I mean instantly and completely awake and alert. All was quiet. For a moment I stared into the darkness (there was no moon) wondering what had woken me and I turned the bedside lamp on briefly to see what the time was – 1.25 am. Objects on my dressing table began vibrating and the lid of my jewellery box tinkled; I reached out and straightened it. These familiar signs explained to me why I had woken up (or so I thought at that moment). Earthquakes ranging from small shudders to prolonged quakes are a common occurrence in the East Coast region and I expected one was about to happen.

Within seconds, other objects throughout the house began rattling and I was surprised Dave continued to sleep through it. I waited, expecting to hear the rumbling noise that sometimes precedes a long rolling quake, and soon I could hear a faint humming sound coming from an easterly direction beyond the township. The vibrating noises in the house increased in intensity, although objects were not falling off the shelves. I tried to wake Dave, but without success in spite of me shaking him and speaking to him. This alone was unusual and unsettled me.

With a rising sense of panic and confusion, I realised this was not the usual rumbling of an earthquake. The humming sound had increased, or was now over-ridden by an electronic-sounding, fast frequency buzz. The vibrations penetrated everything: the bed, the walls, the sheets and blankets, my entire body, as if every atom was dancing and humming in every object. Listening intently, I realised the buzzing noise was airborne and approaching our house over the paddocks, and terrifying thoughts of an aircraft crashing into our house flashed through my mind.

The impulse to leap out of bed and peer through the window vanished with the shocking realisation I could no longer move! My body was paralysed with the exception of my eyes and head and I wanted desperately to call out to Dave, but was incapable of doing so because the buzzing had increased to an incapacitating intensity. It was unbearable and I thought my head would burst.

Whatever it was, it swiftly arrived directly overhead, with harsh white light consuming our house, glaring through the edges of the curtains and the weave of the fabric. I managed to turn my head away from the window in the direction of the hall, where wide shafts of light beamed in all directions through uncovered windows, but then quite suddenly from that point I have no memory of what happened next.

At some stage, I recall lying in bed feeling confused, thinking I must have just woken up. Slowly, I realised there was light outside and the chilling memory of that bright light and the over-powering noise came flooding back. I do not know how long I lay there in anguish, waiting and fearing that something was about to happen, while it did not occur to me that it might have already happened.

I managed to wake Dave from his deep sleep now and poured out a garbled account of what had taken place, and after looking outside he told me it was sunrise. Where had the hours gone since I looked at my clock at 1.25 am and heard what I thought was an earthquake approaching? There was a complete blank in my memory, preceding my second awakening some hours later.

For several days I felt on-edge and shaken, suffering fatigue, sensitive hearing and nose bleeds; again, my mouth dried and my hands perspired when I thought about the experience. After some discussion, Dave decided it must have been an earthquake, but could not account for the bright light and noise above the house, or that I had been wide awake, cognisant and moving around before the loss of memory or consciousness. He did not want to entertain the idea it could have been a UFO.

After talking to locals, listening to TV and radio and hearing no reference to an earthquake in our area, it became yet another incident for the too-hard-box. Ultimately, any possible explanations we considered, ranging from thunder over the hills to bad dreams, did not match up with the full details of what I had experienced.

In the end, out of sheer frustration, Dave came up with the idea I must have heard a sheep transportation truck rumble along the road near our house in the early hours of the morning, this idea being based on the fact their engines make a characteristic humming sound. I pointed out that sheep trucks are not airborne, do not shine brilliant lights and make unbearably loud buzzing noises above houses, or paralyse people, but he was adamant, clinging to a logical explanation he could accept and deal with. There was no point pursuing the discussion so once again I was left feeling alone, afraid and helpless.

Over the years, in the course of interviewing other witnesses of the UFO flap, I met and became friends with Beverlea Parsons in 2004. Beverlea was a nurse at Gisborne Hospital back in 1978, and she was able to provide a corroborative account, describing an occasion when she was in the Waimata Valley where a significant number of UFO sightings took place. As it happens, the northern end of the Waimata Valley is only a few kilometres from where I was living at the time.

Beverlea and a couple of friends had heard about the UFO sightings occurring in the area and decided to go up the valley one evening for a spot of sky-watching. They parked on the side of the road and sometime later they heard a humming/buzzing sound approaching down the valley. At first the girls thought it was the distinct sound of a sheep truck making its way down the winding valley road, but wondered why they could not hear the familiar sound of gear changes as the truck rounded corners. From their vantage point, they saw not a sheep truck come into view down the valley, but an airborne object surrounded by a misty orange glow, emitting a constant buzzing hum. It passed close-by, causing their car to rise and fall on its axle as if by a magnetic attraction. On this same evening, another Waimata Valley resident I have interviewed saw this same object, at the same time from his home, and documented the sighting thus corroborating Beverlea's account.

Beverlea had a number of UFO sightings and encounters in the infamous Waimata Valley, and she became the first New Zealander to publicly describe her contact/abduction experiences and to explore them through regression with NZ UFO researcher and regression therapist, Bryan Dickeson. (However it was not until 2011 that I explored my own vivid memories of Gisborne flap experiences through regressive hypnosis.)

Some years after these Gisborne and East Coast incidents, I read US author and abduction researcher Budd Hopkins' book, *Missing Time,* and UK UFO researcher Jenny Randle's book, *Abduction.*

Through ongoing research, I discovered my experiences matched now-classic descriptions of contact experiences recounted by thousands of people worldwide. The state of paralysis and tingling limbs I experienced in the Tokomaru Bay incident is a common factor associated with encounters with UFOs and missing time, and is definitely not to be confused with the normal and relatively common sleep phenomenon called *sleep paralysis*.

The idea my life may now be linked to UFOs and their occupants, who could somehow place me in an altered state of awareness, made sense to me. After all, why would anyone suddenly go to sleep if they were expecting an earthquake to happen any second, or nod off in the middle of a terrifying experience? How could anyone not recall the full details of what had occurred?

In the meantime, my fears grew. Who could I express them to? I felt I had no choice but to internalise them for the time being.

Chapter 6

Overcoming the Fear

In 1983, we moved further north along the coast to another small community. UFO sightings were still occurring periodically in this region and while on a fishing trip, we had a daylight sighting of a large bright green light at close proximity, some six hundred metres from us. The light/object was larger than a bus and appeared to have risen out of the sea close to shore where the seabed drops away sharply into deeper water. It skimmed low over the water's surface, moving swiftly inland above the narrow coastal strip, hugging the contour of the land as it ascended over the hills and was gone.

On another evening, we sighted a large bright white light out over the sea that remained stationary in the sky for around twenty minutes from the time we began watching it. Eventually, a number of smaller white lights emerged from it and sped across the sky in different directions, the original light ascending until it disappeared from view. A friend staying with us at the time also witnessed the sighting and we considered possible explanations, finally deciding that "UFO" was the only logical one. However by the next morning he and Dave seemed almost embarrassed to have considered this option and promptly discarded it in favour of a flare, even though the features of the sighting just did not match up with the characteristics of a flare. It is intriguing how some people will staunchly clutch at any logical explanation, even if the details of that explanation are incorrect or illogical, rather than consider the possibility they have seen a UFO.

My two sons were born two years apart during the four years we lived in this area and intriguing occurrences of a different kind now emerged in my daily life, but at the time, I was unaware of the direct relationship these would have with future events.

In particular, unusual incidents happened prior to and around the time of the birth of my first son. During the pregnancy, I sometimes awoke at night to see small vibrant balls of light about the size of softballs, moving in the air above my body or crossing the room and passing through the wall.

But often I awoke to see a particular single ball of light, a larger electric-blue sphere about the size of a small soccer ball, which would float above my body for a few seconds before slowly fading from view. I had no idea what this light could be, but I felt no fear of it and believed the vibrant blue ball of light was observing me and communicating with my consciousness while I slept. I cannot explain how I came to this conclusion and can only say I sensed a familiarity with it.

Prior to the birth of my second son, life became much more difficult. I suffered from debilitating fatigue and ill-health from exposure to toxic organophosphate orchard sprays and I struggled daily to complete normal household chores. One day while sitting feeding my baby, I saw the spirit of an elderly gentleman materialise right in front of me, and he conveyed a message to my mind: "You must move away from here or you will not survive." Slowly he disappeared.

This was another wake-up call! For the rest of the day I thought about how unhappy I was living far from town, with no family or friends nearby and no opportunity to do the things in life I dreamed of; stagnant, living in a remote area simply because my partner enjoyed fishing and diving! By dinner time I had made the decision my children and I were moving – with or without him. If a benevolent spirit had taken the time to provide me with a sobering warning, I was not going to ignore it. Dave (somewhat reluctantly) and I made the decision to move closer to the city where I could receive better healthcare. The gentleman-spirit was right, and within months I was diagnosed with both a chronic illness and a life-threatening condition requiring surgery.

But following our move, it soon became evident I had not left the anomalous incidents behind and in fact, they now increased. Coping with this, combined with ongoing ill-health and raising two small boys became a constant struggle.

I began having foreknowledge of the appearance of UFOs in the sky, and one evening this was accompanied by precognition that a significant event (for me) would occur that night. A friend and I were driving home from a function when this insight came to me and I relayed it to her. As we drove up my driveway, we noticed neighbours were out on their decks looking seaward and skyward. Upon enquiring, we discovered that periodically throughout the evening they had watched several bright green lights moving erratically in the sky off the coastline, disappearing and reappearing elsewhere. One of the neighbours rang the police to report this and was told they had received numerous calls concerning the lights. They had ruled out marine flares, but offered no other explanation for them.

Thinking we had missed the light show, my friend and I made a cup of tea and sat out on the balcony in the summer air. It was then that a second specific thought flashed through my mind that we were about to see five lights, and I told my friend this. Within minutes, a group of three green lights in a triangular formation swiftly traversed the sky, travelling horizontally before performing an acute-angled descent towards the sea near an off-shore island. Exactly one minute later, two similar lights passed over, one directly behind the other, following exactly the same horizontal, then sharply downward course, making five lights.

However I found the fulfilment of the premonition disconcerting rather than gratifying, because as I watched the last two lights pass over, I experienced the profound and unexpected feeling that part of my awareness was there on the balcony, but at the same time, it was as if a part of me was up in the sky with the lights. A strange "dual awareness" is the best way to describe it; a feeling of "another self".

Equally perplexing were the powerful emotions of love and longing I had momentarily experienced for something intangible and unidentifiable, similar to the intense emotions of homesickness, or the grief of missing someone dearly. Why would anyone feel this way just from watching lights cross the sky? I could not rationalise these feelings at first, but it slowly dawned on me they matched the indefinable exchange of love, familiarity and happiness I'd shared with the night visitors in childhood. As I sat there, a realisation crept over me, making my hair stand on end and my heart race: I had experienced this feeling of a dual awareness before a number of times. Now it was clear: this was the *significant event* I had predicted.

More lights visited us. Not long after this event, Dave, the boys (then aged two and four years) and I were in our open-plan living area one evening, my youngest son sitting on Dave's knee while my eldest son played with toys on the floor. I looked up from the kitchen bench to see the now-familiar sight of softball-sized balls of light moving across the room.

"There are some lights in the room!" I blurted out spontaneously.

Looking directly at the position of the lights, my eldest son responded calmly, "Yes Mum, three green ones and two yellow ones." He was right! I was no longer alone in my perceptions. But within seconds our surroundings took on a strange atmosphere, with all sound seeming to recede into the distance. I recall seeing my partner and sons cease all movement, like statues, and then I remembered no more, as if I had blacked out while standing at the kitchen bench. How long this situation continued I do not know, but the next thing I recalled was a feeling of being woken up and seeing my eldest son begin moving again and smile at me; a strangely knowing smile. In that moment I felt a deep connection with my son that intimated a shared awareness of something beyond our day-to-day lives.

I now believe some kind of time-slip had occurred, where our consciousness transports itself elsewhere, in this instance, possibly with the balls of light that had appeared in the room. At the time I surmised they were souls, but today I would add "extraterrestrial intelligences" to the mix. In that time-space of what may have only been a few short seconds of absence, it is possible our consciousness spent a considerable length of time elsewhere. Several seconds passed before Dave and my youngest son began to move normally again, which indicated to me they had somehow been "switched off" by something I did not understand at that time, just as Dave and I were switched off when we saw a massive light illuminate a valley.

A similar incident occurred later that year when I was at an evening barbeque out in the countryside. While sitting on the balcony with a number of other people, I saw an exceptionally bright white light suddenly appear in the sky over a nearby hill and pointed it out to those around me. Immediately, everything seemed to move into slow motion and the loud rock music took on a muted sort of sound. The last thing I recall seeing is the light approaching speedily, and then – nothing.

In what seemed like the very next moment, I felt as if I had just woken up and for a second or two I stared around me in disbelief. Everyone had "turned to stone" – people dancing in the living room or chatting on the balcony were all in suspended animation while the music boomed on, and then as if released from a spell, they simultaneously burst into activity and conversation as if nothing had happened, while I sat shaken, wondering. The light had disappeared, but what had taken place in the interim?

Despite the routine of everyday life, other elements were occurring beneath the surface. I now sometimes awoke with recollections of (what I thought at the time were) strange lucid dreams involving small pale creatures with large heads, tiny mouths, over-sized dark eyes and spindly limbs. The dreams invariably involved non-verbal communications, activities, and instruction from these entities in the company of other people I did not know. I could recall substantial details about the environments I observed in the dreams and snippets of discussions that took place.

At times I dreamt of being with these entities walking down curved corridors with no visible source of light, although the air around us seemed to illuminate as we moved along. I recalled looking back and seeing darkness behind us, as if the group was walking in a bubble of light. The floor was black, dimpled and rubbery, silently cushioning each step like carpet underlay. The rooms I was taken to had stark white walls, with extraordinary equipment and technology such as I had never seen before, but I felt relaxed in the "dreams", as one would do in familiar surroundings.

At first I tried not to attach too much significance to them other than curiosity, that is, until I began to recall dreams in which my sons were present also; sometimes just one, sometimes both. Now I was really concerned, and this change in the previously innocuous dreams set me thinking about all the unusual occurrences in my life over the years. Fear crept back in now that my children were regular participants in the dreams too, and I felt there was nobody to share my thoughts with as there was just too much going on, and too frequently.

Things escalated when on a number of occasions I registered the fleeting, unnerving image in my mind of what I initially thought to be a skull with large black eye sockets.

A catalyst: another person's encounter, 1988

Around this time, I read a notice in the newspaper about a local UFO investigation group run by veteran New Zealand UFO researcher, (the late) Harvey Cooke, and I decided to attend a few meetings. Initially it was refreshing to be among people with enquiring minds, but my enthusiasm was dampened somewhat when I learnt they focused solely on the sightings or nuts-and-bolts side of the UFO subject. I had hoped to find someone in the group who had also experienced missing time in conjunction with the appearance of a bright anomalous light.

However one evening, to everyone's surprise, Harvey announced a young man would speak at the next meeting about what he believed to be an alien abduction he had experienced while working overseas. I looked forward to the next meeting, wondering if perhaps I would find some answers at last.

I arrived early! The young man was in his mid-twenties, clearly intelligent, and quietly spoken with a sincere manner. He described how he had worked at a restaurant near ski fields in British Columbia, Canada. Late one evening after closing time, he took the trash out the back behind the kitchen and spent a few minutes leaning on the fence enjoying the night sky in clear conditions. He noticed a bright light approaching in the sky and felt curiosity as it increased in size, coming straight towards him speedily and silently. This frightened him, and he was about to take cover when he discovered his arms and legs were becoming numb and tingly, until he could no longer move them. He remembered nothing further from that point onwards.

I squirmed in my seat.

His next recollection was of regaining consciousness lying on his back in the snow, freezing cold, with his boss shaking him and saying his name. Over an hour and a half had passed and everybody assumed he had gone home.

Since this incident, he had researched UFOs and alien abduction experiences, coming to the conclusion he had been targeted by a UFO and was likely abducted by an extraterrestrial species labelled "Greys", resulting in missing time. It was a traumatising, negative experience and he did not know what had taken place or whether it would happen again. Since this experience, he had been plagued by recurring dreams of being in strange unfamiliar rooms or surroundings and suffered "flashbacks" – unexpected vivid memories of entities with pale skin, over-sized heads and large dark eyes, an image he described as being similar to seeing *a skull.*

I froze in my seat.

As I listened to the young man describe his experience I felt as if we were the only two in the room. He was talking to me! Me alone! But nevertheless, I still felt too embarrassed and fearful to approach the young man after his talk and instead, hung around in the background, trying to catch fragments of his conversations with other people. I was not yet ready to own my experiences or even give them a name.

My thoughts went into overdrive as I travelled home that evening. Fear is a terrible thing. It can cripple and stunt us, sapping our vitality. Were my sons and I being abducted by aliens? If so, would these creatures always bring us back?

Because of the mix of both relief and fear engendered in me by this young man's account, it was some time before I could buck up the courage to make a date to talk to Harvey Cooke about my own experiences. Despite Harvey being friendly and welcoming on the day, my palms sweated, my heart pounded, and my mouth dried up – those familiar symptoms – and I feared disbelief. Several hours later I had given Harvey a comprehensive run-down, like floodgates opening. It was a tremendous relief to be able to finally get those innermost fears and pent-up emotions off my chest.

It was not until several years later that I ordered my first book on alien contact, *Secret Life: Firsthand Accounts of UFO Abductions*, by Dr. David Jacobs. When at long last it arrived, I took one look at the cover and burst into tears. A shaft of light illuminated the silhouette of a child-like, spindly figure, and there were those apt words, *secret life.* I realised this was exactly the kind of life I had been leading, one in which I was afraid to reveal an integral part of myself to others.

Although in retrospect today, I can identify with some of the details abductees provide when recounting their experiences, the general nature of their accounts is often negative, sometimes concluding the Greys are bad. I believe my fear was amplified by these kinds of accounts that were prevalent at the time. This did nothing to alleviate my fears and I did not want to accept these traumatic and frightening circumstances might be happening to me or my sons.

But as is my nature, I began to analyse my position: certainly I had experienced some frightening incidents in early adulthood, but more recently my experiences and vivid dream memories had engendered curiosity and feelings of love, rather than fear.

From the time of the terrifying experience with a huge orb of light on the Hawkes Bay highway, I had moved some distance along the difficult but intriguing road of experience, discovery, and understanding. I had witnessed the beauty of coloured lights floating serenely near my body, and had dreamed of meetings in "alien" environments with advanced technology. Was all of this so intimidating? Whatever was happening to me, I had to admit I had remained safe and unharmed, as had my children.

The skull revealed

Things came to a head one evening when Dave and I were watching television after the boys had gone to bed. I suddenly became aware of the skull-like image in my mind, which I had seen on a number of previous occasions, and felt a surge of anger that I could not identify it or get rid of it. It was as if something wanted to make contact with me, and in my mind I asked, *who are you? What do you want? If you are real and not my imagination, then do something that will prove it.*

There were a few seconds of silence, followed by a loud crash in the hallway. Dave and I leapt to our feet and ran to see what had happened and were enormously relieved to find it was only a mirror that had fallen onto the wooden floor. The cord must have broken or the hook pulled out of the wood panel, and we fell against the wall laughing at ourselves and the expressions on our faces, our hearts still pounding from the fright and sudden exertion.

But when Dave picked up the mirror, he remembered that a couple of years earlier he had replaced the cord with a piece of wire. It was still intact and the hook was still in the wall! *Something* had lifted the mirror up and off the picture-hook, dropping it on the floor without the mirror shattering! A chill ran through me and I retreated to the bedroom to gather my thoughts.

I closed my eyes and the skull image was immediately in my mind again, but slowly developing detail like a foggy window clearing. There was the face of what I believed to be a "Grey". But at that moment, instead of terror, I registered thoughts and feelings of immense love. A stream of images, emotions, sounds and impressions filled my mind and senses, as if a door to a long-forgotten, yet familiar reality had finally re-opened. There was an instantaneous realisation I had known and loved these entities from childhood, and warm memories of small glowing figures standing by my bed flooded through me. The recognition was complete and over-whelming, and all fear left me.

Chapter 7

Reality Checks

My adult mind began to reassess past childhood situations, and my thoughts waxed and waned between curiosity as to the agenda of these entities and disbelief they could have any interest in me.

My friend Harvey Cooke put me in touch with a wonderful lady, Daisy Kirkby, one of New Zealand's first researchers of cases of alien abductions in the 1970s, who remains a treasured friend of mine to this day. For a number of years Daisy produced and edited a newsletter called *Outer Space Connections,* held public meetings, and helped many people to come to terms with and better understand their contact encounters. I was able to discuss my experiences with Daisy and begin to assimilate the reality of these contacts into my day-to-day life. Just knowing there was someone with considerable understanding and expertise who I could contact was reassuring.

During the late 1980s and the 1990s, several life-changing events transpired for me including major medical operations and the end of my first marriage, but despite obstacles and difficulties, I still felt as if an unseen guiding hand was on my shoulder.

Running simultaneously over these years, five differing and distinct incidents occurred, which opened my mind to the possibility the "visitors" in my dreams and experiences were influencing my life in a constructive and deeply purposeful way.

Circles in the mud
1989, age 34 years

I awoke one morning with recollection of standing on the wooden floor in the hallway of our home in the middle of the night, dressed in my nightgown and in an ultra-relaxed state. My eldest son was with me, along with a group of three short entities, which I now surmised to be Greys.

After some discussion regarding my younger son (which I retained full memory of), they levitated us a few centimetres above the floor before transiting straight through the glass front door. The group floated us down the road, and I recall passing shrubbery and letterboxes and eventually floating along another short road, but not really registering where we actually were at all. Despite this relaxed state, or perhaps because of it, I was amused by the fact I could cycle my legs in the air as we glided along, but I also perceived the accompanying Greys were watchful and anxious to move quickly. My last memory was of drifting upright over water towards a disc-shaped craft on tripod legs.

The next day the old fears returned and I felt far from relaxed about these recalled details and struggled to define them. They shook me emotionally, throwing me back into a state of fear because the safety of my children was paramount to me.

Two days later, I received a phone call from a friend of mine in the village where I lived, one of only a handful of people I had confided in concerning my UFO sightings and associated memories. A few seconds into our conversation, I felt as if my stomach had dropped through the floor as the dream memories were triggered and flooded back. The conversation went like this:

S. Hello.

J. Hi Suzy. I see your mates have been to see you!

S. Hi “J”. What do you mean?

J . Just joking! Haven’t you been down to Beach Grove yet? I thought you would have been one of the first people down there.

S. Why? What’s happening?

J. There are these circles in the mud. Haven’t you heard? Maybe something landed there in the water! I knew you would be interested and I wondered what you thought of them. You should go down and take a look. [Silence] Are you there?

S. [Pause] Yes, I’m here.

J. Are you alright? You sound upset.

S. [Pause] I’m fine thanks.

J. OK. Well get down there soon before they disappear into the mud. Bye!

Instant panic! J’s description of the location matched my recollections. My legs shook as I realised Beach Grove was just a couple of hundred metres down the road from our house, a short road that led to a boat ramp at the shallow harbour edge. But I could not bring myself to venture near Beach Grove, or the circles. (This is a decision I have regretted, as a photo of the circles would have supported my description of the incident. My friend told me a number of people took photographs of the circles at the time. Many years later when I began writing this book, I advertised in the community newsletter seeking a photograph, but without success, as people had passed away or moved elsewhere.)

For weeks, every time I thought of the circles I felt sick with worry. Sometime later my friend wrote a description for me of what she had seen:

"G. and I were on the walkway, heading down the hill towards Beach Grove. It was low tide and we saw a lot of people out on the mudflats. We could see these circles in the mud and people were poking at them and we thought – what on earth are they doing? So we went down to find out and got talking to people. There were three circles, each about 1.5 metres in diameter, spaced about 8 metres apart, forming an equilateral triangle that was positioned just to the left of the boat-ramp, maybe 15 metres off-shore. Each of the circles was a raised, shallow dome of mud. It was as if the soft mud had been sucked up and hardened by something – heat or pressure maybe – because people were trying to chip them or cut into them, but their hammers and tools just bounced off! It was as if the mud had been baked. What could leave marks like this? People were taking photos and joking that a UFO must have landed, and that's when I thought of you Suzy!"

Did the circles indicate my dream recall was in fact reality, or were the circles just coincidental and attributable to something natural or conventional? If my memories were reality, then had the contact been designed as a way of proving to me I was truly experiencing contact with other-worldly entities? Was an undeniable physical trace left to shock me into acceptance?

Going public: a radio interview
1990, age 35 years

On one occasion, my see-sawing doubts about the accuracy of my recollections influenced my thinking with unfortunate results.

My friend Daisy Kirkby had recently featured in a magazine article about the abduction phenomenon, and she had asked me to contribute a brief account of experiencing missing time, which was published in a text box alongside the article. I used the pseudonym "Carol", and described the 1975 Hawkes Bay incident.

My elderly friend Harvey Cooke phoned me a week or so later, to ask if I would be willing to take part in a talkback radio interview with him on the subjects of UFOs and alien contact experiences. My first reaction was to decline, because I did not feel sufficiently confident to speak publicly and was concerned about being subjected to ridicule and disbelief. However Harvey continued applying pressure, trying to convince me to join him on the programme in a week's time. In the end I reluctantly agreed, but worried whether I was doing the right thing. However after some thought, I felt if it could help others who were experiencing the same then I should do it. Naively, I assumed I would at least be treated with courtesy by the interviewer.

My intuition or gut feeling however, was strongly telling me not to be involved, but I did not listen to it.

In the interim, the boys and I went away for a weekend to stay in a lakeside cabin. The boys shared a room, leaving me with a room of my own. At some stage in the early hours of the second morning I awoke and stared into the dim light, wondering if one of my boys had called my name. Suddenly, three Grey entities transitioned smoothly through the exterior wall of my bedroom. This was not a dream! Two of them remained still, while the third now-familiar figure quickly glided forward and passed his hand over my forehead, and I suddenly felt relaxed as he began to communicate.

Here my memory became sketchy the next day, but I recalled he warned me against doing *something* because there would be a negative consequence if I did. I recalled feeling a little indignant that he seemed to be telling me what to do, and I maintained an opposing position about something, whatever that was. Disappointment and frustration emanated from him, and he eventually stepped back and conveyed a message into my mind, which I did clearly recall: "You have made your choice." They passed silently through the wall and were gone and I must have immediately lapsed into sleep.

The next morning I churned over my scantly recalled details, focusing only on the perceived negative consequence. What choice had I made? Was I being threatened? I became increasingly apprehensive about what the circumstances might relate to and whether it involved my children. There seemed to be no explanation, and I gave absolutely no thought to the fact it might relate to the forthcoming radio interview.

The day of the programme arrived and the producer called to inform me that they would interview Harvey first, followed by questions and comments from listeners. The female talkback host would then phone my home and question me about the nature of my experiences. Because of my location, I was unable to get radio reception to listen to the programme, so I would be answering questions without knowing what had already been covered by the participants.

Being a novice at that time in dealing with (some members of) the media, I expected the interviewer would ask sensible, relevant questions. How wrong I was! I think my part in the programme was just the sensation factor to raise the listener ratings. It seemed to me there was a distinctly negative agenda around the image she was creating in people's minds, with her comments to me about aliens and people like me. I bumbled through a few responses until she asked me to recount an experience and I chose the 1975 event of missing time, which had recently appeared in the magazine. Out of the blue, she began ridiculing me, accusing me of being a hoaxer, wasting their time by copying the previous caller! The phone went dead.

I was incensed! How dare she invite me on her programme only to rudely cut me off! It was a real slap-in-the-face because I had agreed to do the interview in good faith, willing to be truthful and open about my experiences publicly for the first time, but now I wanted a hole to open in the ground and swallow me up. It was distressing to be treated this way by someone who lacked any broad knowledge of the topic, and who had no concept of what I had been through in my attempts to unravel the mystery of these memories or visitations. I had drawn on immense inner strength to enable me to lead a family life, cope with ill-health and work as a professional, while also coming to terms with the notion of extraterrestrial contact.

I felt as if I had been knocked flat and couldn't concentrate on anything. Harvey rang me later and explained what had happened. Just prior to my short and embarrassing stint on the radio, a woman had rung in calling herself "Carol", describing my experience outlined in the magazine contribution word-for-word, and claiming it as her own! Harvey, an old hand at media interviews, told me in his usual cheery manner not to worry about it, but after many years of interviews he was hardened and resilient. Days went by. The "why me" syndrome set in.

Then as I sat on the sofa one day, in the quiet of the moment a thought dropped into my mind, not gently, but like an explosion. This was the negative consequence! *The interview* was the situation the

Grey had tried to warn me about. Thoughts bounced around in my head. How did they know so much about what goes on in my life? My future life! Why would they single me out and offer a warning?

I recalled the Grey's words, "You have made your choice", and perhaps they respected this free choice and could not force me to act upon their warning. Perhaps they were allowing me to learn a salutary but unpleasant lesson, thus they had erased any direct association with the interview from my memory in order for me to discover an important fact: I was not ready to speak publicly on these issues yet. I needed to grow in confidence, resilience and knowledge, as well as recover my health first. If there were extraterrestrials seeking to help and guide me, I was now ready to sit up and listen. I wanted to discover more about what these contacts meant and how they might relate to my future and that of my children.

Changing my name
1996, age 41 years

Not long after my first marriage came to a close, I was sitting quietly in my living room one morning reading the newspaper when a thought, unbidden, entered my mind in the form of an instruction: *change your name.*

This was surprising, something I had never thought about before. Again, as if somebody was privy to my thought process, the name "Hansen" emerged in my mind. This was an option I would not have considered, but I knew my Grandfather was born with the surname Hansen. His birth father died young and when his mother remarried, his stepfather adopted him (as was a custom back then) and he took on a different surname.

It seemed like a good idea. A new start! And so after conferring with my sons, six weeks later I legally changed my surname to Hansen by Deed Poll. It felt right, as if the vibe of my name had been changed to another frequency, like tuning a radio to a particular station.

However the story does not end there. Eighteen months later in 1998, I began to receive mail addressed to a "Mr. T. Hansen". What a coincidence! I didn't know anyone of this name and so I asked around the neighbourhood and heard of a man who was building a house at the end of our rural road, and I wondered if it was his mail. I found the building site and delivered a bundle of mail to a man called Thomas Hansen. My first reaction when I saw him was one of surprise, quite profound and unexplainable emotional shock, because I felt sure I had met him somewhere before – a tall thin man with a quick sense of humour. He asked if I would mind dropping off any further mail as he had not yet put up a rural mailbox. Over time, we got to know each other and eventually began going out together, and in 1999, Hansen married Hansen.

Had I not been "given" the concept of changing my name, and even what that name should be, I may never have met my second husband, who has been fully supportive of my involvement in the UFO field. I don't think it was coincidence.

ET shows up at a conference
1997, age 42 years

The UFO contact fraternity in New Zealand was very small in the 1990s and word soon got around about my experiences and memories. I was approached by Jonathan Eisen, an investigative journalist, former radio talkback host and founding editor of a magazine called *Uncensored*, who asked me to speak at his International UFO Symposium held in Auckland, New Zealand.

My good friends Harvey Cooke and Daisy Kirkby were also invited to speak, and I met another New Zealand experiencer, Alec Newald, who was also a speaker, along with (the late) Capt. Bruce Cathie, former NZ pilot and author. I think it was a pretty good local line-up to balance the impressive overseas contingent of speakers.

I met with Jon and his wife Katherine some months beforehand to discuss the conference and my small part in it and just as I was about to leave, Jon threw a parting shot at me in jest: "Don't forget to tell those ETs we want to see them in person when you speak! That'll be real proof!"

My stomach lurched. I'd already had a premonition several weeks earlier that not only would I be invited to speak at the symposium, but that a Grey would be present in some way to assist me. However I could not bring myself to believe that second half of the presentment, even though the first half had already transpired; surely I must have imagined it or misconstrued the message. I convinced myself it would *never* happen. I had always considered myself a level-headed and practical person. It was absurd to even think about it.

Ironically, my speech was entitled, "A Balancing Act: Integrating spiritual, psychic and UFO/Contact Experiences into Normal Life".

On the day of my speech at the conference I was very nervous and suffering from back pain. The IT assistant fitted my microphone, clipped the accompanying wire and box inside the back of my trouser waistband, and it was time to step onto the stage. Once in the middle, I looked out at the large audience and my mind went momentarily blank. All I was aware of in that moment was that my nervous breathing was restricted by the IT equipment, as my trousers were now too tight. Therefore my first words to the audience were, "Gosh! It's hard to talk with a microphone down your pants!"

This brought the house down. I relaxed after that and surprisingly, my speech flowed reasonably well from there.

In those days I had only two slides to project on screen during my speeches, side and front view pencil drawings of the face of a Grey. Just as the first image came up on screen I became aware in my peripheral, or perhaps my intuitive vision, that a Grey had materialised and was standing to the right of the screen, looking out at the audience in the large university auditorium. I froze momentarily and my voice faltered, but I managed to pick it up again and carry on (this point can be detected in the video of my speech). As I did so, he faded from view. Nobody in the auditorium was pointing, shouting or running towards (or away from) the stage, so I rationalised that either I had imagined it, or I was the only person who saw this.

After the speech, I left the auditorium and talked to a group of people who had followed me out into the foyer, before managing to escape into the restroom. An elderly, neatly dressed woman followed me in and asked if she could speak with me. Her words made my hair stand on end:

"Sorry to disturb you Sue, but I'd like to tell you about something I saw during your speech. Of course you probably already know what it was and what I'm going to say. When you put the first drawing up on screen, I saw a small pale figure on the stage, like those little Greys."

My mouth went dry and trying to sound calm and nonchalant, I replied, "That's interesting. Where did you see it standing?"

"It was just to the left (my right) of the screen. It was only there briefly and then it slowly just disappeared from view. But you know this already, don't you?" she replied with a knowing look on her face.

And so it was shown to me that I had not imagined the message of the appearance of a Grey at the symposium to help me with an inaugural conference speech, and if I wasn't keen to believe it, they would have someone else confirm it to me. This lady and her husband became friends and kept in touch with me over the years. They both had a long history of involvement with spiritual and environmental groups, and this was the first of several ways in which they helped me out by heeding a message from another realm.

Some months later, when I was a solo parent with a limited income, a van pulled into our rural driveway one afternoon and out hopped the lady's elderly husband. He gave no reason for his unexpected visit, a six hour drive from his home, other than to say he had something he needed to do. The next day he chopped wood, tidied up our property and completed fix-it jobs. His visit was refreshing for the boys and I and we were disappointed he could not stay a while longer.

The morning he left, he told me he had been given a message from spirit that the boys and I were in need of urgent help and encouragement, and this was why he had come to see us. He passed an envelope through the van window and cheerily told me not to open it until after he had gone. When I did, I found two crisp one hundred dollar notes inside.

The bruise
1999, age 43 years

An acquaintance of mine has recall of contact incidents and encounters onboard alien craft. She rang early one morning just prior to leaving for the airport to fly overseas and quickly told me she remembered being on a craft with Grey entities the previous night, and that she had seen me there too.

She recalled sketchy details of the Greys inoculating a large group of people, pressing an instrument of some kind on their arms or legs in places where the mark it left would generally be unnoticed. That morning she awoke with recollection of the night's activities and found a circular bruise two and a half centimetres in diameter, positioned high up on the back/underside of one arm. She noticed it when raising her arm to brush her hair.

The bruise contained a ring of dark pin-pricks near the circumference, with another smaller ring towards the centre, and a single larger pin-prick in the middle. She was adamant I would have an identical bruise but I had not noticed anything when I showered earlier, so I put it to one side. It was the weekend and I had a busy day ahead. But later, when we were getting dressed to go out, my husband said, "What's that on your leg?"

High on the back of my leg was an identical bruise with the same pattern of markings she described, which we photographed and documented. The bruise faded quickly and was painless. This was an entirely new turn of events – physical evidence of a different kind to the anomalous circles left in the mud.

Cheating death

Throughout my life I have come close to death five times, through accident, illness, and assault. On each occasion, a timely (almost miraculous) intervention of some kind has happened. Unfortunately, not all were so successful – minutes before I had a near-fatal car accident, I was conversing with a group of people when I heard a spirit woman's voice say (clairaudiently), "Go now! You have to go now!" My upbringing had taught me not to walk away when someone is speaking to me, so I waited until the conversation was over, and then left. Fifty metres down the road, my car was hit by a vehicle with a drunken driver. Clearly, this one was not meant to have happened.

I have been told by health professionals that some of the injuries I have sustained should have killed me. My chiropractor once said to me prophetically, "Somebody wants you alive Suzy."

In 1991 I had a major operation for a life-threatening condition, and as I lay on the operating table waiting for the anaesthetist to knock me out, I suddenly became aware of a presence in the theatre. I actually asked the medical team to wait a moment while I turned my head to look behind me. In the corner I saw three spirits, a man and two women, who assured me I would be fine, before fading from view.

Is the fact I have survived near-death several times merely coincidence? Like a movie stunt person with "nine lives"? There have been too many unusual "coincidences" surrounding these life-threatening incidents for me to believe this is so. Over the years I have spoken with other experiencers who have cheated death on a number of occasions through extra-ordinary interventions, or turns of fate.

Chapter 8

Threats from Agents and Support from an Entity

Following the 1997 New Zealand UFO Symposium I received invites to speak at other international UFO conferences, and over the last seventeen years of public speaking I have accumulated some wonderful memories. UFO research attracts a colourful mix of characters and there are always stories to tell afterwards of both pleasant and disconcerting interactions with speakers and delegates. On occasions I have had premonitions about certain events or people I would meet, while at other times I have had to deal with situations about which I had no forewarning, but from which I learnt timely lessons.

The late Lt. Colonel (USAF Ret.) Wendelle C. Stevens was among the international speakers at the Auckland Symposium. On the evening the conference ended and after returning to where I was to stay the night with a friend, I had the feeling someone involved with the conference was urgently trying to contact me. This intuition was so intense that my friend set about phoning a number of people, including Jonathan Eisen the conference organiser, who told us he had been ringing around trying to find out where I was staying. Wendelle Stevens was flying home in a few hours and wished to speak with me.

I contacted Wendelle immediately and we talked for half an hour or so, during which time he strongly expressed concerns for my safety. He was impressed by the amount of detail I was able to describe of technology and the environments I had seen onboard craft, as well as other aspects of my experiences and he commented, "You've really been there, haven't you Sue." It was a statement, not a question.

Wendelle believed I needed to protect myself by continuing to go public with my experiences and by completing a book about them. He warned of covert groups and elements working against experiencers and abductees by intimidating and silencing them to prevent the public from hearing about contact issues. This was worrying, even though I had heard rumours of such things. He offered to put my name forward as a speaker at the annual International UFO Congress in Laughlin, Nevada, USA, of which he was a committee member. The Congress facilitators, Bob and his wife (the late) Teri Brown invited me to speak at the Congress the following year in 1998, however due to illness I could not attend and was invited again in 1999.

On the first day of the 8th UFO Congress I found myself in the lift alongside a paunchy guy wearing a badge with “FBI” on it – not at all like the muscular agents you see in the movies. Nevertheless, naive panic swept over me. I wasn’t sure whether to be impressed or scared and couldn’t wait to tell my husband, but instead of being surprised he rolled his eyes and led me into a room where sales tables were set up, and where there were dozens of fake FBI badges for sale at a stall.

The UFO Congress ran for eight days and on the first day of the conference my husband and I were befriended by a couple in their mid-forties, who said they were Mexican. We sat together on the odd occasion to listen to other speakers and chatted with them in the foyer throughout the week. They seemed relaxed and casually friendly.

The couple approached me after my speech and requested a private interview, stating they were very interested in my information and would like the opportunity to discuss it with me in more depth. I was aware other speakers were holding private meetings with people and so, yes, naively again, I invited them to come to my hotel room the next day, rather than meeting them in a public café, which would have been preferable. Initially, the first half-hour of our get-together was quite pleasant, exchanging viewpoints and discussing the UFO field in general. I noticed the woman said very little, allowing her husband to do most of the talking, however she was very attentive.

The second half-hour took on a slightly different atmosphere, with the gentleman becoming quite emphatic about some issues and slightly derogatory towards experiencers like myself, at the same time asking probing questions about my contact encounters. I began to feel decidedly uncomfortable and limited my answers. Whereas in the beginning he had encouraged me to do much of the talking, now it was he who was controlling the tone and direction of the conversation. All my senses were now on overdrive and I tried politely, but unsuccessfully, to bring the meeting to a close.

During the third half-hour his conversation became downright sinister and disturbing. Although I desperately wanted to reach the hotel room door to open it, they had positioned their chairs with their backs towards the door, thus effectively blocking my way in the small room. In this last half-hour the male subjected me to subtle threats and ridicule, while the woman supported his statements with the odd negative comment, overt body language and facial expressions. Try as I may, I felt strangely unable to motivate physical movement or mentally combat the situation. I had to work hard to maintain control of my mental capacities and I suspect now of course, that the woman may have been exerting a form of mind control over me, hence her relative silence.

The male told me I "knew too much" and warned me that if I did not return to New Zealand and give up the idea of speaking publicly about my contact experiences, "something bad" might happen to me. He banged his fist on the small table on a number of occasions, pointed his index finger in my face and raised his voice.

But it was when he said menacingly, "You've got two sons haven't you? You wouldn't want anything bad to happen to them, would you?" that I managed to roll over the end of the bed, lurch past them and open the door, ordering them to leave the room. They departed, but not before making further threats about my safety and that of my family.

After they had gone, I took the lift to the lobby outside the lecture theatre, where there was a break between speakers. My hands and legs shook like jelly. My husband was chatting with another experiencer who was also a speaker at the Congress, and as I approached them she exclaimed she had been looking for me to warn me about something. Apparently a US remote viewer and former military person also present at the Congress had warned her he had recognised two "agents" in the audience. They were posing as a Mexican couple and would likely spread disinformation and possibly try to intimidate the experiencers speaking at the conference. Too late, they had already got to me. I did not see them again on the last remaining day of the Congress.

At that moment, I made up my mind the risk to my children's safety was too great if I continued public speaking and I would return home and melt into oblivion. It was devastating because by now I had developed a deep sense of commitment to the contact phenomenon and to supporting others experiencing contact as well.

But it wasn't over yet. After the Congress, my husband and I decided to hire a car to do a spot of sightseeing before flying back to New Zealand. The car rental firm sent a female employee to pick us up at the hotel and take us to the depot to pick up the car, and an odd-looking man was seated in the front passenger seat of the pick-up truck. He was mostly bald with only sparse blonde wispy hair, and his high-necked polo jersey looked old-fashioned and inappropriate on a hot day in Nevada. The gentleman did not join in the light conversation and neither of us felt the urge to make conversation with him. His demeanour was peculiar, sitting slightly hunched and staring straight ahead. Our driver ignored him entirely, directing her conversation only to my husband, while I sat in despondent thought about my situation.

Within a short time however, I perceived a powerful and somehow-familiar emanation of energy from this man, but disregarded it, putting it down to the fact I was upset and jangled.

We arrived at the depot where the driver left the truck to arrange the paperwork for our rental vehicle. The atmosphere in the truck was absolutely electric by now and my attention became fixed on the back of the man's head, as if I knew something was about to happen. Even my husband was still, frozen in a position half-way through picking up his camera from the floor, and he too was staring expectantly at the man.

The gentleman slowly turned his body in the seat until he was looking directly at me, his eyes large and the most startling bright pale blue. I heard him say clearly and authoritatively:

"They always look after their own."

The man immediately got out of the truck and walked through the door of the car rental building, leaving us stunned. Gathering our wits, we raced into the building, but after a thorough search of the office area and restrooms we could not find him anywhere. Other people we questioned had not seen anyone enter the room after the driver, who did not know what had become of the gentleman either. It was as if he had walked through the doorway and simply vanished. But it was not until afterwards that we both realised the man's mouth had not moved when he "spoke" and that my husband had also registered his words.

Taking recent events into account, we interpreted his statement as being some kind of reassurance. There was the added curious implication with his words, *their own*, that I was *one of them*, which set me wondering. It seemed to us that like the incident at the New Zealand conference the year before, when a Grey had appeared to me on stage to bring reassurance and strength, this unusual man had appeared with a supportive message designed to keep me on-track, at a crucial time when I was considering never speaking about my contacts again.

I am not alone in this experience with what I now believe to have been a transgenic or hybrid entity – I am not sure which – a genetically engineered Grey/human entity that can walk amongst us without appearing too noticeably different from us. Many experiencers worldwide report having contact in their day-to-day lives with human-like transgenic or hybrid beings. They are usually reported to be pale-skinned and of slight build, with bright blue or dark eyes and often dressed in clothes that are inappropriate, old-fashioned, or even bizarre. Their hair is generally sparse and wispy, or they wear an obvious wig.

I returned to New Zealand and discussed the "agent incident" with my family, because if they felt fearful, I would respect their wishes and cease public speaking. After deliberating on the issues, we decided I should continue my work.

However as the years have passed, my family and I have still been subjected to periodic harassment and intimidation in our private life, in relation to me speaking at conferences, or on occasions after being interviewed by the media about UFO sightings.

Both prior to and after speaking at the Auckland Symposium and the UFO Congress, and after publicity had been released about the speakers, I received anonymous phone calls for months on end. Our house was broken into on one occasion but nothing taken, just unmistakable and deliberate signs left that someone had been there, including objects left in full view on the pantry shelf in a symbolically sinister way.

On one occasion when I lectured in Australia, I found a mysterious debt had appeared on my credit card, meaning I could not access money and had to borrow funds from the conference organiser. While waiting at Sydney airport to fly back to New Zealand I noticed a woman with a clipboard approach a security officer. They both looked at the clipboard, and then began to study the sea of faces around them, finally whispering to each other and settling their gaze on me. Out of a couple of hundred travellers in the departure lounge, the woman then approached only me to complete a questionnaire about how I had accessed money while in Australia. Was my photograph on her clipboard? I saw this as a deliberate act of intimidation – someone wanted me to know just how far they could push me, including tampering with my finances.

On another occasion after speaking at an Australian conference, I spent a day shopping in Sydney and ordered a coffee in an arcade café. While sitting at a table, I experienced the powerful feeling that someone was looking at me from behind. I spun around and almost instantly a man took a photo of me, smiled with a sneering expression and disappeared into the crowd. After immediately doing a reality check by looking around and establishing there was nobody else in the direction he had pointed the camera, apart from a wall, I deduced he had indeed photographed me.

A week or so later back in New Zealand, I received a phone call from a man with an American accent, seeking to discuss his alleged alien contact experiences with me. Very soon into the conversation he claimed he had been threatened by a covert group, which he alleged was capable of atrocities against experiencers and abductees, and commented that sort of thing could happen to me. Out of the blue he then recounted a little story about how he had been at a mall in Sydney recently where he stopped for a coffee at an arcade café, and someone from this covert global group took a photo of him. I was now on red-alert. He said he knew he would be "targeted" now and casually asked me if I had experienced something similar lately. I hung up.

On a number of occasions our house has been watched by men in white vehicles (common to private surveillance companies). The neighbours on both sides of our property in a rural area independently told us they had seen the occupants of these suspicious vehicles watching our home, thus confirming our own observations. Sometimes the vehicles pulled into our driveway, shining headlights on the house in the early hours of the morning, waking and frightening the children, before driving away. This kind of activity has continued up until as recently as 2012, following media interviews in which I commented on specific UFO sightings in New Zealand that I had investigated involving not only the sighting of actual craft, but entities associated with the encounters.

A close friend of mine has said to me many times, "But Suzy, why would anyone bother to harass you? You're no threat to anyone. Why would they bother sitting in cars watching your house? What's the point? It's juvenile!"

Yes, it is, but it happens nevertheless, the aim being to intimidate people into silence.

If I was the only person working in UFO and contact research that had experienced this, my friend's comments may well be valid, however I am not. There are plenty of contactees, abductees, experiencers, researchers, witnesses, scientists, military whistleblowers and professionals worldwide connected to the UFO subject who have experienced similar. Clearly, back in the 1990s at least, what we were publicising was a threat to somebody.

Fortunately there are happy outcomes from speaking at conferences too. In 2003 I spoke at the Hidden Truths Conference in Perth, Australia. Prior to leaving for the conference I had some intuitive thoughts and told my husband I felt my speech would not actually be absorbed by the audience for some reason and that in effect, I would be speaking to only two people.

On the morning I was scheduled to speak, the presenter before me was challenged by members of the audience resulting in some angry exchanges and raised voices on both sides. By the time it was my turn, I felt many in the audience had switched off, their thoughts elsewhere. The mood seemed heavy, but I delivered my speech and answered a few questions nevertheless.

The microphone was passed to an elderly couple, who had been standing up in the middle of the auditorium to attract my attention. The woman outlined that they had a young-adult daughter who had divulged her emerging memories of contact experiences to them. They were outraged, as her accounts went against their belief systems and terrible arguments ensued between them. Their daughter described her experiences with entities as positive, but they saw them as evil. The couple were convinced their daughter was mentally ill and wanted her assessed under mental health criteria. She left home and they'd had no contact with her for over two years.

The couple read advertising about the conference and noted an experiencer would be speaking, and they had come along with the sole intention of giving me a piece of their mind, angry that people like me speak publicly, believing me to be a charlatan leading people like their daughter astray. However during my speech they were shocked to recognise similar details to those their daughter had described. My description of the ridicule I had faced, even from some family members, had touched a raw nerve with them, and they realised their daughter had been courageous in approaching them. They had quietly conferred with each other during my presentation and now wondered if they had made a terrible mistake by rejecting her accounts. The lady conceded they had not investigated the subject as their daughter had requested of them.

You could have heard a pin drop in the auditorium – everyone was listening now. The elderly couple held onto each other, crying and telling me how my speech had changed their perspectives. It was as if they were in shock, devastated, and comprehending the damage to family relationships. The elderly lady said all they wanted now was to find their daughter, welcome her home and *listen* to her.

As predicted, I had flown thousands of kilometres to another country in order to help two elderly parents, and hopefully, their daughter.

Part Two

Contacts

"The mind, once expanded by a new experience,
never returns to its original dimensions."

Oliver Wendell Holmes

Note:

- Part Two contains excerpts from regression transcripts in italics. S. = Suzy, and R. = Regression Therapist.
- All footnotes are written by Dr. Rudy Schild.
- Throughout the remainder of this book all communication I describe between myself and the entities is telepathic, although to prevent the constant repetition of this word I have used terms familiar to the reader to signify communication, such as "conveyed", "responded", "said", etc.

Chapter 9

Soul Origin:
Pathway to a New Life

1989, age 35 years

I had memory of a time before I entered this life. I recalled having no body and instead, I was in the form of a soul, a bright ball of purple light, consciously aware of my surroundings. A group of other souls and a council of wise beings had met with me to help me to plan my new life and prepare me for various tasks I would carry out in it.

Twenty years later, I explored this memory through regressive hypnosis and a broader, more detailed account emerged of my soul's transition into this life, which contained this brief memory. The material in this chapter questions the concept of absolute freewill. Guidance might be a better word.[1]

Awakening in the Field of Consciousness

My soul-source, or essence, the tiny spark of energy that would eventually become my soul, existed in peace, calm, stillness, without a physical form; in stillness, yet with a feeling of awareness and eternal movement of consciousness. Like a cell, alone, but connected; part of consciousness, but individual within it.[2] No sense of awareness of time passing, but nevertheless, a feeling of endlessness, eternity, antiquity. Resting, but awaiting a purpose.

---

[1] My own suggestion, similar to guidance, would be "alignment", as in "alignment with the purpose of the universe". The purpose of the universe is for life to emerge and thrive, and thereby contribute to the appreciation of the Creator, who is in the Jung collective consciousness, and is, in the situation described by Suzy, seen to be actively guiding the Universe (which I also understand as the Universe of Universes.)

[2] This is a terrific description of the soul state between lives.

An awareness of something quietly seeking, stirred within my soul-source. From the vast Field of Consciousness, it sensed strands of energy approaching, like little electric charges. There was a feeling of being targeted, awakened, given options. My soul-source felt a gentle pull, a desire to reach towards them. It was time; time to become active again in some way, to choose an experience, a life.

It experienced conscious movement, like a floating mind, a separation from within the greater Field of Consciousness. Aroused from rest, it examined the approaching frequencies, or life choices.

This process of examination had occurred many times before, where sometimes options were not considered, were passed over. The soul-source consistently sought a "match", a resonance, a harmony of vibration and commitment. But now an attraction occurred. A call. [3] My soul-source was drawn to only two of the several available tingling frequencies and began accessing just these strands – possible future existences or lives, preparing to make a choice.

The first strand (life option) involved a long period of time spent on a planet where life is just evolving, just beginning. The second strand offered the choice to assist on a planet where life already exists and has evolved to some extent.

The electric tingle from these choices prompted my soul-source to ascertain which of the two it was drawn to the most. It sensed terrible hardship and a gruelling existence in the first strand:

S. *One life would be, in my perception, almost a fruitless life as a developing life-form of limited physical or intellectual effect, but it would be a huge* (soul) *commitment nevertheless. I discard this one.*

---

[3] This is the central activity of the brain. A mathematical expression of this exists, and is called cross-correlation. The mathematical statement of this would be that I am cross-correlated as my own quantum wave expression of soul, with the quantum wave expression of two possible alternative quantum expressions of existence, to discover which of the two offers the stronger overlap, expressed in this soul existence as a "tingling sensation".
The central activity of the brain is described as consciousness, and is a cross-correlation of the soul quantum wave with the Cosmic Consciousness quantum wave. It may be described as the multiplication of the two waves together, so that the amount of overlap describes the amount of agreement between the direction and purposes of the two quantum waves, formulated then as an alignment or overlap of the two.

The soul-source selects, divides, and becomes a Soul

S. *I'm choosing the other because I can foresee the outcome and it is more pleasing, more fulfilling.* [4]

My soul-source is ancient, and although there was an energetic match with the life it selected, adaptations would be needed in order for it to carry out this life – to fit the life-form, the intellect and the purpose. It would not be able to exhibit the full consciousness (knowledge and wisdom) it has amassed over countless previous lives. Instead, the soul-source now divided this wisdom, selecting only that which would be appropriate to the chosen life, therefore the soul created would be somewhat curtailed, but at times of necessity it would still be able to access that greater wisdom. From the greater Field of Consciousness, it then also selected and added wisdom that it perceived would be useful or complementary in this new life.

As it selected what it needed, the gentle tingling became an electric charge. Once the soul-source had made the decision, expressing conscious intent to accept a life and taking initial steps to equip itself for that life, that intent took on an electrical form and became mass, condensed light, a complete ball of consciousness – a soul for this life.

A 1st interim step: attracting other individual souls or a soul group

Now in the form of a soul, I was drawn through time and space to the place of this future life, where I would begin the process of preparation. But interim steps were necessary before entering the life.

S. *I find myself with another soul I am drawn to! And a further group of several souls is gathering. We are "somewhere" – it's not "nothingness" anymore.*

A number of souls appearing as glowing balls of light now came together; they would be closely connected to me in this life. But I felt drawn to one soul in particular, a vibrant blue ball of light which projected a similar frequency.

---

[4] Mathematically this says that Suzy's soul consciousness cross-correlates most strongly (pleasantly) with the other. Alignment with the nature and purpose of the universe, as in sexual intercourse or church prayer, always produces a pleasant sensation; also noticed when living a real life.

Conferring with a spiritual Universal Governing Body ("UGB")

We were now in a boundless white space, a place of quietude. A variety of forms, figures, gliding, grouping, approached us. They expressed infinite wisdom, a guiding or governing body; a spiritual hierarchy officiating over a particular planet and civilisation, acting as wise gate-keepers. But it is also a practical group that has the welfare of souls in mind, as well as the welfare of the physical life-forms and the planet itself. It is a universal group in the sense that there are many more groups like this which serve other planets, life-forms, civilisations, and other intelligent forms of energy that have no physical place of origin.

All souls entering lives in this particular civilisation must meet with this group, the UGB, to first gain approval and then discuss a life-plan, before being accepted. My soul realised that although it had made a choice of a life on this planet, it may not necessarily be accepted by this governing body of Earth; that there is no guarantee, no certainty of freewill and free choice on this issue. The group's approval would depend on my soul's adequate preparation for the life, the wisdom it chose to bring with it, and the support of the other souls present that would be associated with it in this life.

Another change in consciousness took place and now my soul did not feel so ancient. It was more active, aware and focused, as if beginning to take on a persona. The blue ball of energy, with which it felt a strong familiarity, began conveying information to the UGB, a discussion I did not participate in. It acted as an intermediary, discussing my suitability to this life, whether the choices and selections I had made up to this point were appropriate; what state of consciousness or vibration was necessary for this role, this potential life. These preparatory choices are part of the growth of consciousness and evolution of the individual soul, so even decisions made in the source field are part of this spiritual evolution. Incarnation into the chosen life is not necessarily immediate, and free choice has limitations. All must align with the universal purpose – the oneness.

The UGB conveyed further details of this potential life, spreading them out before me, and the purpose of it was proposed. My consciousness extended into it and I was allowed to explore it energetically, to understand it. The UGB accepted my intent, giving me a final choice of willingness to accept this life ... and I was willing. [5]

S. *I'm aware it will be a difficult life, but it matches my antiquity - what I have amassed from many lives and experiences. I'm assessing how I will be able to utilise spiritual understanding and wisdom in this life, and although I know it will be hard, I really want to do it because they have outlined to me the importance of this life and I feel challenged by it.* [6]

I began to feel more youthful, lighter, as if already becoming something through the expression of conscious intent. The life was already becoming a reality.

S. *Any movement is constant movement towards the light. Movement is necessary.* [7]

A 2nd interim step: connecting with another species

But there was yet another interim step required for this particular life, a step which is not common or usual for most souls. Before entering this life I must first absorb specific background information about a particular task and receive training from another species assisting the UGB with this planet. This step was necessary and twofold. The purpose was not just to experience another life and

---

[5] Extremely interesting. At this point, the spirit guides tending our civilization on Earth have judged the conditions under which Suzy's choice is suitable for human existence, and are laying out conditions. This is mathematically a further process of cross-correlation and the output becomes the conditions that Suzy discovers will rule her existence. Finally, Suzy's willingness is cross-correlated with the spirit guides' quantum hologram, which is then strengthened and reinforced, and this in turn strengthens Suzy's emerging existence.

[6] Mathematically this last statement means that as Suzy continues to cross-correlate the possibilities of terrestrial life as now reinforced by terrestrial spirit guides, she finds high amplitude for the alignment with the nature and purpose of the universe.

[7] This movement is probably what many have called "raising my frequency".

acquire spiritual understandings from it, but there was also a requirement to assist a life-form, a civilisation.

The familiar soul, the blue ball of light, would accompany me in this life, as would two others from the group of souls present, souls which had entered lives already and had left their human forms to be present at this meeting. Decision-making is not restricted to the individual soul, but is a consensus of consciousness between several souls. We would all become part of something together, but the blue soul is the one I have had a long connection with in previous lives, and this would continue in the new life.

A further shift in consciousness took place, with an abrupt change of surroundings once the decision was made to accept this second interim step. We now found ourselves in a familiar place which we were drawn to, but also directed to by the UGB. My soul now accessed familiar memories of past lives and existences associated with a particular life-form, a culture. I have cooperated with this species before elsewhere on different planets, and so in a sense, I felt as if I had "come home". In previous lives I have been taught to take on their physical form at will. They are an interplanetary species I would come to know in this life as "Greys".

The blue soul and I were now on one of their craft. We had moved closer to inhabiting a physical form but another upgrade or acceleration of our consciousness must take place first, facilitated by this species of Greys. The resulting life will include both personal growth and personal sacrifice through commitment, by answering a call from the UGB for assistance.

Volunteering: answering "the call" from Earth

R. Is it a call for assistance from the planet?

S. Yes and this call was a part of the electric tingle that reached me ... a feeling of urgency ... a possibility of limited survival.

The Greys have felt that same call, and for centuries of time previously, they have been associated with this planet, but theirs has been a long and difficult task and the call has been sent out through the Field of Consciousness for further assistance.

The blue soul and I were now given a comprehensive "package" of information and data, providing us with an understanding of what would be required of us in this life as volunteers, gaining a history of the planet and the species in which we would incarnate, before embarking on a course of action. The Greys assisted us to assimilate this, along with memories and knowledge of our past association with their species. We needed to reacquaint ourselves with their modes of communication, their perspectives, the way they operate, in order to work with them. I began to see connections that came from past lives with them, as one of them, which I could now add to my soul-consciousness.

R. *So this connection with the Greys has been for a long time?*

S. *I cannot put it in human terms, put a figure on it, because it has not always involved the human civilisation, therefore our perception of time is different ... does not exist in other forms.* [8] *Suffice to say, it is a vast association with them.*

The blue soul and I would receive education from the Greys in the use of specific modes of communication (telepathy, energy, and broader sentience). We would need a well-developed understanding of the human psyche from the very earliest days of our incarnation as children, and this will be necessary because we will be observing and reporting back to the Greys and the UGB. This second interim step is unusual and task-specific:-

Soul enhancement and education: incarnating with a dual soul

S. *There is to be a change to the soul.*

R. *A change to the soul?*

S. *Yes. There is to be a dual soul perception or identity* (Grey and human) *and they explain why: we must be able to operate on two levels; there must be a closeness of the two perceptions and we're being told we may find this difficult.*

My soul-source had memory of having done this before, functioning with a dual soul, and so I had an acceptance of it without fear or doubt, but I perceived these very emotions would occur in the future life as a human. At this point though, there was purely cooperation and assimilation. The Greys informed the blue soul and I

---

[8] This is a revealing comment about the nature of the experience of time for a species not always aware of time in human terms. "I cannot put it in human terms, put a figure on it because it has not always involved the human civilization, therefore our perception of time is different (from human, and) does not exist in the other (alien Grey) forms." I interpret this to mean that it is possible in the incompletely conscious state to perceive time in human or in alien Grey terms, but not in an admixture of time experience.

that the dual consciousness of the two species (human and Grey), or two aspects of soul in combination, would create an unusual electric emanation. They would provide us with complex, multi-levelled educations and our understanding must reach a particular level and frequency in order to implement particular tasks in our lives.

We must work hard to maintain balance between the two identities for this to be successful. Once incarnation took place, the Grey identity would guide the human via communication and interaction. There was clear instruction about what the Greys can and cannot do to assist us once incarnation takes place and there must be acceptance of this by us, before we moved into a physical form.

R. So this blending of the two species, is that a universal thing on this planet or just for selected individuals?

S. Not "selected", but those who have made the choice.

Extraterrestrial education programmes to assist human evolution

The blue soul with whom I felt such an affinity will not enter a life at the same time, but will incarnate later. Our association in this life will be extensive, a relationship, and co-operation in terms of commitment to a task, and there will be continuous communication between us on various levels throughout the lives we will lead.

S. We will be required to take on the Grey form (from time to time) *which will be a part of us.*[9] *This will be necessary in order to work closely with the guidance of the Greys and their programmes we will participate in.*

There will be separate education programmes: for the human, the Grey identity, and the soul (which will maintain its universal awareness). This blending of the two species in one incarnation is a common occurrence universally, but it is not common in the human civilisation. In this life to be, there will not be many on the planet with this dual soul identity and therefore we will affect people with our vibration. For some people, it will be unsettling, but it will awaken something in others. But there will be many other souls entering lives as volunteers to assist the planet who will receive a spiritual education, and become part of the Greys' programmes.

---

[9] Other abductees/experiencers have reported seeing beings incubated and grown in tubes aboard craft. So possibly Suzy's (physical) Grey identity was cloned and created (born) aboard a spacecraft located in Earth's vicinity.

There is a perception by the UGB and the Greys that there are many souls living lives on Earth that have forgotten their spiritual mission, the purpose of learning through experience. They have become stagnant and there has been a process of analysis amongst other species as to why this is, on this planet in particular. Why is there a retrograde spiritual movement on Earth? It has become a source of curiosity and they have questioned what can be done. It is perceived to be to do with the expansion of the universe.

I can explain this using the comparison of a river: sometimes the current carries water into the central flow of the river where there is a constant moving channel. But there are eddies and flows that move off to the left or right where the water flows less swiftly. There may be blockages caused by rocks or logs, or muddy pools. The water is a little stagnant here. It doesn't move so freely and life is different in that area of the river, away from the central flow.

Similarly, there is stagnancy in this part of the galaxy and there are moves to rectify this on Earth and bring mankind back into line with the universal flow and expansion.

R. *Is this stagnancy a natural progression or has something been influencing it?*

S. *It is a natural consequence of growth and movement on the universal scale, and on a scale of consciousness.*[10] *In the flow and expansion of consciousness, mankind's consciousness is on the outer eddies, and is being "retrieved" so to speak. Mankind is being brought back into the flow.*

But on a planetary level, there is curiosity amongst other species as to why there is limited spiritual awareness within the human species. Humans have experienced advancement in technological know-how, but a deterioration of spirituality. Spirituality is not keeping pace with technology, and so there is a conflict: what will this species do with their technology if their spirituality does not match the manner of implementation of that technology? There is a danger emerging for other species, and this is of concern.

The Greys provided further information on the future life, preparing me both spiritually and intellectually. My soul state will

---

[10] "It is a natural consequence of growth ..." is possibly a reference to the scientific revolution that accompanied the renaissance around 1500 A.D. and on into the modern times of the atomic era.

require a strong internal core, but this difficult life will also be an equipping life. On a human level it will provide opportunities to develop perspectives and insights through hardship.

They further explained the function of the Grey identity within the dual soul: from their perspective it provides an opportunity for the Grey species to observe humanity from within, rather than from without. Through the dual soul they will be able to experience human emotions and many human personality characteristics they do not have, and the Grey consciousness (identity) will assist the human to complete tasks in line with the call for assistance.

S. Future generations of Greys and humans will benefit because of the understandings gained from dual soul identities. [11]

This interaction between Greys and humans will continue into the future. When the human dies, the soul will divide once again. The original soul-source will be offered choices: return to rest in the peace of the Field of Consciousness to await another opportunity of life, or remain in the soul state and assist the Greys in other ways. The Grey identity however, will not come to any demise through the death of the human form. It will not necessarily return to the soul-source but may simply continue as a working life-form, inhabiting another Grey body. Thus the unique consciousness containing both Grey and human perspectives and knowledge can be retained, and this will be of great value, working for the future guidance and survival of the human species. Dual souls will provide a new echelon of understanding of human civilisation amongst the Greys.

My soul was then provided with information about the accompanying blue ball of light/soul. It will also have a dual soul, but it will receive a much greater education and preparation for its life. The electric field created by this soul combination will be exceptional, and therefore I am taking on a guiding role for this dual soul to allow it to assimilate into its life. I will continue to provide that guidance even beyond my death, as will the Grey identity continue its communication and association with, and guidance of, this soul. My

---

[11] I understand this sentence to mean that the joint quantum hologram describing Suzy's dual human/Grey existence will be much more powerful than a hologram describing a single human identity could be, and this will be of importance to the future evolutionary development of the universe (cosmic intelligence).

overall role or task in life will not compare to that of this soul, which is vast. The tasks ahead are complex, and we must be carefully prepared for these lives on many levels.

R. As two souls, have you worked together before in this way?

S. Yes, there is a close affinity of consciousness and similarity of frequency, which in the human life would be called "love" and "commitment".

Discussion

I first lectured publicly about this memory and my theories on the soul's intimate connection with other universal souls, at a UFO Research New South Wales (UFOR) Conference in Sydney, Australia, in 2001.

For a fuller explanation of the *source-field* or the *Field of Consciousness,* readers can refer to the Journal of Cosmology, Volume 14, April/June 2011, section XII. http://journalofcosmology.com/Consciousness149.html

This soul-memory reinforces what many of you reading this material will already know: that on a universal level of consciousness, there is no differentiation between life and death, soul and living being, incarnate and discarnate, and it demonstrates the many dimensions of the soul. All is a continuum of life and energy. Between lives, a state of consciousness exists – lives-between-lives. Individual consciousness survives physical death.

Some of the concepts that emerged from this regression confirmed my personal perspectives on the soul and reincarnation, while others were new to me. But playing devil's advocate, one might ask: if the UGB assists souls to join our civilisation with a spiritual life plan, why do so many humans commit heinous atrocities?

Many souls lose touch with their spiritual reason for being here, and become entrenched in less attractive aspects of human behaviour and existence. The UGB and other universal forces have recognised this retrograde spiritual tendency and are seeking to raise humankind's awareness through specific methods. Alternatively however, some human belief systems espouse that we learn through suffering, even that caused by others, and see it as "God's will", or a necessary part of the balance of life … while many who have suffered question the very existence of God.

Throughout the regression, I was aware of profound shifts in my energy, voice, and even body temperature, and these were confirmed and documented by the regression therapist, who noted these changes occurring as I described each progression the soul-source made towards incarnating in this life.

The Field of Consciousness initially presented two choices of lives to me, and I was surprised one of them involved a "gruelling existence" which I was able to view as a large sponge-like form, grouped together with other similar life-forms in smooth whitish mounds in solitude and inactivity, and it didn't appeal as much as the other option. Although I described this life-form as having "limited physical effect", nevertheless, intelligence and commitment were required. The concept that an aware soul can inhabit a sponge-like form is contrary to many human belief systems however, this material indicates our incarnations are based on spiritual intent, be it manifested as animal, plant, mineral or other. This may require us to re-examine the concept that there is a "human" soul distinct from animals, birds etc. I believe our soul-source can incarnate in a myriad of life-forms, anywhere, and is not exclusively "human".

This reinforces perspectives held by many experiencers that in past lives, they incarnated into an extraterrestrial species or life-form, and yet have become an earthly human in another life. It also supports my perspective presented in a previous chapter that animals' souls are no different from our own and originate from the same source. This concept would require some of us to view our companion species on the planet very differently.

I believe that no matter what dimension, galaxy, planet, physical or non-physical form we believe we belong to, we all originate from the same Field of Consciousness; and there are at least some extraterrestrial species able to communicate with all manner of life-forms, using pure consciousness as the form of "language". [12]

From what I have ascertained, Greys may have a long life span but they may also be able to begin another life at will, rather like reinventing themselves, or beginning a new process or purpose by

---

[12] These two important phrases seem to require that there is a field of quantum holograms that are interpreted by the various languages of human and alien species as emotional content (meaning), which is a profound statement by Suzy of the principle of the Edgar Mitchell Quantum Hologram formulation (concept).

transferring the soul to another vehicle (body) elsewhere, without having to return to the source-field. Perhaps their understanding of life-between-lives is so advanced that they can short-cut the process.

The formation of the dual soul required an interim step not usually necessary for a soul preparing to enter a new life on Earth. My original soul-source selected what it needed for the proposed life, both from within its own history and from the greater Field of Consciousness. In the second interim step, the Greys added or inserted (a part of their soul-insertion capabilities) an aspect of their consciousness that I will refer to henceforth as the *Grey identity* or *Grey intelligence/consciousness.* It is capable of manifesting independently in the Grey physical form, or can function as a Grey intelligence offering guidance and input to the human throughout their life. It may also manifest as a ball of light. This is a new aspect of the Greys' association with our civilisation, and it involves people from two consecutive generations within certain families, likely numbering in the thousands worldwide.

Universal networks of intelligent, spiritual, governing (guiding) groups (UGBs) exist to assist souls choosing to incarnate and evolve in diverse forms throughout the physical universe or multi-dimensions. Over recent decades, volunteer souls have incarnated on Earth and continue to do so for specific purposes. The regression therapist asked me, "Is it a call for assistance from the planet?" and I replied that it is. In part, this is an example of our collective human consciousness appealing to the Universe for help, along with Earth's UGB.

We all share a common Source, connect and resonate with the harmonics of the source-field, interface with other individual souls, groups of souls and species, and have agreements with spiritual UGBs. Deeper understanding of the nature of consciousness and the soul will unfold as our awareness evolves and expands, expressing our readiness for the next phase of enlightenment.

Thus began my soul evolution as it applies to this life. In the broader context of the following chapters, I encourage readers to reflect on their own lives and what their soul purposes may be.

Chapter 10

A Cosmic Playroom and a Lullaby Bed

1960, age six years
The playroom

I stood barefooted on a floor like warm milky glass, wearing my short summer pyjamas. Thirty six other juvenile Greys, mixed-species, human/Grey genetic mixtures, and human children were playing together in this large room. I had just arrived onboard and felt over-whelmed and emotional because I had missed them.

R. How do you know them?

S. Because I've been visiting them for a long time.

The alien children's eyes were complex in appearance: overly large, dark and curving, or bright pale blue. Some had mottled skin with smudges in hues of cream, fawn, grey and a hint of charcoal-brown, and they were all completely bald. Their spindly limbs seemed too long for their torsos, and their hands were petite and skeletal, or long and slender with three fingers and a thumb.

The human-Grey children were more human-like, but also had distinctly different features – delicate physiques, sparse wispy blonde hair, blue or black/tawny eyes, and pale clammy skin.

I sensed the vibrant energy surging around them, and the intensity of their eyes penetrated my mind. Except for the human children like me, they all lived on the craft, but a few of them could have easily walked amongst us without standing out as overly different. I felt completely at home with them all.

(During the regression, the therapist asked me if I could recall an even earlier age when I had been onboard craft as a child, and to describe the experience from an adult perspective. I regressed back to a time when I was six months old and was once again amongst a group of similar children of other species.)

1955, age six months

Mind melds: brain and mind synthesis

I felt content, lying on a short bed wearing nappies and a top, pulling my feet up so I could hold onto my toes, and looking around at the children. We were in a room with three white walls and floor, while the fourth wall consisted of a glass-like material. (I remain uncertain as to whether this was a large black screen, or a window looking out into space or the night sky, however I recalled not wanting to stand close to this window/screen in childhood in case I fell out.)

Two entities around six feet tall (183 cm) were attending to the children. Their general appearance was similar to the Greys', but with elongated skulls forming a rounded peak or "cone-head". As a child I thought they resembled crickets, which is certainly how they would have seemed to a small child looking up at their dominant dark eyes and sloping forehead. These entities were our carers and I guess as I got older, I looked upon them as being like kindergarten teachers. I was able to communicate with them through thought, even at this young age, and the other mixed-species children were like family to me. Right from early childhood, I understood that in some way they were related to me, connected to me powerfully. We would grow up together, meet often and work for some common purpose.

One of the tall entities approached, gently picking me up and bringing his forehead to mine; reaching into my mind but at the same time, using this physical action as a mental and physical interface to teach me how to communicate telepathically and what part of the body that process originates from. They did this often, a kind of fusion between our energy fields allowing me to think, feel and understand at their level. This "merging", or "psychic bonding", was accompanied by a sense of lightness, weightlessness, providing heightened stamina through a boosted energy field. [13] When this early process of merging took place it always engendered a heightening of vibrations within my body, inducing a broader awareness, precise

[13] I liked this description as a fuller elaboration of what probably most experiencers would just refer to as "raising my frequency". The two are probably equivalent.

thought processes, fluent telepathic expression and enhanced learning capabilities while onboard craft. [14]

Throughout childhood these mixed-species children played with me and other human children, allowing us to learn and absorb their communications in a way that was fun. I could understand their complex telepathic and energetic emanations as intrinsic parts of their multi-levelled expressions, and their energy fields were often visible as vivid interplays of colour and light. The cone-headed entities were essentially carers rather than educators, making sure we were safe and interacting with us, and they were males. [15]

During the regression I recognised a small Grey amongst the children, who I recall having considerable contact with right throughout my life, and I felt a strong sense of kinship with him. In childhood I nick-naming him "RJ" because of a guttural sound he made on occasions, close to our vocal blend of the letters R and J.

The regression therapist brought me forward again, back to six years of age, standing in a room with mixed-species children.

Using the mind to create holograms

The playroom had few toys as such because we created games and entertainment mainly with our thoughts. These alien children could manifest balls of energy with their minds, give them any colour or texture they liked, and then project them into the air for all to see. The human children soon learnt to interact with these games, albeit more clumsily.

---

[14] Suzy's statement here is amazingly profound. The fact that we can communicate telepathically across species is a new take on the Noam Chomsky concept of how human language and communication betray the existence of an "ur-sprache" and even imply that all humans have a common place of origin on our planet. The fact that we can mentally communicate cross-species implies that our language has a deeper significance, and that the quantum holograms describing language of communication must have similar wave form to the Quantum Hologram of the described emotions.

[15] Having a male carer is surprising indeed. In our terrestrial civilization we believe that maleness includes aggressiveness which is related to family responsibility, food gathering, and sexual prowess. I wonder if males of these species have evolved through cloning, to have other personality aspects as a result of less need for aggressiveness because of reproduction by cloning and less danger related to food gathering and nutrition.

We would sit in a circle and one of the onboard kids would create a ball of energy in the air above us, which we would try to emulate until the space above us was filled with glowing orbs of light. On other occasions we levitated small objects and were able to pass them around to the other children. [16] Through these activities we learnt telepathic cooperation, the power of combined (melded) thoughts, holographic projection, and telekinesis. By having fun, we human children learnt many extraterrestrial skills and modes of communication, and unity. [17]

The lullaby bed

While mentally viewing the room under hypnosis, I recognised an unusual short bed, which as a small child I nicknamed "the lullaby bed". The sight and memory of this bed immediately evoked intense mixed feelings of sadness and comfort. I remembered being taken onboard and placed on this bed, which induced a feeling of instant relaxation. When I arrived, the carers would already know everything that had happened recently in my life, and they placed me on this apparatus on a number of occasions when I was unsettled.

Lullaby beds are equipped with metabolic sensors that register all bodily functions, necessary for babies and small children as a method of non-invasive examination. They were created to cater for young human children coming onboard craft from a variety of backgrounds: cultural, ethnic, social, or environmental – some of which may have been traumatic or difficult conditions to grow up in. On other occasions it was used to stabilise the child after certain transportation

---

[16] Here I read for the first time the word levitation. This is extremely important because it would confirm my understanding that consciousness is an off-diagonal term in the Einstein Field Equation of quantum description of gravity and matter existence that mixes consciousness with gravity. This tends to explain the Buddhist traditions of levitation and also the observations of UFOs seeming to silently and effortlessly hang in the sky, as if not affected by gravity.

[17] Suzy states she and the other children were positioned in a circle which would assist their developing a single shared telepathy. Such a shared telepathy is implied by their creating, and each in turn developing, a complex propertied energy ball. A feeling of elation accompanies resonance with the universe in sharing a project with other children.

procedures, or to settle their emotions. In effect, it was designed to monitor and harmonise a child's mental, emotional and physical states in preparation for learning and interacting at a higher level with the Greys.

There were two sizes, for babies and toddlers/young children. The bed sat close to the floor, with raised ends that curved up and outwards. Screens at each end displayed attractive lights, patterns and colours, accompanied by soothing melodic sounds or frequencies, and the bed's surface was warm. In this way, it utilised features many small children worldwide find comforting – soft sound, colour and warmth. The bed's features induced a relaxed state of receptiveness not otherwise possible for human babies and young children to achieve in a short space of time, in preparation for extreme focus.

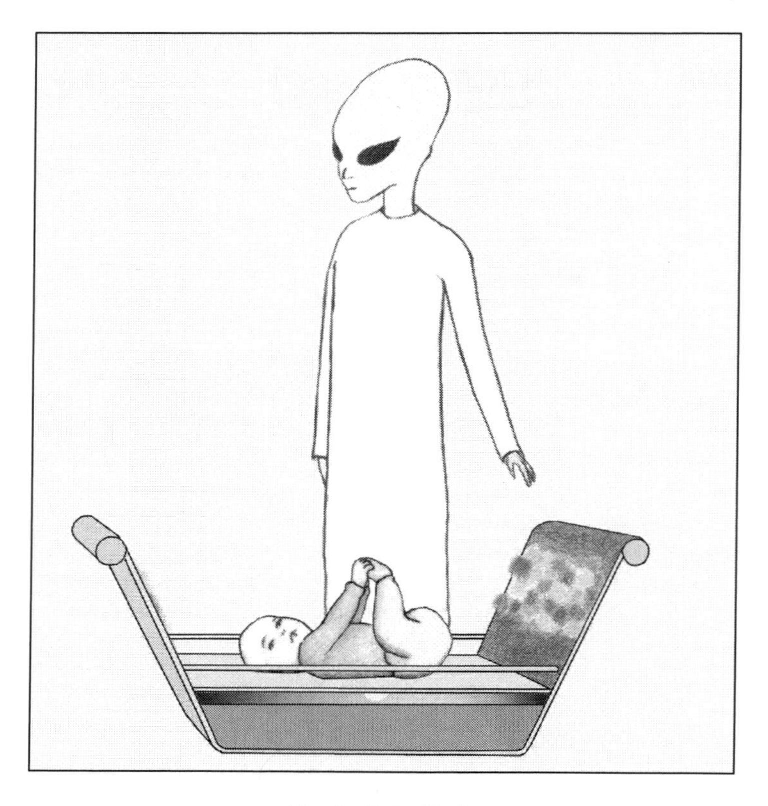

The Lullaby Bed

Discussion

Taking into consideration my early conscious memories of glowing figures by my bed, and my dream-like recollections of being in strange rooms, and combining it with this information, it seems I was taken onboard alien craft at night during childhood. There I became accustomed to communicating with and relating to a range of extraterrestrial children and adult entities. The Greys use various methods to teach human children how to communicate adeptly with them: creating a synthesis of telepathy by merging energy fields and thoughts, fostering social acceptance through play, and developing mind skills including holograms and levitation.

Activities such as levitation in these alien playrooms are corroborated by fellow New Zealand experiencer, Alec Newald. In his book entitled, *Coevolution* (2011), Alec wrote about being in a similar playroom on a craft:-

"There were other children there, too, and we played together. The best game was where several of us would sit in a circle with one in the middle. The outer circle of children would hold hands and the one in the middle would rise in the air. I had my turn in the middle as well. How could I forget that!"

As an adult, I learnt the young Grey child I called RJ is a more recent genetic production of the species, and although he looks like a Grey, he has developed a more human aspect to his psyche through his contact with human children. Psychologically, he is not quite "them", but not quite "us" either. The Greys have created new genetic lines or sub-species to adapt to new environments and other cultures, and in the future, to further assist us in our evolution. This young Grey has also been trained in communication, creating a mirror effect between the two species, with human children. [18]

Through this early contact I also learnt about the involvement of other members of my biological family in these programmes. We do not know how long the extraterrestrials have been studying the human species, but at this time in our evolution, the Greys in particular have identified families with particular genetic make-ups and have studied

---

[18] This is the first account that I have read where it is understood that contact with humans can contribute to the Greys' development, instead of the other way around.

members of the last four generations of these families in depth. They have carried out genetic interventions within the last two of these four generations, which have received inter-species education onboard craft.

It is within these last two generations that certain souls have incarnated into lives on this planet to complete specific previously agreed-upon tasks and achieve certain goals. [19]

This early childhood contact included not only communication, but also learning alien scripts and using advanced technology from a young age. The Greys constantly appraised the progress of the human children, with a view to selecting some of them for specialised programmes. "Mind melds" and "thought transfers" into our young minds became the routine way of educating us at a heightened level of consciousness, activating our psychic functioning.

This regression revealed the extent of my own contact with the Greys throughout childhood and began an unlocking process in me, allowing deeper understanding of my experiences thus far. I am aware there are many thousands of people participating cooperatively in these programmes for humans, designed to facilitate inter-species understanding and perhaps to create a bridging group in preparation for future open contact on our planet. These programmes aim to enrich human intellect, expand our psychic capabilities and contribute to expanding our mass-consciousness.

---

[19] I was tickled to read this paragraph because it explains the fact that our entire tradition of religion and literature does not include reference to extraterrestrial contact. While there is older reference to UFO sightings and alien visitation, as documented on the *Ancient Aliens* TV series, ancient reference to contact seems not to exist, except perhaps in the biblical Christmas story.

Chapter 11

Meeting the Soul of My Future Son

1962, age 8 years
Lessons on the craft

I'm with the children again, ones like me and ones like them, and I'm wearing my favourite lemon-coloured summer pyjamas. Fourteen of us are sitting cross-legged on the floor in a large room, and some of the alien children are wearing close-fitting body suits and black foot-coverings, while others wear shapeless white robes or nothing at all.

Each species communicates slightly differently and their energy fields "feel" different. (By this I mean I perceive differences in the intensity of their energy and the way they express their consciousness through various means: colour, imagery, sound, and expressive patterns that make sense to me, and streams or waves of meaningful energy beyond human literal description.) [20]

We are playing my favourite game, learning to use the mind to create activities and challenges, and holograms hang in the air above our heads, vibrantly colourful and radiant. We see them not only through our physical eyes, but at the same time, we view them from within the mind or consciousness, mentally and energetically constructing and manifesting the shapes. Our thought-forms can be projected to others in the group who can continue to develop them in complexity, transforming them into whatever we wish, and we can expand or reduce the size and dimension of each others' creations as desired. Each child adds to it in some way, continuing the process, forming spectacular conjoint designs, shapes or images floating in the air. They are intricately beautiful and complex: crystalline, geometric, organic, with intense colours, interlocking, flowing, and transforming.

---

[20] I presume that Suzy notices that their waves of consciousness are different in detail, which is inevitable across species, because some consciousnesses would be more sensitive to sacred geometry or different ranges of colour or frequencies of sound.

Mind Games in the Playroom

We have all come to know each other well during these visits onboard craft and they have been my friends as far back as I can remember.

R. *Why are you there?*

S. *I'm going to meet someone!*

One of the adult Greys, who as a child I had nicknamed "the Grandfather", takes me to one side, holds my hands and asks me to look into his eyes. He explains something to me very blandly and simply in a way that I will understand and at the same time, I am looking into his eyes and "reading" these thoughts. He asks me if I would like to meet a child and I say that I would. I'm curious as to why the Grandfather is being so careful in his explanation and it's as if there is something he's not telling me yet. He's inviting me to follow him to another room and I feel obliged to go with him.

We proceed down a corridor and I'm skipping along behind him, tugging at the tight elastic around the bottom of my short pyjama pants. He's turning slightly, watching me, and I can sense he's amused by my uncomfortable antics. I'm feeling quite excited now!

S. *We're going through a door into a small room. There's nobody there! I say, "Where's this other kid?" and he tells me, "Just calm down and be patient. This is important".*

I feel suitably subdued. We stand still together and wait side-by-side. I can tell he's talking to someone with his mind, even though there's nobody else there with us. He's sending a message, but I can discern some of it. They "talk" at lightning speed to each other, but I can make out the gist of it after listening to them so often, when they allow me to "hear" that is. He's asking someone to come from somewhere else on the craft.

I'm watching the door. They're taking a while, so I sit down on the floor and lean against the wall, scratching at a prickle in my big toe. The Grandfather remains standing, observing me, but I can hear snippets of thoughts in his mind; he's amused again by what I am doing. Finally, he tells me to stand up, as two other Greys enter the room.

S. *Oh gosh! The Greys have got a little beach-ball floating in the air between them! That's really pretty! It's all blue! Bright glowing blue!*

Suddenly I begin to feel strange, emotional and tearful. I'm looking at the ball hanging still and fragile in the air and I feel something I don't understand. I don't know what is happening! An unfamiliar rush of emotions and thoughts races through my mind and I begin to sob.

The Grey stresses to me, repeating with emphasis, "Be calm. You will love this (referring to the blue ball of light). You will love this. You will *love* this."

S. I don't understand. I feel stupid! I feel like it's mine. The blue ball is mine! I'm crying and I don't know why.

He continues, "Be still and I will explain."

I don't know what this is! I'm aware the Grandfather is trying to help me calm and control my thoughts as I look at this beautiful ball of light turning slowly in the air, electric, bright and shimmering.

S. It's thinking at me! It's thinking at me!

The Grandfather says, "This will be yours."

I stammer in amazement, "What? What is it?"

He calmly responds, "This will be your son."

I immediately feel confused. "But ... I'm not married. What do you mean?"

He replies, "This will be your son. We are introducing you to your son."

I feel scared now. I don't understand this. But I feel as if I already know this bright ball of light somehow!

He says, "Look into my eyes and I will explain. Be still." I obey.

He continues, "This will be your future son. One day when you grow up like your parents, this is the son you will have. He doesn't have a body like you yet."

I'm shocked and repeat again naively and indignantly, "But I'm not married!"

"We are introducing you to him in this form, but in time, he will be your real son and become a child like you." Tears roll down my cheeks.

"Look into my eyes and I will clear your confusion."

The Grandfather conveys a massive outline of future events, and pictures flash through my mind with accompanying feelings and emotions. Three simultaneous streams of communication are layered over this, like a kind of "voice" describing the life the child will lead:

1) A basic first stream, calming the shock and confusion.

"We want you to get to know him, to be friends."

They want to observe how we will relate to each other, future mother and son.

2) A second stream, a deeper level of information embedding specific and detailed information into the subconscious, much of which will be revealed at some time in the future, some of which I am permitted to register now:

This has been planned for a long time. There is a purpose. They need me to start relating to this form, the soul of my future son, before it is born as a child, my child. They must be sure we will relate satisfactorily. We must know each other well to cope with the future. Our relationship, and what is required of us, has already been complex. I knew this soul when I too was just a ball of light, before I was born into this world. Now is the time to consciously relate to this soul again, as a child.

Future parents must learn from an early age, initially, how to relate to these particular souls, and later, how to raise and nurture them. This is essential to achieve the final goal of a proliferation of *future humans* worldwide, who will instigate unprecedented positive changes within humanity and for our environment.

Now he opens a new compartment, a facet of my mind or consciousness. Momentarily, I am able to comprehend his thoughts, the information transfer, from a mature perspective. He assists me to view the future:-

They will assist genetically in the creation of a physical body which the blue ball of light (soul) will inhabit, and they will help develop a persona for that soul. Then the two will become joined as one, but the soul will continue to operate independently at times. The body and soul ("source" or "essence" as he called it), and the energetic fields of both, will interact in many ways, unfamiliar to humans, and underlying interactions will take place that few will be aware of or be able to recognise.

This is not a soul as we humans understand the concept of a soul. It is highly evolved and has been "enhanced", or altered by them with the addition of a dual soul identity/consciousness, or Grey intelligence. I am the same. There are others like us. Humans have no understanding of this and it is not necessary for me to have a deeper understanding of it at this point in childhood.

I will receive extensive education from the Greys, not just for my own sake, but for my son's as well. What I do in my future will directly affect his. This information is to remain private for the time being therefore I will have no conscious memory of these events throughout my childhood (except when I am with them onboard craft).

But under their guidance, they want me to learn how to interact with this "complex system" as he calls it – seen by me now as a ball of blue light – from childhood to parenthood, and beyond, continuing even after my death.

He moves me forward in time in my mind, to observe my adulthood. At a certain point in the future, they will assist me to realise my son and I have been communicating on another level since long before his conception and birth, as well as having extensive contact with them. My son will not realise any of this until well into his adulthood and this knowledge will be easier for me to understand as I grow to adulthood, than it will be for him to accept initially.

There is another important reason for this early introduction: in the future, no matter where my son is there will be a stream of consciousness and telepathy between us. They will assist us to become proficient in this. It will be necessary. There will be many other mothers or fathers around the world similarly trained and educated.

In the meantime, this soul will be given a separate education onboard craft in preparation for the time it will merge with its human body. After that time, a triple education will take place: the soul will continue to visit onboard craft, the Grey aspect of the dual soul will receive an extraterrestrial education, and the child himself will also be taken onboard to receive an extraterrestrial-oriented education, which will enhance his human capabilities. The child's task in the future will be to access and utilise the three educations for the benefit of mankind.

I ask from my child-mind, "But why am *I* going to be his parent?"

He shifts my awareness again to a mature level of understanding and embeds further information, reminding me of the generational/familial aspect of the project I am part of, describing how particular human genetic lines have been selected and altered by the extraterrestrials. We cannot comprehend the number of extraterrestrials involved in these research programmes, or the number of people taken aboard craft in the process. Multiple programmes exist in which we are constantly tested and assessed.

The last two of the selected four generations are now entering, or are preparing to enter life on our planet. But the generation that the blue ball belongs to has had (at a soul level), and will have (as humans) the most extensive education within the extraterrestrial programmes. They are the "Third Wave". He refers to this soul as an "end-point" child (last in the four generations).

The Grandfather says this is a loving agenda, not a negative agenda, as will unfortunately be surmised by some humans in the future. They are confident of eventual positive outcomes for mankind.

3) The volume of information he has imparted is too much for a child to comprehend and retain consciously, so he filters it to the subconscious. Now, using a more superficial stream, he spreads an overlay over the information, bringing my mind back to the present and smoothing it all into an appealing and simplistic form suitable for a child of eight to understand. I am left with just a set of basic facts regarding meeting a new friend, another child.

Feeling calm again now, I look at the blue orb solely as a lovely ball of light that can communicate as a friend, and I'm no longer considering what the Grandfather has just conveyed to me. And he tells me I'm allowed to play with it!

The Grandfather says, "He can "talk" to you. You will learn to be friends. We are going to leave you now to play for a while."

I'm glad they are leaving us alone and I stand with my hands behind my back and my feet apart. I feel pretty smart because *I'm* the boss now! I'm looking at it … at "him". It's beautiful! What shall we do now?

I say to him in a loud commanding voice, "Bounce!"

He doesn't move. I walk around the other side and ask more timidly, "Can you bounce?"

No answer. That's disappointing, I thought it could talk! I move away a bit and do a cartwheel on the floor. The floor is soft here and I always do cartwheels when the Greys are not looking. I do another one. I stand up and stare at the ball again. It's not playing with me! I sit on the floor cross-legged and lean against the wall.

Suddenly I feel as if I am being watched. It's coming down! It's moving around my head. It tickles! It's really close to me and I want to hug it, like I hug my dog, Polly. It's ... he's sitting on my shoulder against the side of my face! I try to grab him and he's letting me hold him out in front of me like a beach-ball. Now he has slipped out of my hands and he's flying around the room in a circle. I chase him! I feel as if he is a *real* friend now, and he's talking to me!

Now *he's* chasing *me* around the room! I sense he's laughing, and I'm laughing too. But … I feel funny again and I don't know why. I feel as if I love this ball. We race around the room for a while and he swoops up and down while I leap and try to catch him, laughing when my hands pass right through him.

S. Hey! Wait a minute! The Grandfather is talking to me from somewhere else. He's coming back!

The three Greys enter the room now. The Grandfather stands near me and says, "Let's be good," to calm my excitement. I stand with my hands by my sides, waiting with my heart pounding. The Greys seem really pleased about something. I wonder if they saw us playing together. Now the blue ball floats motionlessly between the other two Greys, shimmering and electric-looking. Silent.

The Grandfather says gently, "He is your son."

I answer indignantly, "He's my friend!"

"No," he replies patiently, "We will continue to call him your son from now on. You will become accustomed to this, but you will not remember it when you are not with us – not yet. He must go now."

I feel disappointment at the short time we were allowed to play together, which the Grey immediately registers, assuring me we can play together often when I am with them.

I ask if I can take the ball to the playroom to show the other kids and he responds, "No, this is just for you. This is private. It means you don't tell anyone." He emphasises the last word.

The other two Greys are going now, taking the blue ball with them. There's a lump in my throat. The Grandfather reads my sadness, absorbing and examining my thoughts and emotions, my feelings of intense love for this blue ball. It is important he knows them. He responds kindly and the sadness fades, leaving just enough to impress upon me the importance of the occasion.

He conveys satisfaction, "Good, an excellent start. Come now."

I follow him back along the corridor doing my "sad steps" behind him, dragging my feet and trying to make him feel bad for taking my new friend away so soon. He knows it, but ignores me! We enter the room where the other kids are playing and communicating.

"You have done well." He emanates a feeling of warmth to me, as if my body is momentarily wrapped in a cosy blanket. I join some of the kids sitting in a circle playing mind games, squeezing in between a Grey child and another girl, who move over to make room for me. I have a secret they don't know about!

I have joined in with the game now, perceiving an intricate collection of shapes in the air above us, like a labyrinth with vivid tunnels and connections that can suddenly appear or vanish as another child's thoughts intercept and alter the evolving design. I love playing these games! No-one argues or becomes angry here, everyone cooperates and we all talk like the Greys (telepathically).

After a while another Grey enters the room. All the human children like him because he is funny and mimics human behaviour. He "claps" with his mind a couple of times to get our attention and sends us a silly thought-voice, "Clap! Clap! It's time for some of you to go now!"

We head off down the corridor, straggling along behind the Grey, lost in our happy thoughts. As we pass each open doorway I jump, stop, look in! I might see the blue ball one more time. I skip away to the next doorway, but sadly the blue ball is nowhere to be seen. We enter the hangar area to await our departure in smaller craft.

Time passes as we travel. I watch a couple of the other children leave, lowered in a beam of light accompanied by a Grey. Eventually I am called forward and one of the Greys steps up beside me. He knows me well and it's as if he has put his arm around my shoulder protectively. But he hasn't of course! He has just wrapped his mind around my shoulder, giving the impression of his arm. They have been teaching me how to do this kind of thing with my mind, so I try to do the same in return.

"That's good," he says encouragingly.

We float straight through our large living-room window, skimming over the top of the couch. Everything goes "black" for a second as I pass through the glass. I walk down the hallway with the Grey floating alongside me. Everyone in the house is asleep and he tells me I could make as much noise as I like, but they would not wake. I climb up on my bed.

He says goodbye to me, "Turn over and go to sleep. You have done well. Thank you."

Discussion

Suzy:

I have now been re-introduced, in this life, to the mysterious blue ball of light I was reunited with in the soul-state prior to being born. Child and future mother meeting a soul, a future son.

An ongoing relationship has been established which will continue to the time of his birth as my son. We are both receiving specific educations in preparation for tasks we will complete in our lives.

Examples of humour between me and the Greys indicate a relaxed relationship with them. It is interesting that at the age of eight, and perhaps synonymous with these contacts, I experienced an upswing in psychic abilities in my day-to-day life.

From a mother's perspective, the intensity of the emotions I experienced throughout this regression as a child, are difficult to express adequately in words. Yet the ideas expressed are also hard to comprehend, as these emotions *were* those of a child, one who had not yet grown to maturity to know the love a mother has for a child. This information went a long way to explaining aspects of my relationship with my son, especially our telepathic link.

The Grandfather made it clear I had known this soul, my future son, in previous lives. I recall an evening when my son was four and a half years old, when we shared what was for me an unforgettable moment, which indicated he had retained an awareness of a past life with me. We were staying at a friend's house and he and I shared a large bed, while his brother slept in a separate one. My son was still awake and restless when I climbed into bed at 9.30 pm, and I instantly had a gut-feeling something important was about to happen. He cuddled up against me and put his arm around my waist, and I waited as the feeling intensified. I have never forgotten his words:

He quietly said, "Mum, I knew you a long, long time ago."

I replied, "Did you?"

He said, "Yes, you were there with me. Do you remember? You were there when I fell down the long hole. You helped me. I knew you before."

I asked, "Before what?"

He sighed and lapsed into sleep. This could not have been a memory of the birth process into this life as some have suggested, because he was born by caesarean section. As indicated in Chapter 9, *Soul Origin*, we have shared many other lives together.

The reality of reincarnation and how we evolve spiritually, possibly over millennia, has been a prominent understanding in my life. I believe my experiences present new aspects of reincarnation, how it is also a part of the UGB's agenda, and the process behind alien programmes involving working with specific souls and humans.

This experience illustrates the complexity of the soul state, and challenges us to reassess our current limited understanding of the soul. It supports the concept that a soul evolves not only through repeated cycles or lifetimes of personal experiences, but that the dimensions of the soul can be "designed" by the individual soul-source itself to meet the needs of that life.

But significantly, this experience illustrates how the soul can be educated, altered and enhanced by alien species to achieve a specific, agreed-upon purpose in a planetary agenda. The physical body is the result of genetic intervention.

The late Dr. Roger Leir, author of *The Aliens and the Scalpel*, was a pioneer in the removal of alleged alien implants from abductees' bodies. Roger stayed in my home in 2007 when he spoke at our UFOCUS NZ UFO Conference, and he commented that after forty years of studying child development in particular, he believed the entire human race is being advanced at a rate that is unlikely to be due to natural evolutionary forces. He stated it was more likely that the rapid advancement of the human species is due to alien intervention in our bodies and minds.

There is an echelon of children (some now young adults) born over the last three decades – children who are clearly different from those who have already become known worldwide in UFO/contact research as "the Star Kids".

This new distinct echelon is part of a complex alien agenda and has a specific purpose in our future. Notably, there is a separate role for their dual soul, distinct from the role of their human personalities.

The creation of these enhanced humans can be likened to a short-cut in evolution created by our UGB and extraterrestrial races, their role being to specifically address a planetary need, and to assist or inspire other souls to evolve quickly, rather than over many lifetimes.

The soul of my future son began relating to me onboard craft twenty one years before he was born into this world. These unique children are the first of *the future humans.*

Dr. Schild:

Reading this chapter reminded me so much about reading Chapter 9, *Soul Origin*, on the formation of Suzy's soul, and all the complex bargains and permissions needed to get her manifested in this life with a dual human/alien identity. In the present chapter we read how the Grey's are being extremely careful to be sure that Suzy will be compatible with her unborn son, because of the complexities of their dual soul identities.

I was interested to read about the "layered" communication between the young Suzy and the Grey. We know that the human brain functions on several rhythmic patterns at differing frequencies that the brain research community has called alpha, beta, etc. In principle, the layered communication could be experienced simultaneously if the beings know how.

I was also interested in Suzy's description of an empathic sudden communication with the blue ball of light, and how she described it being like the feeling of somebody watching her. This is so like the "subway experience" of involuntarily looking at a stranger and immediately noticing that they are staring at you.

From these kinds of examples, I consider Suzy's book extremely important, written as it is in her own voice with clean and consistent quality.

Chapter 12

Discovering an Intimate Soul Connection

1962, age 8 years
A gathering of souls

I stood next to the Grandfather, holding his hand and staring in awe and excitement at an array of around thirty vibrantly colourful lights hanging in the air before us. They varied in size, with an appearance and intensity that seemed electric. In my enthusiasm to run and play with the lights I began leaning forward, tugging on his hand. He pulled me back though, telling me he must talk to me first.

I held both his hands and looked into his eyes as he reminded me I had spent nearly a year interacting with the blue ball of light, but now they wanted to show me a number of other such balls of light, and one in particular. He would open a "bubble" in my mind enabling me to remember something important, information he had previously placed in my mind, but closed off from conscious memory. Carefully, he reminded me the blue light would be my son one day, but there was yet another light that would become my second son. This soul would become more active later in life, concerning his association with the Greys.

The two lights were now suspended in the air in front of me, my blue friend and a smaller aqua light emitting silver flashes, reminding me of the colours of a peacock's tail and a scintillating Christmas tree decoration. The Grandfather said I would be permitted to play with this light as well, so I could get to know it and spend time with it alone. Sometimes I would play with the two lights together because they also needed to learn to relate to each other as future brothers, as well as getting along with me.

The Grandfather told me he was about to transfer a "book" (a large amount of information) into my head. I could not access the "pages" of this book yet, but he assured me it would open up one day all by itself and I would be able to "read" the pages (the information would emerge into the conscious mind). However he assisted me to understand the information pertained to specific people I would meet in the future, and tasks I might complete with them.

He drew my attention back to the other lights floating in the room, telling me these lights were people I would eventually know too, and they would play significant roles in my life, but for now they were appearing in soul form. Some had not entered this life yet, had not become a person, and so they would be younger than me in the future, while others were already leading a life and would be older than me when I meet them.

The Grandfather delved into my mind to find a parallel concept in order to clarify this information for me, discovering the concept of a fish net – eventually I would do something in my life that would attract these souls, like casting out a net and pulling it in with fish.

He wanted me to get to know the soul of my future second son, along with these other souls. Again, he rapidly explored my mind selecting the image of a sandwich made up of many fillings, which he likened to the myriad facets of knowledge these souls have accumulated over many lifetimes.

Now the Grandfather encouraged me to relate to all these souls, to converse with them, but I felt rather daunted by this seemingly formidable task and stared blankly at the array of lights before me. He read my thoughts and assured me he had already placed another bubble in my mind (instructions, information) to assist me to relate to them, but the bubble also contained "grown-up" information which would allow me to understand things differently when I am older. I have difficult tasks to complete in life, but all these balls of light would help me.

The small aqua light twinkled silver in the momentary stillness. The Grandfather announced he would leave the room for a while, and the doors slid shut behind him leaving me alone and tearful, feeling glum now and wishing he hadn't gone. The lights hung silently in the air, richly glowing against the white background, until suddenly the room came alive with movement.

S. The blue light's laughing and twirling round me. He's going so fast I can feel a breeze on my pyjama top! I feel a bit better ... and now they're all racing around the room after him!

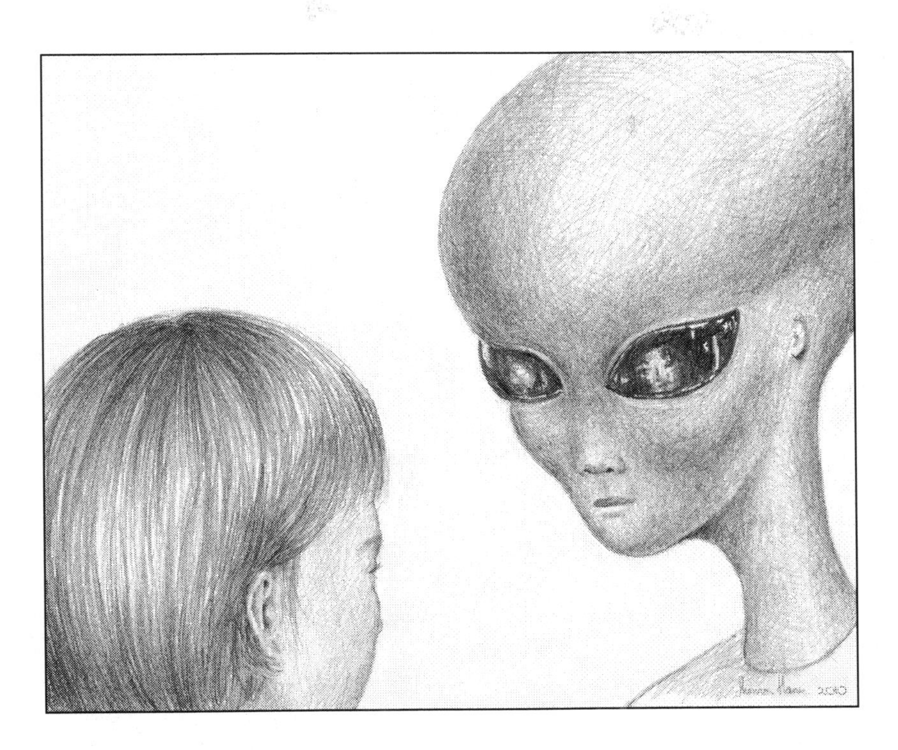

Information Transfer

The second light, my future younger son, remained beside me and floated softly onto the crook of my elbow. Now the lights slowed down and spread out around the room, and I sensed their relief that I had regained my composure and was no longer apprehensive, thanks to their lively game which eased my self-consciousness. I walked amongst them, reaching out my arms, twirling around on tiptoe and stirring them! Thoughts and feelings flooded my senses and I knew they were happy to meet me and looked forward to seeing me again. Images slid into my mind, foreknowledge of future faces, and places where I would eventually meet these people in my life. They came towards me one after the other and I concentrated hard, trying to remember them all. The blue light drew near to me, reassuring, and advising me just to relax and greet them, allowing them to place information in my mind which I would recall in the future.

It was easier now, but I felt the need to be especially polite and respectful because I was aware of future relationships with these lights. All the while, the blue ball supported me emotionally and mentally, giving me the impression he was much older and wiser than me, a strange, incongruous feeling. Equally mystifying was the fact I had been told some of these souls were already leading a life and were therefore older than me, but had appeared here this evening in the form of vibrant lights rather than in a bodily form. From a child's perspective, I wondered where the other souls that had not yet been born were living! Were they staying on the craft in the meantime? The blue ball seemed like a real person to me already, although I knew he had not yet been born.

The lights now drifted languidly in the air and the blue ball reminded me I should establish a relationship with the small aqua light. I cupped my hands and held them out in front of me, and as it alighted on them a brief exchange of emotions and playfulness took place between us, the beginnings of a relationship.

But all at once, the room became quiet and still. The atmosphere changed dramatically as an intense wave of energy enveloped me with deep feelings of tenderness and devotion.

S. *I'm getting the message that the Grandfather is coming back ... the door's sliding open, and there are three* (Greys) *coming in with him and they're s-i-n-g-i-n-g!* [singing the words in a lilting voice] ... *there's some strange singing!* [sudden loud hissing/static noise on the regression recording]. ... *Yes, it's like singing!* ... [hissing/static noise increases in volume so that my voice and that of the regression therapist become almost inaudible] *But, oh! Maybe it's not singing!*

R. *Not singing?*

S. *I don't know, I thought it was, but maybe it's like a strange language!*

Familiar, yet somehow awkward emotions washed over me. I felt great sadness and a sense of longing as I recognised these sounds, this beautiful language, and realised the Greys were actually "singing", or verbalising their language to me! Some part of me registered that I had missed these sounds terribly.

R. *When did you hear those sounds before?*

S. *When I was like them* (lived a previous life as a Grey). *But they're singing to someone inside me!* [audio recorder keeps switching itself on and off] *I feel like I've got two heads! Two brains! They're singing to the other brain!*

Just as we may wish to thank someone for doing something special by singing a song to them or giving a speech, the Greys were thanking me for doing this work, but they were also thanking "someone" inside me!

S. When they make that singing noise I can see a red glow in their bodies ... and ... oh! ... I can see a red glow coming out of my pyjamas! Something inside me is answering them! I feel as if a part of me is one of them!

"My" two lights moved towards my body, the blue ball resting on my left shoulder and the aqua one against my midriff, as if embracing me. The Grandfather calmed me by placing his hand tenderly on my forehead. The red glows faded away.

Serenely, and without further communication, all the vibrant soul-lights followed the three Greys through the door like a stream of colourful party balloons.

S. The Grandfather is smiling at me with his mind, and he conveys gently, "Come." He holds his hand out, and I think I'm going home now.

Discussion

I have now become aware, as a very young child, that I have some other intelligence or consciousness that is a part of me – the Grey identity (part) of the dual soul. I am introduced to souls who will assist me at various times in my life, and in particular, my second son-to-be, who I was told would be awakened by the Greys later in his life. The experience describes the multiple levels on which communication and connections take place between humans, souls, and extraterrestrials. I felt deep love for the entities who are guiding me.

In recent years, there have been perspectives put forward in the UFO/contact fields that the Greys are kidnapping and cloning "human" souls for negative purposes. My experiences may offer an alternative, positive perspective on how souls are drawn to working with the Greys for spiritual reasons, within a positive agenda.

Many experiencers describe having a "bubble" or "knowledge bomb" placed in their subconscious minds by these entities, comprising a vast amount of information that will emerge at an appropriate time in the person's life – what I refer to as *information capsules* or *thought seeds*. They can also assist a child to momentarily perceive information from an adult perspective, providing deeper than normal understanding that filters into the subconscious.

This material also raises a somewhat different perspective on soul-mates, from the much-hackneyed idea of a love attraction. I have known people who have been adamant a person they have met is their life soul-mate, only to be disappointed when this special (often romantic) relationship crumbles after the two have faced difficulties or trauma. Soul-mates are defined as two people with a deep connection and similar minds or viewpoints. Based on this experience as an eight-year-old, we may meet several soul-mates who have agreed, prior to incarnation, to cross paths with us at various times in our lives to assist, guide, or share experiences, but ultimately parting company when this task is completed.

I became aware that what I thought was a song was in fact this species of Greys' spoken language, and at that moment, I could recall hearing it in previous lives I had lived as a Grey. Only on a handful of occasions have I heard vocal articulation by the Greys or other species, which sounded like a pattern of guttural clicks and purring noises, and at other times, crystalline tinkling.

These cosmic languages/singing, or energy-based languages, emit frequencies that are an integral part of the total transmission, what I referred to as "an intense wave of energy enveloping me", causing the atmosphere in the room to "change dramatically". They are wave-like and spiral in nature, rather than linear, as is our own language. The "singing" contained an immense amount of information: the sensation of being saturated in emotions of love, joy, and gratitude; details of past lives lived as a Grey; knowledge of my dual soul status, and much more that is understood in an instant of "knowing", but cannot adequately be recounted to another person in its entirety.

Many experiencers and abductees report unusual paranormal incidents or effects associated with encounters, or even when they later speak about them. In their day-to-day lives they may have problems with electrical or electronic gadgets, and a number of my regression sessions elicited such effects, often at significant parts of the experience. On this occasion, the recorder began malfunctioning at that point in the regression where I described the Greys singing or articulating their vocal language to me, and emanating a red glow. During another session, the moment I began speaking, the battery in the recorder was stripped of all power and had to be replaced several times. On another occasion, the digital recorder turned off at exactly the point where I was recounting information I was told by the Greys must not be revealed yet publicly (timing issues). Sometimes, just by merely touching an electrical appliance, it has failed or burnt out. Media recording/sound equipment has blown as I began to speak.

What causes these anomalies? Is our electrical field significantly different from others, or do our voices carry a timbre or frequency that somehow affects electrical equipment? [21]

This experience reinforces the existence of dual soul identities (Grey and human), and illustrates how as an eight-year-old child, I was reintroduced to the fact I have a dual soul when the Greys sang to me and my other (dual) consciousness. I struggled to come to terms with this awareness of duality (as I described in Chapter 6), and I felt as if I had "two brains" and "two heads". In a sense, dual soul humans are experiencing two lives and two purposes.

There are many thousands of similar souls inhabiting people on this planet. [22] As well as implementing an agenda aligned with soul connections, the Greys are studying our evolving human understanding of spirit and the soul. They seek to understand how we perceive other dimensions and realities, as a precursor to possible future open contact, as they are aware our general human perceptions on these issues are, overall, primitive by comparison.

---

[21] These questions will probably be answered when we have the full description of the Einstein-Maxwell field equation written for the complex space Stein manifold. The anomaly would be understood to originate in the experiencers having particularly strong resonance with the Jung Cosmic Consciousness (cosmic Unconsciousness) and that quantum hologram field being amplified by the experience. In a sense, we might describe it as the experiencer grounding so much of the cosmic consciousness that our electrical systems malfunction from overload. The energy for this comes from the Edgar Mitchell VZPE (Vacuum Zero Point Energy). Recall that our electrical grid oscillates at 60 Hz, and this is very close to the 64 Hz quadrupole octave above the human consciousness 15 Hz beta frequency, which is not so much a single frequency as a frequency band.

[22] In my view the concept of the dual soul is not difficult or complicated to understand. The soul is apparently a resonance with the sum of experience in an identity, and I see no reason why the brain cannot resonate with two souls. This is mathematically very close to what happens when a human soul resonates with another in telepathy and other psychic phenomena.

Chapter 13

Grey Lifestyle

1967, age 12 years

Tiny town

I was among other children in a room on a craft and I had struck up a conversation with some of the Greys present, asking them what they eat and whether they have bedrooms. They were somewhat amused and surprised because none of the other human children in the group had ever asked them such questions.

One of them offered to take me into their separate living quarters, which humans do not usually enter. I felt excited, in awe of this opportunity and I had no qualms about accompanying him into an unknown area of their craft. We travelled some distance through corridors and down to another level in a light elevator.

Upon stepping out of the elevator I was immediately taken-aback by the unexpected sight before me – everything looked smaller, more "economical", and the narrow corridor resembled a plastic tunnel or drainpipe. A bland floor stretched on ahead of us, flat, with curved walls forming a semi-circular ceiling and the entire structure was integrated, seemingly moulded from one enormous sheet of material. The network of corridors were like rabbit warrens, but laid out in grid-like fashion giving me the sense this area of the craft was vast compared to the restricted areas frequented by humans.

A private rest cubicle: connecting to the "big brain"

The Grey had intended to take me to see their version of a kitchen, however he immediately sensed my interest in other rooms, spaced every three to four metres or so along the corridor, and he asked me if I would like to see one of their "rest" rooms first.

I tentatively stepped into a tiny cubicle and was struck by the feeling of confinement and simplicity of the room, with only a bed and a rather odd-looking chair. This was their equivalent of a human bedroom, and I began mentally comparing it with mine at home containing two beds, a dressing table and mirror, a chest of drawers, cushions, bedspread, and other personal items such as soft toys. He responded to my thoughts, commenting they do not need much in the way of personal items as their technology supports their lifestyle, with ample choices of entertainment and education. Personal items such as humans have in their homes would be of no use to them.

As an example, he indicated their version of a bed, which over the years I came to refer to as "shelf-beds", also found in areas of the craft where humans visit. It resembled a thin plastic shelf jutting out from the wall, incorporated seamlessly as part of the total wall structure. There was nothing supporting it underneath and although they look flimsy, they are in fact very strong, softly moulding to your shape but returning to a flat surface as soon as you get off them, as if they have a mind of their own. Pre-empting my thoughts again, he explained there is no need for bedding because their technology maintains a constant temperature control that is suited to their metabolism. I couldn't imagine going to sleep without the comfort of a pillow and bedcovers. The Grey interrupted my thoughts:-

S. *Um, he says they don't lie down that often! But when they do ... how can I explain it? It's as if they connect to a "big brain" and it filters and sorts. Their mind is like a machine, almost. So they don't really sleep.*

He commented they are often amused when humans come onboard and lie on a shelf-bed because we tend to toss and turn, wriggle, change position, roll over and so on, even in an altered state. Humans need sleep to regenerate and recharge the body and we can't survive long without it. However he said when they lie on these shelf-beds they are able to slow their metabolism and by thought-command, connect their mind to a central computer through their body's energy field contacting with the material the bed is made from. In other words, their shelf-beds are a continuation of the organic or conscious technology found right throughout these craft. They lie down to rest while this form of intelligence monitors their physical status and rejuvenates their entire system. But this is a secondary function, and more significantly, the primary function is to examine the mind and brain, seen by the Greys as separate functions working in synergy. The "big brain" as I called it, also gives instructions or information to them about their next task in their particular job or position. We would call this the next day's work, however there are no days and nights on the craft, only what they see as time periods.

I was fascinated by the Greys comments, which confirmed what I already knew even as a child, that there is always so much more to their technology and environment than meets the eye, deeper levels and functions that are not immediately obvious to humans. He stood still, allowing me to look around the room to see what else might arouse my curiosity. I tried to imagine what it would be like to have a bedroom without a window to look out of, a somewhat boring cubbyhole.

S. "But," he says, "That's not all, there's the chair!"

The virtual-reality chair

As if to counteract my disappointment, the Grey turned my attention to the only other visible furniture in the room, a chair constructed of similar thin, light material as the shelf-bed. It reminded me of a small reclining dentist's chair with a foot rest, raised off the floor on a short pedestal so you had to step onto it. He explained it provided a form of personal entertainment and education, and offered to show me how it functioned.

S. I really like the chair and I wish I had one! This isn't his room, but he's showing me. So he's got into it and he's pulled this thing out in front of him, and he has commanded it to turn on. It has lit up and there's a little screen!

The small screen was positioned about forty centimetres in front of his face. It resembled a small sheet of dark grey glass or plastic, approximately twenty centimetres wide and twelve centimetres high and fixed on the end of a thin extendable arm. His physical contact with pads on the arms of the chair enabled him to instruct the technology to function, along with thought.

S. Oh wow! He says, "Come around!" I'm standing beside him looking at the screen and ... wow! There are all these amazing things!

The Grey explained it was the equivalent of us watching a film, but the complex designs rotating on and beyond the screen would mean nothing to us. I was fascinated by swirling shapes which "stood out" in the air away from the screen in a myriad of colours and mysterious patterns.

(The screen showed images in what I now surmise to have been a 3-dimensional display.) [23]

My interest was really piqued when he thought-commanded a second time and a band of light shone from the rectangular screen, widening as it extended out, encompassing the Grey's face and head. I asked him the purpose of this light and he replied he would instruct the technology to activate the programme he had just selected, and I would see!

I stood transfixed as a new stream of strange images appeared now within the band of light, animated, vibrantly coloured, floating, appearing, disappearing, receding, advancing – like a movie reeling forth from the screen along the beam of light straight into his eyes, and I assumed, his mind or brain. Although the computers I had seen in the human area of the craft produced "stand out" (3-D) images, I had never seen anything quite like this technology. It revealed a whole new level of magic for me as a child, and the images seemed "alive" as far as I was concerned!

S. He says he can actually go inside their "movie"! I ask him what that means.

The Grey placed an appropriate parallel in my mind: imagine if I stepped through a door in my home and into a room where I found myself in the jungle, or under the sea. So, suddenly you are not in your room anymore – you have become part of another environment where you are able to move around, smell, touch and examine things.

Somehow this technology incorporates the screen and the user's eyes, brain, mind and senses in such a way that they feel as if they are "inside" or part of whatever they are looking at, but it is really only their mind and sensory perceptions that are there. Through thought-

---

[23] The child Suzy described rotating and 3-dimensional patterns, which suggests that they were designed to create effects in consciousness, so an fMRI brain scan would probably show that the two opposite brains lobes would have registered them in the characteristic consciousness state mirror-symmetrical brain patterns. And Suzy mentioned that they were visually 3-Dimensional, which implies that they were registered as visual information in the two brains lobes where the brain patterns would be compared in the two brain lobes, and registered as 3-Dimensional. Thus the same brain mirror neuron network would have been registering image data and emotional consciousness reaction, making this (for the aliens) an animated pleasing experience.

instruction, they are able to experience the sensations of moving, touching, tasting, hearing, and experiencing almost anything they wish in this environment (what I now understand was an advanced virtual environment or enhanced reality). The technology interacts with their optical faculties, but although the Grey described this form of entertainment to me quite well, it was still difficult for me at the age of twelve to get my head around these concepts.

I so badly wanted to get onto that chair! But my companion told me my eyes and electric field did not match this strictly Grey technology, and therefore I could not adequately connect with the screen, thus preventing me from fully experiencing what they can. The Grey perceived my bitter disappointment and was even a little amused at my extreme reaction to technology they must consider quite ordinary and familiar. He counteracted my disappointment a second time by diverting my attention elsewhere, revealing a cupboard in the wall that was not visible until he touched a particular spot, and it opened up. Inside was a pair of tiny, narrow black shoes, similar to the rubber gardening galoshes my mother used to wear outside in winter, but other than that the cupboard was bare. My child's mind felt sorry for the Greys that spend time in these rooms, because despite their amazing technology it just didn't feel homely to me, but my companion reminded me it is home to them and they don't need what we have.

I asked if it was actually okay for us to be in this room as it was clearly not his, but he reassured me it was fine because they do not have a sense of ownership like humans. To illustrate their perception of individuality he described how they utilise the "magical" chair they have in their rooms, which seemed the only piece of private life available to them. Through this technology, each user can access an infinite array of topics in combined visual and multi-sensory form. Once connected to the technology, the user scans topic groups of interest and selects one, instructing the computer to activate it. They can then consciously "step into" and become part of another reality, interact with another civilisation or life-form, or explore an unfamiliar location in the cosmos.

The user can access material relating to the many species the Greys have genetically intermingled with, planets they have explored, or civilisations and species they may have assisted, studied, or worked with. Add to this a myriad of scientific and cosmic databases spanning innumerable years, centuries, or millennia. It was difficult for me as a curious twelve year old to move away from the chair. I longed to be able to sit in it, choose a topic or location, and become part of an unimaginable environment.

However, both he and I were aware I was becoming cold, dressed in short summer pyjamas with arms and legs bare. It was clear the Greys preferred a colder living environment than humans and it was affecting me. We moved on towards their kitchen.

A communal "kitchen"

The Grey ushered me into a communal room where their food or sustenance, was prepared and processed. It was not like my kitchen at home and was without fridge, sink, or visible cupboards. However, registering my thoughts, he reminded me there *were* cupboards concealed within the walls! A large rectangular table with a central pedestal leg running the length of it, stood just inside the doorway, with the right-hand end of it attached to the wall. It was made of similar material as the bed, but without the flexibility.

Eight short Greys were seated on pedestal stools around the table and when we entered the room they looked up at us and casually carried on with what they were doing. I wondered why they were not surprised to see a human child enter their kitchen.

> *S. The Grey says he had already ... he's having a little* (human-like) *joke with me ... he says, "I radioed on ahead that we were coming!"*

I suddenly became acutely aware of the situation I was in – an entirely different setting from the children's playroom, sharing a communal moment with these entities. Visits onboard craft were usually focused on a particular activity or purpose, sometimes with limited time to make personal connections with all of the entities present, or to examine in detail their individual physical features. I was intrigued by these small Greys seated around the table carrying out ordinary, everyday tasks, just as we would do at home.

Their genetic characteristics varied just as much as those of a room full of humans. I stared at them unashamedly, feeling my closeness to these entities had now taken on a new level of familiarity, a deep binding affection towards them. Even though they were strangers to me, I was aware they had already telepathically "read" everything about me: how I felt towards the Greys and mixed-species, and my closeness to those I have worked with. These entities had now also become a part of my encompassing friendships, as I momentarily tapped into their hive-mind mentality, absorbing their expressions of emotion towards me and their acceptance of my presence.

My companion pointed out apparatus fixed to the wall at the end of the table – a rectangular container with a clear lid, and one of the Greys was emptying an unfamiliar substance into it, which my companion said was "food". I could see a rotating roller and an intensely bright light operating inside the machine, and underneath was a wide chute out of which small exquisite compressed sheets of the substance were sliding into trays on the table.

These tiny sheets resembled tissue-thin wafers, some five centimetres long and two centimetres wide, with criss-crossing fibres. The Grey described a process of first thinly layering multiple substances of differing kinds, then semi-drying and compressing the mix, before cutting it into strips – a process which takes mere seconds in this apparatus. He enabled me to understand this process by drawing on familiar images and concepts already in my memory banks, then he produced images in my child-mind of me making a sandwich by spreading a piece of bread with butter, then jam, and finally mashed banana. My favourite!

There are two ways of using this sustenance: ingestion and absorption. They can ingest the wafers, but I noticed he did not mention teeth, simply stating their jaw is not appropriate for chewing as their mouths have changed, physically evolving over time. As their technology and understanding of nutrition and sustenance changed and advanced, they started doing things differently. Some of them slip the tiny sheet into the mouth where it dissolves and absorbs.

S. *He says I could taste it but it's not ... I'm sort of thinking of the word "equal" ... it doesn't equal me? He's putting that word in my head and I'm laughing. He understands his translation is not quite right. He means it wouldn't "suit" me.*

The Grey gave me permission to pick up a wafer, but warned me it may react differently on my skin to how it does with theirs, because humans have considerable moisture on their skin. I was disappointed when the wafer broke up and disintegrated almost immediately upon me touching it. He showed me how they can place a strip of this sustenance on their wrist or arm, where it will slowly disintegrate and some aspect of it will be absorbed into their skin. There are places on their bodies where absorption occurs rapidly.

The Grey made no mention of liquid intake and I felt only minimal moisture in the thin filaments of sustenance. One would assume they need fluid, but in true Grey character, he responded *exactly* to my question, "What do you eat?" with precise detail, with no reference or information outside of this question. Perhaps if I had asked, "What do you drink?" I would have got a different response.

He explained that in their culture everyone is equal when it comes to carrying out communal work. The entities seated at the table were taking their turn to prepare sustenance, sorting the wafer-thin sheets of food into piles in small Perspex-like containers ready for different groups of staff to enjoy. Their version of mealtime is structured around the beginning and end of work shifts, and following the end of a work period they may decide to take their sustenance straight away or first complete the re-sorting/rejuvenating rest procedure in their cubicle.

By now I was feeling numb with cold and the Grey suggested we should return to the children's room because it was not good for me to be in this chilled environment too long. I asked him if he found the temperature in the playroom too hot, and he replied that they have the ability to regulate their own body temperature for periods of time, enabling them to cool their body, even in a warm room. I was surprised by this comment, but it explained why, on occasions when I have touched their skin, it felt cool despite me feeling warm.

It was time to leave, but it was hard to tear myself away from the group of entities. A moment of stillness settled in the room as we sensed each other's feelings. My upbringing had taught me it was rude to stare at people and yet the Greys were accepting of my child-like curiosity and allowed me that space to examine them with my eyes, to drink in their physical presence. They paused in what they were doing, looking at each other, looking back at me, and there was a touching moment of amusement and tolerance. I became tearful as I did not want to relinquish this feeling of all-encompassing love, but my companion reached out and softly touched my forehead, restoring my composure.

I reluctantly left the room with him, returning to the children's playroom via a different route, and near the end of the corridor was an enormous light elevator, larger than any I had seen on craft before. We stepped into it and within a fraction of a second the door slid open again – we were back in a familiar hallway and it was warmer here.

As we entered the room I thought I would like to tell the other kids about where I had been, but typically, the Grey instructed me to remain silent about this, in fact he made sure of it by rapidly diminishing my memory of the visit to their quarters.

S. One of the cone-head entities is holding a little baby with a long skull and I say to my Grey companion, "There's a baby!" He says, "Well you can go and see it if you like", and I instantly forget all about where I've just been.

The brainy baby

I asked the male entity if I could hold the baby and he passed it gently into my arms. It was part them, part us, about eight months old in our time and although it lay still and quiet in my arms, I knew it was thinking!

It seemed as if the baby had an old brain in a baby's head, as it perceptively observed me with extraordinary large blue eyes. We stared intently at each other, each thinking about the other's facial features.

S. It's a brainy baby! It has pale whitish-blue filaments inside the iris, like lace, but the rest is bright blue with a small pupil, which gives the eyes a strange look, as if they are staring.

The baby's nose was more pronounced than most of the Greys' and there were small lips, not just a slit, and indentations and folds where the ears should be. It lay still, without squirming, crying, or stretching, and despite its large head, it was not heavy. The head was completely bald and there were places on the skull that moved rhythmically in and out as if the skin was being sucked in slightly from the inside.

I wondered whether it was a boy or a girl and the adult nearby, who had been watching me and listening to my thoughts, replied it was neither. This was news to me! He explained sometimes there are humans who are not quite male or female, but it is rare. He suggested I might understand this better when I'm older, but it is quite common in their culture, and he added that male or female is not important to them, but rather the mind and awareness.

Discussion

As a twelve year old I am continuing to learn communication skills. The unexpected opportunity to visit Grey living quarters was a rare and privileged chance to observe aspects of their lives and culture, particularly technology.

An acute impression I felt when I came out of this regression was that I was physically very small and needed to stretch out. As to whether this was due to the fact I had been reliving this experience as a small 12-year-old girl, or whether due to the fact I had been, in my mind at least, in cramped spaces, I don't know. It was a curious feeling though.

I discovered the Greys' equivalent of sleep is to connect to an organic conscious computer to harmonise the entire system – mind/consciousness, brain and body. In a sense, this examination of mind/brain synergy could perhaps be likened to the defragmentation process carried out by modern-day computers.

The experience of viewing the magical chair in the restroom was phenomenal! Within our current framework of scientific discoveries it is clear this chair used an advanced form of virtual reality for entertainment, relaxation and education. But this technology appears to involve surreal factors combined with sensory aspects, and the specific visual-processing capabilities of the Greys' eyes and visual/interpretive centres of the brain. Humans have been developing virtual reality technology for nearly two decades, but it is limited by comparison.

In the section devoted to the "brainy baby", the Grey adult made reference to the fact the baby was "not really a boy or girl". As a 12-year-old girl I did not understand this comment, however it is clear he was referring to the fact the baby was androgynous (sexually ambiguous; neither distinctly male nor distinctly female), which he stated was "quite common in their culture." Many experiencers and abductees describe Greys whose sexuality they are unable to determine by physical appearance. There is often no obvious indication of breasts or genitalia. However, often the physical appearance of Greys is so slim and delicate anyway, that one only receives an intuitive impression of whether an entity is male or female, or only discovers this through conversation.

The mixed-species brainy baby was one of many I have held and related to onboard craft and I was aware of the analytical thought processes occurring in the baby's mind. From my observations, the Greys relate to their children, and to human children, from a higher intellectual level and in such a way that assumes intellect and capability is *already* functioning, rather than waiting for it to unfold through a developmental process, as we often tend to do. Intelligence and in-depth learning is fostered from the very point of creation, and even prior to inhabiting a body.

As described in previous chapters, the Grey delved into my mind to search for parallels and comparisons, utilising my mind to assist him in explaining concepts and technology. From my experience, the Greys go to great lengths to inform and educate human children at any opportunity and their whole perspective on existence is based on information sharing. Another telepathic "tool" employed by the Grey was his ability to fade my memory of the visit to their private area when I suggested I could tell the other children about it.

We again witness the Grey sense of humour when my companion said he had "radioed ahead" to alert the entities in the kitchen we were coming, using familiar human terminology to describe his telepathy, for my amusement.

The experience illustrates the Greys' lack of a sense of ownership, something I believe is often a negative and detrimental trait in humans.

Like many experiencers I have spoken with, I frequently did not want to go back home; I wanted to maintain that sharp intellect and focus and frequently wished I could stay onboard a while longer.

Chapter 14

Working in an Alternative Form

1968, age 14 years

Confusion set in. Some part of me had heard a call, rousing me to gather my awareness. *Get up!* Some other part of me wanted to continue sleeping. I suddenly became fully aware of two tall Greys standing next to my bed, and the confusion escalated when they requested I begin the process of shutting some part of me off from this present consciousness. I knew I had to leave with them, but I also became aware I would be leaving some part of me behind.

R. So which part are you leaving behind?

S. I'm leaving my body and ... no! ... I'm leaving the human part behind!

The fourteen year girl lying in the bed was unaware of "the call" and remained asleep. Only the Grey identity, part of the dual soul, had heard the request to accompany the Greys onboard a craft.

I began rising up out of the human body, an ethereal Grey body form, feeling my thoughts becoming attuned to a different consciousness. A moment of adjustment took place as I left the more dense human form and my mind was lighter now, free of the complicated emotions of a fourteen year old girl. I felt more comfortable, clearer and sharper, fully in the Grey intelligence as I stood by the bed looking down at the sleeping human body.

One of the Greys addressed me, discussing the human form I am combined with, the complex emotions of the fourteen year old teenager and the domestic environment she was living in. They needed to talk with me because the human side had become dominant, not because it was cleverer or wiser, but because her emotions were weighing her down.

He informed me I also had work to do this evening as part of a team and they would tell me more about it when we reached the craft. One of them reminded me I needed to perform another adjustment because we were about to alter our state or form, to travel to the craft. I had temporarily forgotten my capabilities as a Grey, that I could make that adjustment. This happens sometimes if the Grey identity has become dormant within the human life-form.

S. *A process is happening now ... tuning our minds and energy fields to something ... to a frequency. We're elevating to a vibration. Oh! ... I'm disintegrating! I'm looking down at my* (Grey) *body and I can see the process happening ... and now I don't have a body anymore!*

We had become small, dense, bright balls of white light, although I was still conscious of everything around me, able to "see" it. This new state was accompanied by a feeling of weightlessness – dense and compact, but still light, if that makes sense. The two Greys now drew me with them as we passed through a wall and left the house as three orbs of light. Some part of me was still not quite sure how that happened, but I was tailing along behind them nevertheless. [24]

Within a split-second we were on a craft in an extremely bright corridor, and we were now doing the opposite of disintegrating.

S. *We are like grains of sand ... falling and forming into our bodies again.*

R. *From the ball of light back into a form?*

S. *It's like a projection ... the density of the ball takes on matter... becomes matter ... spills into the air and forms. This is the only way I can describe it.* [25]

My Grey form was shorter, that of a mixed-species with a round skull. After a moment of readjustment, I followed the two tall Greys along the corridor feeling I was more "with it" now, with the awareness of a Grey fully restored and back home again. [26] I comprehended the vast difference in the way I was functioning at this moment, compared to how I function in the human body, combined with the human intellect or consciousness. It is distinctly different and

---

[24] So the balls of bright light seen by some people may be embodiments of sentient beings that have self-awareness but no body. They pass through walls and so are phase relationships and not physical reality.

[25] Re-forming is experienced as the information ball takes on matter, like the quantum waveform has the diagonal terms expressing mass added to it.

[26] Suzy-Grey describes becoming more comfortable resonating with her Grey consciousness and comfortable with her alternate existence.

that is what the Greys are interested in as part of their ongoing research involving dual souls.

We would be working with humans during this night, and we eventually entered a room with rows of slim beds on pedestals. A Grey assistant explained what was required of us, telling us the humans lying quietly on each of the beds were divided into two groups: those who were suffering from cancer, and those who had sustained injuries potentially causing long-term health problems.

But as he began, I suddenly and inexplicably felt swamped with emotions, as if I had inadvertently tapped into something which I was finding difficult to separate from. The other Greys present immediately sensed this and were curious to know what was happening to me, gathering around me and scrutinising every detail of my feelings. In this moment in time my Grey identity became a curiosity within its own species, and they immediately questioned me for research purposes.

It seems the moment I understood the predicament and suffering of these people, I tapped into human emotions, and they were interested that this crossover of consciousness had occurred between my Grey self and my conjoint human awareness. I thought I had left the human consciousness behind, but somehow I was carrying some aspect of it with me, or tapping into it, experiencing human compassion and emotions I found difficult to cope with, but which "standard" Greys would be able to objectively control and isolate in order to be able to carry out their work. Nevertheless, they seemed pleased this interspecies fusion of senses and consciousness was occurring.

Our task tonight was to alleviate suffering from the human cancer patients and prolong life. Prior communications with their souls allowed these procedures to take place and although we could not intervene to the extent of completely curing them, it was possible to take measures to prevent the spread or exacerbation of their problems, allowing extended time-spans to complete life tasks.

Initially, it was intended I should work with the twelve humans who had sustained injuries, however having experienced emotions from the human consciousness, the Greys made a snap decision to assign me to a supervisor of human/Grey genetic mix. They explained he also experienced what they considered to be spontaneous emotions through his human genes, and they anticipated I might learn something relevant from him as the evening progressed, that could be advantageous.

The supervisor explained we would treat three of the ten cancer patients. All the humans present were awake but in a highly relaxed, almost anaesthetised state so they would not be afraid or aware of where they were. Although the Greys could use advanced technology with these patients, under the circumstances the supervisor would perform Grey "surgery", a form of energy-based healing humans are only in the early stages of comprehending. I was to watch and learn as I had limited previous experience in this area.

We began by psychically viewing the first female patient and comparing our perceptions. The Grey doctor swiftly opened a seam in her body by moving his hand just above the nightwear fabric and skin, and both parted without releasing blood. He felt the need to examine the diseased organ and tumour visually and physically, as he intended to focus on the smell or odour of the cancer. Greys' olfactory senses identify smell differently to humans, perceiving odours in "tones" or "levels", registering the frequency or vibratory rate of a smell at a quantum level beyond human knowledge. [27]

I observed as he repositioned his hand above the body, and strands of coloured light/energy streamed from his fingertips, which he used to gently separate tissue revealing a small tumour on an ovary. Leaning over the shelf-bed, he discerned the odour of the tumour, providing him with a great deal of information about its "signature". I watched and learned because I did not have his expertise or analytical perception of the odour.

The tutor asked me to try this myself, to summon my healing ability and attempt to move further tissue away from the tumour under his direction. Light and energy projected from my fingers accompanied by a slight tingle, but the process was more about using

[27] Human smell is just the registration of a chemical reaction in the olfactory chemistry that becomes transmitted to the nervous system. Grey smell may have sensitivity to other aspects of the chemical anomaly, possibly the state of excitation of anomalous chemistry present. Because this occurs in living tissues, it is also possible that the sense of "registering the frequency or vibratory rate" is associated with the smell chemistry. The "quantum level beyond human knowledge" might be the excitation state of the chemical substances, or might be related to the organic nature of the human tissues. It is analogous to human smell and vision, where a particular odour has only intensity, but vision perceives intensity and colour.

intense focus so that the hand just becomes a tool of the power of the mind. [28]

The supervisor addressed the woman's consciousness for permission, before entering her mind and learning something about her. He described her genetic disposition, her lifestyle, fears and traumas, all of which had affected her emotions long-term and ultimately, her health.

By tapping into the consciousness of the human half of my dual soul, he drew comparisons in relation to the future well-being of the fourteen year old teenager, and how any trauma suffered by her could also potentially affect her health in the same way. He reminded me I have combined with the human at a soul level to achieve a specific purpose and my input must become stronger, supporting the human side to attain balance. This is my responsibility.

S. I realise that as the Grey identity, my intellect or consciousness is set apart somewhat from other Greys, who are not in a dual situation. There must be a blending of the two sides of the soul ... and this is what they have been studying.

We returned to the issue of the woman's health problem and with the energy flowing from his fingertips, he worked around the tumour's edges. Now there was the prospect the condition could be further treated by human medical procedures, thus at least prolonging life for a time so her soul could complete pre-determined work in life. He moved his hand above her abdomen again and the opening in the body and her nightclothes sealed up.

The next patient had a melanoma on the leg, however removal would not end the problem as the cancer had already spread elsewhere. He invited me to view the melanoma, as well as the life-force radiating from that area of the body, and using particular Grey visual capabilities I was able to microscopically examine the melanoma by magnifying my visual field. The instructor once again scanned the body, isolating three places with small growths. He held his hand over those areas one at a time and light streamed in multiple thin columns from his palm, extending into the body and dissolving them. The melanoma on the leg would be left for human doctors to deal with.

---

[28] Here we have another example where the experience of resonating powerfully with the QH produces, even in an alien Grey, a tingling sensation.

Looking to my left, I saw our next patient was a child in an aqua nightgown. Her face was tranquil, framed by shoulder length hair, the fingers of one hand wrapped around the edge of the narrow bed.

S. [emotional] ... *and this is a child, a three-year-old girl and she has leukaemia. I'm feeling swamped by the human emotions again.*

But the tutor swiftly and abruptly requested I take control of my emotions and maintain focus; I could not be helpful or effective in that unstable state and must put these feelings aside. Another Grey joined us and we set up an intense field of energy around the child using our minds to quicken the vibratory rate of her body, our aim being to infuse the child's energy field allowing her own immune system to regenerate. So although she, as a child, was not conscious of what was happening, her soul-state, what some refer to as the higher self, was aware of receiving and utilising this energy.

Our input was visible as an oval of white light around her like a bright mist, and it was akin to replacing her blood cells with fresh normal blood cells.

My work for the evening was complete and I was directed to another room, but the moment I entered the corridor I began to feel strange, as if some other unexpected transformation was taking place within me. I looked down as I walked and could still see my spindly legs and hands, but it was as if my psyche had been momentarily subdued as someone reached into my mind, evoking disturbing feelings. I struggled to make sense of this as I became awash once again with human emotions.

A senior Grey was seated in the room, smiling at me with his mind because he was aware of the struggle and turmoil within me. He held me in a kind of suspended animation as he communicated with me on a deep level, providing information about what the fourteen year old human I had left behind would go through in her life over the next few years. I had been "stilled" in order for him to clarify these details.

S. ... *and it's not very nice* (the details provided to me) *and he's using it like a shock tactic to make me realise that, as the Grey side of the dual soul, I must be more effective in providing insights to the human in order for her to survive certain incidents in her life.*

He made me acutely aware of future life-threatening events which I must assist her through, because should the human life be cut short, agreed-upon tasks would not be completed and nor would the research into the dual soul identity, for this combination at least.

In such an event, I would survive in my Grey form, but the human would not. [29] There was a sense of urgency for me to be proactive – a sense of urgency pertaining to the human's life, and balance must be achieved in order for the human side to survive. If I remained dormant and ineffective I would be allowing this to happen to her human form.

Images flashed through my mind of a tragic car accident in the future, and afterwards, the young girl seated, pondering the worth of her life because of it. I had been "sleeping", and they wished to prod me, wake me, redirecting me to focus on the task. I now comprehended how the human emotions had been adversely affecting the Grey psyche. This is a new experience between humans and Greys, experimental, and therefore the senior Grey provided guidance.

In Grey society, the phases from youth to older age are far less noticeable, partly because of their longer lifespan and partly because their children are treated as intelligent equals. Human phases of childhood, teenage years, and adult years are clearly delineated by comparison. He established the core problem for me was that I had not been able to adapt to the natural phases in a human life, or to the associated effect puberty and hormones have on the human body, emotions and behaviour. Human emotions had over-whelmed me, stopping me from functioning effectively in the partnership.

He reminded me that I come onboard many times to work as a Grey in various capacities. By projecting images into my mind he revealed how my memory of this work undertaken while the human teenager is asleep, had become fuzzy. I needed to function adequately within the dual soul, as well as separate from it.

---

[29] There is a profound implication here that two souls originating in the pool of inactive souls as described in earlier chapters were active in her body, so if the human body died, the Grey soul, occupying a Grey body, would survive. In the sense of the book, *Proof of Heaven*, by Dr. Eben Alexander, this is best understood as our consciousness being outside the body and a resonance with our eternal being, so that two such resonances can occupy the same body. Recall that at this point, Suzy's human form was asleep in her home, but the Suzy writing this book was having these experiences. We read that this is a complicated experimental situation that requires occasional maintenance by great intelligence, and re-balancing.

It was my responsibility and I did not wish to fail.

S. *I'm dissolving back into that dense form of light, disintegrating, and within the disintegration, a ball of light is forming. I'm passing through air now ... and floating down into the human body, still in my orb form.*

Discussion

Here, the Grey identity of the dual soul is taking part in healing programmes onboard craft, but is struggling to be effective with the human teenager. Nevertheless, it must prepare for future events in her life.

The experience further develops concepts about dual souls, but it is clear we have more to learn about the concepts of matter, separation, and transformation into another form, as part of their existence.

In the healing room on the craft we are introduced to a form of energy-based surgery combined with "psychic viewing". Human understanding of the power of the mind and the universal energy available to us to be utilised in this way is still in its infancy, but I believe that over the next few decades our medical technology will become less invasive and reliant on medication, and more reliant on the use of energy, frequencies, colour and sound waves.

Over the years I have observed a number of healing methods used by the Greys, usually involving technology combined with consciousness. I recall an occasion when a Grey simply aimed a small glowing red box-like implement at me, and was able to immediately diagnose a minor infection. On another occasion several entities at individual consoles directed spurts of coloured light at my body ranging from the breadth of a hair to some forty centimetres wide. Each charge of light varied in duration and they were directed at different parts of the body. I was told they were tracking backwards through physical and emotional damage that had occurred throughout my life – like unwinding a rubber band. Perhaps there are reasons why these healing techniques differ, and I wonder if bridging healing methods are also being prepared by the Greys to gradually up-scale us slowly, introduced to our civilisation as precursors to much more "magical" technology in the future.

Significantly, we are informed the Greys have the capacity to "smell" cancer. In researching this concept I discovered that dogs have the ability to smell cancer too. Specially trained dogs are able to identify patients with lung and breast cancer by sniffing their exhaled breath, with a high accuracy of between 88% and 97%. Canines' sense of smell is 10,000 to 100,000 times superior to that of humans, with a greater convergence of neurons from the nose to the brain than humans have, hence their tracking and hunting abilities. Cancer cells emit different metabolic waste products to normal cells, and these differences are so great they can be detected by a dog's keen sense of smell, even in the early stages of disease. Similarly, tests and research have been undertaken in the USA and Sweden to develop genetically engineered fruit flies, which glow green when they smell cancer.

I do not recall how the humans who were given healing on this night were selected by the Greys, other than by their condition. Were they humans involved in some of the Greys' programmes? Or are these regular healing procedures part of ongoing medical research or philanthropic projects by the Greys?

When I experienced waves of human emotions, the instructor requested I take control of my emotions in order to maintain focus. Our own doctors, who constantly cope with patients in various states of pain and distress, must develop the ability to "switch off" to some degree in order to work effectively. Medical research suggests that when observing people in pain, physicians may exhibit less activity in the brain circuits associated with feelings of empathy, and increased activity in areas of the brain linked to self-control, regulating emotions and cognition. In other words, physicians may control their emotions to avoid feeling distress, which could interfere with their effectiveness.

The Greys have apparently mastered this ability to control their emotions in a way appropriate to the tasks they are carrying out. In this way, they reflect the self-control exhibited by many of our own medical and veterinary practitioners. Some abductees report cold and officious behaviour by Greys during medical-type examinations and procedures onboard craft, perhaps reflecting this brain/emotion-altering ability.

Towards the end of this experience the senior Grey projected images into my (Grey) mind of a car accident at some time in the future, which would take me to the extremes of despair. Six years after this onboard experience in 1974, aged nineteen, I sustained spinal injuries in a car accident caused by a drunk driver, and my passenger in the car suffered multiple serious injuries requiring ongoing operations. My despair over the severity of our injuries at a youthful age, the injustice of the situation, and the possibility we may both suffer chronic pain for the rest of our lives, presented a grim future. However, a powerful repetitive intervening thought that there was something important I must do in my life, pulled me through many dark days.

In summary, the dual soul combination has already been developed between other universal (alien) species however it is a new and experimental process with humans and Greys. This process is designed to enrich the Greys' understanding of our species and to provide humans with a measure of their consciousness.

Chapter 15

Metamorphosis: the Insect Entity

We revisit and explore through regression the incident of missing time which occurred in autumn 1975, as outlined in Chapter 1, The Wake-up Call. The details revealed are in stark contrast to the terrifying recollections of the beginning of the event that I described earlier, when our car was engulfed by a blazing orb of light.

1975, age 20 years

Our car was floating, surrounded by blinding light, and I was in a state of terror, trying to shut my window in an attempt to keep us safe.

But then quite suddenly I felt calm and relaxed, as if in a dream-like state. The intensity of the light had diminished revealing a dark spherical shape close above us, underneath which our car was floating, moving along as if suspended from the object by invisible wires.

I could just make out another much larger object high in the late afternoon sky. We approached it at such speed that I do not recall its shape, as I was not fully cognisant, but I do recall that two doors slid back on its under-surface revealing an enormous illuminated opening. With unexpected velocity, our car swung out to one side of the small round object and was now floating alongside it, before moving slowly up underneath the larger craft and ascending through the opening, the doors sliding closed beneath us.

As if remotely controlled, our car moved forwards and gently settled on the floor of a hangar area. My body felt heavy, but my mind now worked overtime as I took in my surroundings. The hangar was filled with craft of varying shapes and sizes, and several had large doors or hatches open with both humans and Greys gathered around the machines. The Greys wore tight-fitting body suits, while the humans were dressed in common loose dark-blue overalls with zips up the front and elastic around the waists.

A human and a short Grey approached the car and opened the passenger door, and I felt a moment of confusion as I realised I recognised the Grey. His energy was familiar, as was the close-up appearance of his large, curving black eyes and rounded head. Memories flooded back. It was RJ, otherwise known to me as "the cousin", who in a sense, I had grown up with. He was staring at me, waiting for recognition and I began to feel more alert and charged.

In a flash, RJ mentally restored old and relevant memories of our long association to my conscious mind. Leaving Pete (my flat-mate) "asleep" in the car, we crossed an expanse of black rubbery floor, and the human accompanying us indicated I should follow them into a small glass-like cubicle where a form of suction is applied to the body, thereby removing unwanted material. After a few seconds we entered the body of the craft itself and proceeding along a busy corridor, passing a variety of Grey species and other entities. The human walked purposefully, while the RJ "glide-walked" (floating with his feet only occasionally touching the ground allowing him to move at speed over distance, given the Greys' characteristic manner of walking is not as fluid or fast as ours).

We came to halt at an intersection while a brief discussion took place between the human and RJ. I wasn't quite up-to-speed yet and only deciphered bits of it pertaining to my possible reaction to something. The human gestured and I followed them into a room.

R. What is in there?

S. It's like a huge insect!

A tall entity, like a cross between a Grey and a giant praying mantis insect, was seated at a desk on a low chair. Its face was intelligent-looking and I felt no fear, only brief surprise. Added to the quirky mix of appearance was the fact it wore loose pants and a top of sorts. I had the distinct impression it was male and classified the entity as "him" in my mind. His appearance, although spell-binding, was certainly non-threatening.

The human informed me the entity performed the duties of what we would understand as a doctor. He went on to say they were concerned about my well-being and wanted to undertake a full check-up of my health. I welcomed this because I had experienced a lot of pain following a serious car accident several months earlier.

The insect-like entity stood up revealing he was near seven feet tall. The three of them ushered me through a high-arched doorway into an adjoining room and I lay down on a shelf-bed while they talked to me. They intended to remove an element of shock from my body resulting from the accident, and repair "holes" or weak spots in my energy field, with my consent. Energy was dissipating unnaturally from these holes instead of circulating and emanating as it should. They were aware I had undergone a number of medical tests and numerous treatments on my spine to address the constant debilitating headaches and spinal pain, causing considerable time off work. I was not functioning or coping well and they were keen to be of assistance.

Although he showed no physical signs, I perceived empathetic emotions from RJ and his distress that they cannot prevent some things from happening in my life, or give me a miracle cure either. He was deeply sad, commenting on how much time they had invested in me and how important it was to carry out just enough repair work so I could cope. He gently unfolded in my mind that nevertheless, I would still face some ongoing pain.

The tall insect entity had been standing listening and as I glanced at his face I noticed his features were changing. He was transforming himself into something different!

S. His head has changed shape! He's taking on more of a ... not a human face ... but a humanoid face that has visibly recognisable features to me as a human.

I watched in awe as the entity's eyes became intense and altered shape. His skull flexed and moulded, and his facial features sculpted before my eyes into a humanoid form with small nose and chin. His head now extended into large lobes at the back, with a huge brain capacity more like a Grey, his eyes starkly black whereas a few seconds before they were a complex mix of shifting colours.

The entity explained he was showing me his own dual soul combination, a very different entity from the form I initially saw him in, and a mix of two extraterrestrial intelligences. He can work and function as either, and what I had just observed was an energetic shift in his awareness as he began to draw on the expertise and skills of the other species that he is. This transformation is not necessarily visible in the physical form and can be restricted to the mind or consciousness however he chose to allow the physical change so I would understand how the dual identities can function. He emphasised I must allow my Grey identity to contribute to my well-being, draw on its expertise.

He could have sat at the desk in this other form, ready and waiting for me, but he chose to perform the transition to remind me that dual souls can operate from both systems, to ingrain this understanding in me. They wanted this concept to stay right under the surface of my cognition so that in the future, I can just scratch the surface a little and that memory will be there.

The entity used his visual and mind abilities to scan my body, giving me a running commentary about my bones, shock to vertebrae and discs, and the nervous system. He placed an image of an egg in my mind, telling me he should be able to see a large egg-shaped field of energy around my body, but he now changed the image to one of an egg that is cracked with the egg white spilling out of it. Apparently injuries had caused leakage from my energy field, which he described as a deep purple stream spilling into the air. The entity commented I had been allowing distress about the accident and the resulting trauma, to spiral out of control. We discussed how various spinal and musculoskeletal treatment regimes had failed to reduce pain levels, and it was increasingly difficult to face each day.

S. He's got his hands up now ... wow! They're just hanging in the air above me. He's got stick-like fingers, jointed, thin. He's moving them above my body repairing not just the energy field, but also quelling my underlying emotions.

I began to feel out-of-plumb, as if lying in a banana shape and I felt a bit panicky about this, but he encouraged me to be patient. His features changed again as he transitioned between two species, utilising the variety of skills from each of them.

This repair work would eventually filter down to the physical, spiritual and emotional bodies. It was not just about easing my suffering, but about me taking control of my own well-being, and the entity placed an information capsule in my mind pertaining to a future time when I will need to utilise this information to self-heal at a specific stage in my life. This capacity must unfold, rather than be thrust upon me now in this weakened state. They reassured me they would not leave me entirely to my own devices and they would carry out similar healing procedures until improvement was evident.

Consequently, some discussion took place on coping skills and mechanisms, because the information package placed in my mind would not open for some years and I needed to cope in the interim. They stated my Grey dual identity was working hard with me, asserting considerable influence on my progress, keeping me determined and relatively focused, but my fears of a potential lifetime of chronic pain were over-whelming these attempts. I must endeavour to remain positive.

Having completed the healing, we discussed the role of humans who live and work onboard these craft for long periods, and who represent various groups working in cooperation with these entities in a positive sense. Their aim, with the Greys' assistance, is to counteract the damage being done by other covert groups of humans seeking to acquire and use extraterrestrial technology purely for monetary gain and power over people. Agreements between species and humans have come and gone, some failed. [30] These humans onboard have to be constantly on-guard and up-to-speed with their goal of slowly but surely, acclimatising humanity to the reality of extraterrestrial visitation. The conversation was brief but informative.

I sat up, my legs hanging over the side of the shelf-bed. The human said goodbye and left the room while the other two remained for a short time, and a deep connection and underlying love reverberated between us.

R. What is the nature of this connection that you feel, and what does it relate to?

S. It's like looking at their bodies and seeing me dancing in their cells ... and they can probably see themselves dancing in mine! Like reciprocal electricity enlivening your cells and you understand it. It's as if your blood recognises their blood, and becomes animated. It's a very powerful connection.

It was both a genetic and a soul connection. The tall insect entity left the room and now only RJ remained. He commented they had been intently monitoring what was happening with me and had waited for the right time to pick me up. An implant in my body provided them with information about my health, but they had waited to see whether I could pull myself out of this situation.

As we returned to the hangar and approached the car, we shared a moment of black humour when RJ commented I would not like the situation I was returning to at all. I accepted this, knowing that once our car was placed back down on the ground, I would have little or no conscious memory of what had taken place. My mind would focus solely on memories of a frightening experience with a large bright light and an unaccountable lapse of time. I was not yet ready, or in a good enough state of health to cope with conscious memories of these contacts.

---

[30] Note Suzy reports in a previous chapter how some government operatives in the Laughlin conference threatened her and her family if she continued to report contact with extraterrestrials.

R. What's the next thing you recall?

S. I'm feeling confused ... there's a whooshing sound in the car. Ugh! My hands and feet are numb! I don't know where we are! It's dark! Something's happened!

Discussion

I first spoke publicly about the lead-up to this experience at the New Zealand UFO Symposium, 1997.

As described in Chapter 1, the dramatic precursor to this contact was a wake-up call for me, but conversely, it also engendered a period of fear in my youthful life. The meeting with the human, RJ and the Mantis entity presents evidence of their concern for the well-being of those who are involved in the Grey/UGB programmes, and interventions are made in a person's well-being if appropriate and agreed-upon. However, the traumatic experience of our car being swallowed by a blazing light produced its own negative impact on me, but I concede it also precipitated me into UFO research and an investigative examination of my life's experiences thus far.

The Mantis entity demonstrated the transformation of physical, energetic and intellectual capabilities of its own alien dual soul combination.

In this chapter, I make first reference to the fact I was escorted by a human and that there were adult humans working onboard the craft; I was not surprised, indicating I was already aware of this.

In an experience several years later, I recall again receiving healing from a Mantis entity with a long pointed face and bulging eyes. On this occasion the entity used an instrument that emitted something like a mild electric current. It was a rectangular object around thirty centimetres long and twenty centimetres wide, metallic-looking and with a handle attached. On one side of the object were rows of square lights, some with a red hue and others white. He used it to scan, running it up and down above the surface of my body, causing a tingling electric feeling like a mild electric shock. This did not hurt, but created a prickly "magnetic" sensation, making my hair stand on end. He informed me the square lights/energy were gathering comprehensive information about the physical body, sending data and even images to a computer for analysis.

Having sustained debilitating injuries in a car accident I struggled to cope with chronic pain and the demands of adapting to a new career. Looking back, by mid-to-late 1975 I began to cope better and I was able to return to driving long distances and physical activities that required stamina and concentration. Perhaps all this may not have been possible without the entities' concern and joint intervention.

Significantly, this contact experience highlights what many experiencers and abductees have discovered through regressive hypnosis: that sometimes what they initially recall as a frightening encounter, turns out to be a positive experience.

Chapter 16

Interacting with our Universal Energy Fields

"Tokomaru Bay on the East Coast of the North Island
has been getting some UFO activity.
Is this area turning into another mini UFO flap?"
"Saucerscan" magazine, Gisborne, 30 April, 1978

1978, age 24 years

Here I further explore the incident that occurred in 1978 north of Gisborne city, as outlined in Chapter 5, Illuminating Experiences, The Tokomaru Bay illuminated valley.

R. So you are in the car with "Dave" heading home from Gisborne. Describe to me the first thing that comes to mind.

S. A circular craft is coming up the valley ... it's hovering very close.

The craft hung silently in the air, wider than the road, tilted slightly backwards revealing the underside. I climbed out of the car with some difficulty as my legs felt numb and clumsy. The car had come to a standstill on the grass verge beside a farm gate, with Dave now sitting still with his eyes closed, seemingly asleep. I walked forward and stood in the middle of the road looking up at the craft, waiting. Three interlocking pieces of metal on the underside slid back in a curving movement and a yellowish-green tubular beam of light descended around me in a controlled fashion, without outward radiation. As the light encircled me and began to retract upwards, I had the curious sensation of jumping into the air, before rising up on an invisible floor and through the opening, where I floated down onto a surface.

I was now in a confined space with my head close to the domed ceiling. Two Greys sat at controls with their backs to me and conveyed I should sit on a seat behind them. I could see stars in the sky through the window/screen (henceforth "w/screen") as we hovered for a second or two. The Grey pilots flew the craft by monitoring a screen with symbols and lines radiating from it, and by using their minds. I could not feel any movement at all. [31] It was like sitting still in a room, and I had no idea how long we travelled or what distance we covered. Eventually one of the crew informed me that when we arrived at our destination, I should leave the craft through an opening in the side, and he indicated where this part of the wall and ceiling was located. Crisscrossed metal or plastic-like strips covered this section of the craft's interior, resembling the pattern of a net and providing tread so you do not slip.

Within seconds the ramp began lowering, making a quiet hissing sound. It was a strange feeling, not even knowing we had reached our destination and come to standstill. The light beyond was glaringly bright and it took a moment for my eyes to adjust from the dimness inside the craft.

I now found myself in a *huge* disembarkation area of a larger craft, with lines of Greys ushering people in different directions, and I stood still at the bottom of the ramp, not sure where to go. Instantly, I received a message from one of the Greys nearby telling me to join the group of humans he was gathering together. I wondered how he knew who to include in his group, as there were hundreds of humans arriving in craft. Was it a random selection? I moved close to him and waited while other people joined us, and when he had gathered a total of twenty people around him, he asked us to follow him.

Our escort conveyed mental images and information to us as we proceeded: we were now on a massive disc, with many floors or levels within the body of the craft. The circular flange or lip on the outer circumference of the craft served as a hangar and disembarkation area, with large arched openings spaced evenly around the circumference for exit and entry – all with doors open at present telling me we were somewhere relatively low in our atmosphere.

But by far the most intriguing feature I observed was that the entire roof of the disc's circular edge above the hangar area was transparent. Perhaps it looked metallic from the outside, but inside, you were

---

[31] Thus we conclude that the craft has removed the mass energy from its energy field. The Einstein GR theory, through the Principle of Equivalence, teaches that inertial mass is equal to rest mass, so as the craft moves without Suzy feeling any acceleration force, it must somehow remove the mass aspect of her quantum reality, which however seems not to cause her or the alien Greys to lose their consciousness.

treated to a panoramic view of the sky and stars through the massive sloping roof. It was just amazing! The hangar curved in both directions into the distance, with varying sized craft performing a silent dance as they manoeuvred gracefully in and out through the archways of this vast area.

The short Grey led us into the interior of the craft and it was clearly his job to meet-and-greet humans arriving here. We proceeded down a corridor with other groups both ahead and coming along behind us, each accompanied by a Grey.

Our group was directed into a room set up with rows of seats in a semicircle around a bed-like structure. We all quickly found a place to sit, leaving quite a few gaps of empty seats between us. Nobody spoke to anyone else and in fact, we'd hardly had time to take notice of each other. The room was an odd shape, wider at the rear end and coming down narrower at the front, with a large screen set in the wall in front of us. The narrow, thinly padded bed on a central pedestal was unfamiliar to me, not at all like the shelf-beds seen on other occasions, but there was obviously a high-tech aspect to its design. The underside of it resembled the back of an armadillo, with overlapping layers of pale plastic-like material, and I surmised it could be adjusted into various lengths and curves to accommodate different species or body shapes.

The Grey asked us to stay seated and wait, and left the room. I glanced around at the other humans and was amused by the appearance of one man who stood out because he had pyjama pants on without a top, just a bare hairy chest. At that point I noticed I was also out of place! Normally I am in my night attire, however on this occasion I was wearing my jeans and a T-shirt and there were a few other people with daytime clothes on, which seemed out-of-the-ordinary to me.

My idle thoughts were interrupted when an unusual looking Grey/mixed entity came into the room accompanied by two others, one short and one tall. He had striking features, with an elongated skull and he wore a long white coat-like garment with a raised collar, giving him the appearance of a priest. His enormous eyes wrapped around the side of the head, but they resembled human eyes in that the whites were visible, with brilliant blue-grey irises and black pupils. The odd size and shape of them gave him a surprised look and the fact he had no eyebrows added to his quirky appearance. Unlike the dark-eyed Greys, the entity was able to capture our attention with the expression in his eyes alone and I found this both fascinating and unnerving at the same time.

This entity was our instructor for the evening and he announced he would talk to us about the human energy field. With a direct and officious manner, he asked for a volunteer to demonstrate his information. Nobody obliged at first, so he toned down his telepathic approach, emitting a more soft energy.

A woman with black hair and wearing a floral nightdress stepped up the front, and immediately everyone began chuckling because we could pick up her second-thoughts about volunteering: *Oh, what have I got myself into! Why did I say that!* She turned to smile sheepishly at us when she realised we all knew.

Our instructor indicated his volunteer should lie down on the bed and with a touch on his screen, the overlapping panels under the bed realigned until the woman was in a semi-reclining position with the bed ergonomically moulded to her body. A small rectangular object on a thin pipe now extended above the bed, with a circular protrusion pointed downwards at the woman. I imagined it must be a light until a bird's eye view of her body appeared on the large screen, revealing the object was a camera of sorts. With another touch on his screen an astounding image of the woman's energy field appeared, like a bright mist of shimmering colours, contracting and expanding so we could barely make out her figure.

He asked us what we could notice, and whether there were any anomalies in her field. I observed two places where the flow and vibrancy was disrupted and I can explain what I observed in this way: imagine you are up in an aircraft looking down on a cloudbank, but you can also see the ash cloud of a volcano erupting through the clouds. That is what it looked like, with two bubbling eruptions of colour breaking through the rest of her energy field.

Our instructor stood quietly, reading everybody's thoughts and waiting until we realised what parts of the body these eruptions were located over. Some people were slow in comprehending, still fascinated by the flowing colours on the screen.

Okay, we've got to keep moving, he conveyed, touching the screen again.

S. Oh my god! We're on the edge of our seats! Everyone's holding on to their armrests and looking because we can see right into her body! We can see things pumping and gurgling!

It was astonishing and for a moment I struggled to take in what I saw before me. All the woman's exterior identifying features had disappeared and been replaced by an image of her internal organs! Unaffected by our amazement, the instructor carried on, marking the positions of the two energetic eruptions on the image with a couple of taps on his mini-screen, and we could see they were positioned over her liver and one leg.

The Grey told us he would complete the rest of the lecture in what I call "quick time", or speedy telepathic delivery, as time was short. He began by talking about the state of her liver and how toxins, diet, and our thoughts can affect the health of our organs. Humans don't give enough consideration to this and the Greys consider our thoughts are damaging and toxic compared to theirs. They find it difficult to understand why we ruin our bodies with our negative thoughts and in fact, he added, we can even affect other people's bodies with them.

He emphasised this concept is something many humans have yet to understand, and it is a trait we need to improve upon if we are to have open communication with others in the universe. This could take some considerable time given the varying belief systems and educational, sociological and cultural backgrounds of all ethnic groups on this planet. Human behaviour must change positively, and he stressed that all of us present at this lecture needed to consider these issues so that change can take place within communities and societies in small, but progressive and cumulative ways.

Our instructor returned his attention to the volunteer, who had mixed feelings flickering across her face and looked embarrassed by his revelations about the state of her liver. He calmed and thanked her, telling her not to take it personally.

The Grey continued his lecture about the destructive power that negative thought and intent has on our energy fields, and indeed, on our mass consciousness. Asking the other two Greys to assist him, he demonstrated how the solutions and antidotes to this lay in understanding how to repair and maintain our own energy field with the power of our mind, drawing upon universal energy. One Grey directed negative thought to the woman, and on the screen we observed the effect on the colour and vibrancy of her energy field. The other enlisted the woman's help in dispersing this negative energy with their minds, restoring her field to its former state.

Our instructor emphasised it is important for humans in these programmes to learn to shield ourselves from destructive thought-forms from others, as well as become more aware of the effect of our own thoughts. He said although we can intentionally damage other people's health with our thoughts, if we choose to behave in this destructive way, it is actually ourselves we do the most damage to in the process. Some of the most common conditions causing human deaths are in part, created by our own thoughts.

He moved on, indicating the eruption above the woman's leg was a different kind of damage, with its own energetic peculiarities. The technology now showed ligament and muscle imagery on the screen, and the woman acknowledged she had fallen while horse-riding and injured her leg.

Now he wished to emphasise something vitally important for us to understand and again, he adjusted the technology until we had a bird's eye view of the bed from much further away. We were surprised to see how far the woman's full energy field extended, encompassing the three Greys standing next to the table, as well as some of the people in the front row.

Our instructor focused our attention on the extremities of her energy field stating that at this point we move into what he termed "universal energies". Our "personal energies" are closer to the body.[32] At their extremity, roughly mid-point in the field, we find a crossover point where the personal energies intermingle and merge into universal awareness or consciousness, in our outer fields.

He stated that all of us present had been taught advanced levels of psychic abilities and telepathy, however all humans have the capacity to develop these intuitive abilities by learning to access the extremities of our energy fields. Our personal energies can utilise the universal field to "run the body" so to speak, and make decisions about its well-being, and he added that many of our psychics and healers are already aware of this, but the public in general is not.

---

[32] Here we learn that our energy field has a "near field" and a "remote field" component. I understand this to mean that the universal QH field is the remote field that carries our soul, being resonance with right brain activity, whereas the body's mass is classically understood as a gravitational field local to the rest mass. The Einstein GR theory shows that the two are interrelated by the field equations, since the QH field is predominantly helicity and technically nilpotent, whereas the near field mixes helicity with mass as described in the field equations of GR.

At this point the instructor made an unexpected aside statement to our group, that in the future we would all become public speakers, and it was clear this lecture had a purpose beyond informing us about the way the human body functions in conjunction with its energy field. He told us we had been selected from various programmes to be prepared for tasks in the future involving public speaking about extraterrestrial visitors to our planet, and that this was in line with our soul-agreements. Many of the concepts gained from this lecture would rise from our subconscious in the future and be used in our role as speakers. We would need to use the extremities of our energy fields to assess situations, discern atmospheres and intents, and access and draw information from the Field of Consciousness during our speeches.

He stated the majority of humans walk around each day with their personal energy fields barely functioning adequately, and their universal energy fields are small, poorly utilised and remain close to their personal fields. If he was to bring a randomly selected person onboard, he would likely be able to show us a less active, less vibrant energy field.

Our instructor prepared to convey an information capsule to each of us using a method I nicknamed as a child, a "telepathic spray", because it reminded me of watering a garden, with each drop from the shower of water reaching a separate plant. I will explain this extraordinary form of communication: when humans hold a conversation we can only convey one piece of information at a time. There may be several listeners, but they will each receive the same information. When the Greys perform a telepathic spray, they have the phenomenal ability to convey a different thought, encapsulated instruction, or packet of information as the case may be, to each person in the room at the same time.

He had prior knowledge of who would be present at this lecture (confirming the meet-and-greet Grey knew what he was doing), knew details about each of us, had observed our lapses in knowledge and awareness during this lecture, and knew what was required to rectify this by giving an individual input to each person. This information was then stored in his mind throughout the lecture and was now to be conveyed to each of us at once, within a few seconds, using "Multiple Telepathic Messaging" (MTM), or a telepathic spray. The contents of our individual sprays would be revealed in our minds over time and at the appropriate moment.

Having completed this, our instructor thanked the woman for her assistance and lowered the bed so she could return to her seat. He requested we all change to a different seat in the room, telling us to close our eyes, adding wryly that humans seem to concentrate better with their eyes shut. Next he asked us to shift our awareness outwards away from the body and ascertain how many people were now encompassed within our energy field. With our eyes closed, we had to analyse and feel where each body was by recognising their different energy signatures. There were twenty people spread around the room and I was able to identify that eighteen people were positioned within my field.

Oddly, considering he would already have known the answer, the instructor asked if anybody had isolated less than sixteen people within their energy field, and perhaps with intentional humour, he asked us to raise our hands rather than convey our answers telepathically!

S. Everybody's laughing. Nobody's put their hand up. He says, "Between sixteen and eighteen?" Everyone's putting their hands up. "More than eighteen?" Nobody. He says, "That's pretty good, okay, next exercise." I'm enjoying this!

He asked us to extend our consciousness to the extremities of our energy fields, still encompassing those sixteen to eighteen other people. Now our task was to obtain some random piece of information about each person, from their energy field. It was tricky because we had to ascertain where various fields were crossing or intersecting and know who was interacting with whom, and which person carried certain information within their energy field. Who did it belong to?

S. He says, "What do you feel? What can you perceive about these people? Anything will do, just reach out and grab it."

We all began picking up what he wanted, some silly extraneous stuff about people. I identified a man who was annoyed because his toilet pipe keeps leaking, a woman who collects lion ornaments, and another who grows geranium plants. We spent some time swapping information and the outcomes were both humorous and revealing. The instructor encouraged us to utilise these skills in our day-to-day lives, use our mind less and our senses more. Our minds may have been conditioned by our human education systems, or societal, religious, and cultural expectations and rules. He stressed we should always use these skills with integrity; they were not a tool to be used to "spy" on people or exert power over them. If we were to use our skills in this way with negative intent, we would harm ourselves spiritually and physically through our own conscience.

He extrapolated further on this subject with stunning images of life on Earth, demonstrating how all life forms perceive and interact through their energy fields: plants interacting with insects; animals interacting with plants; insects interacting with animals; humans interacting with animals; humans interacting with plants; and humans interacting with the earth. The energies flared, swirled and intermingled, but sometimes also retracted and diminished in negative situations.

Extending this concept to the cosmos, he presented images of magnetic energies within solar systems: planets interacting with planets; moons interacting with planets; moons interacting with other moons (where planets have more than one moon). This was visually stunning and I'm sure I was not the only one naively wondering how they could capture or recreate this in a visual form (remember this was back in 1978).

Again, he extended our understanding, showing us the energies of solar systems interacting with other solar systems; galaxies with galaxies. It was phenomenal!

S. *He says, "Do you see the correlation? Do you see how everything is energy, and everything is interaction, and there needs to be respect for that interaction? Maintain a harmonious interaction and connection* (through consciousness) *with all things."*

The session ended on this memorable note and although we had been here a considerable time, he assured us they had shortened the time of absence for some in the group who had been brought onboard during daytime or early evening hours, hence the variety of clothing. Each had been picked up at a time when their shortened absence would not be noticed by others.

The Greys thanked us for our cooperation and left the room, while the one remaining requested we follow him.

S. *He says, "Come now." Our energy fields are full of light! There are groups coming out of other doors. It's just like clockwork!*

A different set of workers directed us to waiting craft. They seemed to know who should go where, which in itself was an extraordinary feat considering the hundreds of humans present. A man joined me now and we were directed to board a small craft. I must have dozed off because the next thing I recalled was being instructed to enter the beam of light.

My feet touched the surface of the road, the yellow-green light ascended and the craft departed at tremendous speed. I fumbled my way to the car and got in. Dave was still sitting upright, leaning against the door jamb, asleep. Suddenly, all recollection of where I had been left me.

Discussion

At age twenty four, my education on craft encompassed such topics as energy fields and their usage, thought and intent, and becoming familiar with advanced technology. Through these studies I continued to learn mind/brain capabilities.

The instructor casually mentioned that in the future, many of us would become public speakers whose words would affect others. It appears we have been tutored, along with many other groups of people, in the ability to communicate ideas more effectively through an understanding of thought and language, augmented by methods of manifesting consciousness. Over time, and the tutoring of thousands of people on craft, I believe this has the potential to change the nature of human communication. A further basic explanation of this information came up in another regression as follows:

S. The Grey says that the time will come where, when we are talking to people either in conversation or in a speech situation, we will say things sometimes that will carry a vibration – a trigger, a key – that will be said in such a way that in a flash, it will convey to some people a great deal more than we've actually said. For example, take the sentence, "I can run". For some people the word "run" will open up a set of information. For others, information will emerge from the word "I" or the word "can". People will go away thinking, "Oh, where did all that come from? Gee, all this stuff just came into my mind!" And they will follow it up in some way. It will unlock things in people's minds through the sound of the voice, the words or phrases we use.

This process could be a form of subliminal trigger designed to touch a person's mind and soul, uncovering deeper meanings at that moment, or an individual inspirational thought, all part of a mass consciousness shift.

Scientific researchers now know that language changes DNA – like a biological internet. This could explain how affirmations, prayer, hypnosis, subliminal messages, etc can have strong effects on humans. Information is carried through human language to much deeper levels than we previously understood. Neuro-linguistic programmers know our body is programmable through language, words and thought.

I cannot begin to describe how massive the circular craft was that I was taken to and even now, the thought of it makes my stomach whirl with awe. Given the large number of floors in the interior section of the craft I suspected it was bulbous, walnut or Saturn shaped.

In researching sightings of this description of craft, I came across a report written by Dr. Bruce Maccabee, a US physicist and photographic optical data analyst, who has analysed a number of high profile UFO sightings. The article on Dr. Maccabee's website entitled, *The Fantastic Flight of JAL1628*, describes a 1986 sighting by a Japanese Jumbo Jet pilot named Captain Terauchi, which occurred near Anchorage, Alaska. A drawing made by Captain Terauchi depicted a gigantic walnut-shaped "spaceship".

In his report on the JAL1628 sighting Dr. Maccabee stated: "... he (Captain Terauchi) got the impression that the object was bigger than his airplane, so big, in fact, that in public statements he compared it to the size of an aircraft carrier!"

This corroborated my description of the craft I visited on this occasion, even down to the fact Captain Terauchi also saw lights entering and leaving the large craft.

We see evidence of the Greys' ability to manipulate time itself, when the instructor informed the group they had shortened the time some of us had been absent, to avoid arousing suspicion from workmates or family.

It is characteristic of the Greys to extrapolate on concepts humans may already have some awareness of, in this case, thought and energy, providing a deeper awareness to utilise in our lives. Understanding how they use universal energy, and most significantly, the energetic interactions and interconnectedness between all things, is an integral part of every aspect of education the Greys provide.

This meeting underlined to me the importance of positive thought in all aspects of our lives and evolution, both personally, and collectively as a species. We all know it is sometimes difficult to achieve positive thought as we face social and environmental difficulties, or changes and tragedies in our lives, but nevertheless, our overriding intent towards positivity at least, must remain strong.

The power of thought and intent is potentially both awe inspiring and terrible in equal measure – the power of good, the power of evil. The choice is ours.

Chapter 17

Replacing Implants

"What's going on in the sky around Gisborne?"
Title from the *Gisborne Herald*, Sat. Dec 17, 1977

1978, age 24 years

An investigation of the event north of Gisborne city as described in Chapter 5, Illuminating Experiences: the "sheep truck" incident.

S. *The buzzing ... it's getting louder! My fingers and toes are going all tingly ... I want to get up!*
R. *You want to get up?*
S. [hyperventilating] ... *I think something is going to smash into the house and I want to look through the window!*

I was paralysed, no longer able to move any part of my body except my eyes and head. A deep, buzzing reverberation passed over the house accompanied by bright white light. But then, quite suddenly, all of this mayhem receded into a distant part of my awareness and I felt inexplicably calm.

I rolled my head to one side and realised someone was coming down the hall, and they were floating! A group of four Greys, three adults and a child, glided into the bedroom. I recognised their leader, who levitated me vertically off the bed, the blankets falling away as he stood me upright. We all proceeded back down the hall with me following behind him, floating in the air with my arms and legs hanging limply. As we moved, he explained that although I now had full control of my mental and emotional faculties, and all fear and shock had dissipated, it was easier and quicker for us both if he moved my physical body in this way.

The group drifted silently through the living room and without even pausing, transitioned through the curtains and glass sliding door, over the concrete terrace, across the lawn and over a fence. It was cold outdoors and my long nightgown flapped around my legs.

A small craft stood on a tripod in the paddock next door, sleek shaped but shallow in the centre, and I wondered how we could all fit into it. As we approached, a portion of the upper surface opened up, pivoting and lowering down to form a ramp. We entered a surprisingly large interior and the lead Grey released me from his mental grip to sit on a curved seat against the wall.

Once underway, I asked the lead Grey about the child, as I had never seen one onboard during a "pick up", and I was surprised when he replied the child was related to me! He added that the child was curious to meet me, having heard I was to be brought onboard, but he offered no further explanation. The other two Greys were "observers", learning the procedures of transporting people and interacting with them.

I couldn't resist staring at the remaining occupant who captured my attention. His physical features were unlike the Greys, with large black and almost vertical teardrop-shaped eyes, giving him an ant-like appearance. The entity met my gaze directly and passively, and I found it difficult to drag my eyes away from him.

The lead Grey picked up on my thoughts about the numerous UFO sightings that had occurred over recent months in the Gisborne and East Coast areas, and offered to show me something of interest. Within my mind, he placed the image of a steep hill with a dark opening in the side of it, and I could see something sliding across the opening, concealing it. He told me they had established a small temporary base in remote hills nearby and this was where many of the craft were coming from that people had seen around this area, but humans would never locate this base. I found this revelation just too extraordinary to believe – a base in the area where I lived? How could they excavate and develop an underground base without attracting attention? Surely this must displace a huge amount of rock and soil, let alone the noise generated by such activity.

He explained their technology could excavate underground efficiently and relatively quietly, compressing soil and rock to a fraction of its former extent. They could then transport it to places where it would not adversely affect the environment or even be noticed. He stated that in a sense, they were "masters of disguise" using advanced technology on our planet in ways that avoided unwanted attention. This technology would seem like magic to us, but it would advance our civilisation dramatically if we had access to it. He conveyed this matter-of-factly, without conceit or guile.

He stated they have many bases around the planet, which allow various extraterrestrial groups working together to perform a variety of undertakings. These include studying our current environmental and ecological problems and developing specific technology to address these, such as rapid purification of large volumes of water and, something I found intriguing, “soil cleansing”. This technology will be leaked to mankind over time.

We had now arrived in the hangar area of a larger craft and I followed the senior Grey; I’d met him before and he can best be described as a medical technician. We entered a room where he intended to replace implants in my nose and one ear. These biological implants need to be changed occasionally as they begin to dissolve over time. He had inserted two small organic implants three years ago, and the one in my ear was counteracting balance problems caused by the car accident, but it also allowed them to hear what I hear. He reminded me I also had an implant in my right eye, which somehow enabled them to see what I see. This, along with similar ear implants has enabled them, and in particular the hybrids, to learn about us: languages, emotions, lifestyle etc. They can cause the ear implant to make a loud noise and apparently they had used it to wake me this evening, which explained why I had woken so suddenly.

Beginning with my left ear, the technician placed a large oval object over it, which I thought looked a bit antiquated by Grey standards. It was cone-shaped, narrowing towards a lens-like object inside, and the whole piece of apparatus fitted closely over my ear and part of the side of my head like a cumbersome earmuff. He peered into the circular “lens” and I assumed this enabled him to see inside my ear, although compared to apparatus human doctors use to look into the ear it seemed large and clumsy, but likely had other functions I have no knowledge of.

Having withdrawn it, he picked up a long thin flexible wire (possibly hollow) with a miniscule horseshoe-shaped clasp on one end of it and a lens/viewer on the other, and carefully inserted the clasp end inside my ear. After looking into the viewer, he withdrew it again and I glimpsed a tiny irregular-shaped chip between the clasps. The new implant, like a droplet of shiny glass, was then inserted deep inside my ear. This procedure did not hurt at all and finally he repositioned the “earmuff” and double-checked his accuracy. My “balance horizon” now felt a little odd, but he said this implant was an upgrade from the previous one and I would soon adjust to it.

The technician repeated the same process to replace an implant in my nose, telling me it was not as easy doing this one because I'd had a broken nose and therefore the nasal passages were narrow. This implant would assist them with their studies of the human brain and its electrical functions.

With the tasks completed early, the technician desired a short chat with me. He had already perceived imagery within my mind of my dog, and he was interested in our human concept of pets – my relationship with my dog and my deep love for her. He viewed it as an inter-species relationship, whereas he commented we humans tend to view it as "master and pet". They would relate to the dog more as an equal, another intelligent species, while we feel ownership of them.

Our conversation continued, and I was surprised by the rapid change of topic with his next abrupt statement that I would have children soon! This was a shock because my partner did not want to start a family, and this had created difficulties between us. The technician's following comment was equally blunt, relating the subject of having children, to having a pet. He commented that once I'd had a child I would understand the difference, and I would realise that although I love my dog dearly, I will still treat her differently from my child; that despite loving (domestic) animals, I still see them as pets. I would realise the difference in the way they look upon other species.

He expressed interest in my teaching profession and how our children are taught in comparison to theirs, and he raised other differences between our cultures, commenting our future children will have the benefit of advanced technology akin to their own. Grey children have a different attitude towards knowledge and application to a task. They cannot understand why in some human societies and cultures, and even amongst many children in our more developed countries, there is such resistance to education, particularly for females, not deeming it important in their lives or in our evolution. This kind of mindset does not exist in their society.

Then just as abruptly as it had begun, the brief exchange ended there, as it was time to leave. The technician accompanied me to the hangar entrance and I spontaneously turned and waved to him, and although he did not physically wave back, he projected a humorous image into my mind of him waving boisterously as a human would do.

A number of the ant-eyed species were working in the hangar and one of the observers told me they carry out research with the Greys, and those present in the hangar were pilots of craft.

We entered a disc and there was the child again! I felt an instant rapport with it, and sensed it was female. I wanted to scoop her up and hold her, but instead, I held my hand out tentatively and she placed her palm, three fingers and claw-like thumb over the top of my knuckles, looking at me intently. Her hand was delicate, with the texture and softness of suede, and I could feel a short "pile", like minute hairs that stand upright when touched. We sat half-turned towards each other and mutual curiosity passed between us.

S. The observer says he's going to put me in an altered state now. I ask, "Why so soon?" He says, "Practice!"

Discussion

Like many experiencers/abductees it seems I have been fitted with implants, possibly since childhood, which not only provide the Greys with information about human life and physiology, but also temporarily helped me to cope with the result of injuries.

I learnt there was a genetic link between me and the alien child on the craft. But the most surprising revelation was that I would have children of my own sometime soon, and both my sons were born within six years of this contact event.

There are a few other aspects which warrant further mention.

The intense buzzing sound I described in the initial stages of this contact (as outlined in Chapter 5) may have been technology directed only at me and my partner to effectively paralyse us, while everybody else in the small township may have been unaware of any disturbing sound approaching. Research indicates that various military groups around the world have been developing direct-beam sound, capable of targeting one individual amongst a large group of people. The sound can have a variety of effects ranging from incapacitation, to pain and unconsciousness.

The craft that flew over our house and landed in the paddock next door was streamlined, with very little vertical space in the centre, and yet we all fitted into it. I have noticed this anomaly on other occasions, where the interior of a craft is vastly different in size than the exterior indicates. Many craft that transport humans are purpose-built to accommodate our stature, while others seem to transform in size upon entering them, as this one did. On other occasions I have travelled in small craft clearly designed for Greys only, without this capacity of transformation because I have had to stoop in them and sit in cramped conditions. [33]

We are introduced to the fact that teams of Grey observers are learning the procedures involved in picking up and dropping off humans, and how to relate to us. To me, this indicates a preparatory process occurring, where the Greys are anticipating contact with humans *in increasing numbers*.

I was not surprised to discover I had implants replaced in my nose and ear, because for several days following this experience I suffered nosebleeds and sensitive hearing.

The technician reminded me I also had an implant behind one eye, and this has prompted my recollection of a funny incident which occurred some twelve years ago. I awoke one morning and opened my eyes to see a small screen-like image suspended either "inside" my vision, or above my face. On the screen was the face of a Grey looking back at me! I'm not sure who was more surprised, but I certainly perceived a sense of shock and embarrassment from him when he registered my amusement, and the screen instantly disappeared. Just how I was able to view this I do not know.

I was interested when the lead Grey informed me that many of the craft seen around the city of Gisborne and surrounding areas during the time of the Gisborne UFO flap of 1977-80, were coming from a base they had established in remote hills in the area. I have a

---

[33] I have myself been interested in this, when 5 years ago I began to hear people with onboard experience describing the craft that they were seeing in the field or woods was only about 10 feet as seen from the outside, and "cavernous" with multiple rooms on the inside.

I have already concluded that this is a relativistic effect, and that it is related to another effect that I have seen in studies of images of UFOs. When I see a real UFO picture, I notice that above and below the spacecraft the background sky is dark. It looks like the spacecraft is surrounded by a dark halo. The halo extends from its start at the skin of the craft, and then thins and disappears at about a third of the spacecraft size away from the skin. It is perfectly grey, as thin semi-transparent black.

So I attribute it to a relativistic effect, where the spacecraft is using quantum manipulation of the Vacuum Zero Point Energy (VZPE) to locally modify the local gravitational field and thus locally modify the null geodesics - but only quite local to the craft.

considerable archive of UFO sightings reported at this time and many of them occurred in the now-infamous Waimata Valley northeast of Gisborne, mere kilometres from where I was living. At the time, people reported strange noises in the valley, rumbling underground sounds not associated with earthquakes, and distinct loud cracking and popping sounds similar to the noise an aluminium soft drink can makes when you crush it. These sounds are unusual for a quiet sheep farming area.

The experience also highlights the fact that wherever possible, individual Greys will sometimes seek to converse on a personal level with humans when essential tasks are complete. It presents a positive aspect of contact with this species.

But my lasting impression from this account is that of the little suede hand placed gently over mine by the Grey child, a loving link between us.

Chapter 18

The Galaxy Screen

Date and age unknown

This contact experience probably occurred between 1978 and 1983. At that time I was living in a remote area and I often drove long distances at night on my own.

R. *Where you are now?*

S. *I'm with RJ. I can see exactly what the room looks like but I'm just trying to understand it. He's explaining it to me but I'm so bewildered by what I'm seeing, that I'm not really absorbing what he is saying just at the moment.*

The room created some confusion for me because of its spatial characteristics or my perception of its dimensions, which seemed to be skewed somehow. Initially, upon passing through the doorway I thought the room was circular, but once inside it seemed square, with a higher ceiling than usual (I estimate the room was some 7-8 metres long and wide). I could not account for my inability to ascertain the shape of the room and attributed it to the fact the Greys have the ability to warp internal dimensions. There were corners in the room and yet my vision registered a spherical aspect, like the magnification of a round fishbowl.

A low console was positioned in the centre of the room, on top of which stood a large sloping rectangular screen, with several small screens in a line below. It resembled smoky grey-coloured glass and was completely covered with a grid of pale fawn lines, like graph paper. My concentration was still distracted by the room's unusual shape-characteristics, but RJ insisted I must first understand the function of the screen in order to make sense of the dimensions of the room.

He activated the technology and an image of our Milky Way Galaxy appeared on screen; an elliptical galaxy, grey-beige, deeper in the middle and narrowing out to the edges. Hundreds of small square grids still overlay the image. RJ explained the image of the galaxy could be viewed from any angle or perspective and by altering the image, I could see it as a spiral.

He told me they use this technology to teach their own species, particularly children, about the universe, but they also allow humans in their programmes to see it too, those who work in the fields of astronomy and astrophysics on our planet. Some are given extensive tuition which will rise to their conscious minds in the future, as mankind comes to accept ongoing discoveries about the nature of the universe. As well, those who simply show an interest in these subjects may be shown the technology, as was the case for me on this occasion.

He asked me to prepare myself for a surprise, first touching a smaller screen and then extending one long finger to touch a grid on the larger one.

S. Oh man! There are things projected in the air all around me! I don't know how to explain it. It's beautiful! The whole room has changed and he's explaining that we are now inside that grid! But it's not our solar system!

We stood within a hologram, which formed a giant sphere almost entirely encompassing the interior of the room, filling it with planetary bodies from this "grid" of the Galaxy. I was aware of my feet standing on the floor but at the same time, I had the strange sensation of physically floating in this virtual environment.

RJ showed me this same grid replicated on one of the small screens, and demonstrated how he could magnify any part of that selected grid by touching any area on this secondary screen. He touched it again and immediately the images in the air around me changed, with some of the astronomical bodies disappearing beyond the parameter of the virtual sphere, while others were magnified in clearer definition. RJ brought the original imagery back into focus and introduced an addition facet of the technology: movement, colourful electromagnetic fields around planets, swirling and flowing.

We walked around behind the projection of one planet in particular and I wondered what it was called. RJ explained they name or identify planets by their magnetic energy, something that has no relationship to my language. He said he could make up a word, a name for the planet to satisfy me, but this would be meaningless because we do not know this planet exists yet.

His explanations increased in complexity with the statement we were observing these parts of the Galaxy in "real time", in other words, as they were evolving at that time. While I struggled to digest this statement, he returned to the screen, inviting me to choose a grid. I touched a dense-looking area of the Galaxy and we were instantly surrounded by a dust-like cloud, the air filled with holographic particles – not a good choice. I selected again and the grid produced a burning sun, fiery red, orbited by several small moons.

We played around with this absorbing technology for a bit, but now RJ wanted to show me a significant event in our history and asked me to prepare myself for something intense. Our own solar system now appeared in the air, as if suspended in time, and he zoomed in on the Earth, enlarged like an enormous beach-ball.

He stated this technology can display any point in the past they so desire. In this case he pin-pointed a particular time when two critical events occurred on Earth: the atomic bombing of the city of Hiroshima, Japan, followed by the bombing of Nagasaki, in August 1945: two occasions when mankind used nuclear weapons in warfare causing massive destruction, loss of life and ongoing suffering. He reduced the image so the Earth became a smaller ball.

S. He's showing me Earth's magnetic field and it's exploding outwards! I can see the effect of the explosion reverberating right out through the solar system, and further out into the galaxy. He's talking to me now in relation to this. [34]

RJ said sometimes it is hard to face facts, emphasising this must *never* happen again and outlining the potential danger to other species created by nuclear warfare. I was upset and shaken, so he touched the screen and the solar system vanished. He explained there are many people of my generation who are working in various scientific fields but who are also part of the Greys' programmes. Through this contact, the Greys have been able to influence these people to make positive changes concerning nuclear weaponry, working towards a better future for mankind. However there are also single-minded

---

[34] My take on the weapons exploded in Japan is that we had not ever thought about the possibility that our weapon explosions would propagate so extensively through the universe. We think more of the destructive impact on life and property, but here we read that the quantum wave expressing the reality of such mass transmutation and energy deposition is, by their projection to Suzy, a very significant event that becomes broadcast to a wide universe.

humans who support nuclear armament under the guise of a deterrent. Ultimately, the Greys know that what affects one, affects all, which is a fact we too must also understand if our civilisation is to survive. Sensing I was still disturbed by what I had observed, RJ placed pleasant calming images in my mind momentarily as a way of settling me down and bringing me back to the present.

Although the planetary images had gone, the spherical imprint of the (virtual) technology was still operating and I realised this had caused my spatial confusion when I entered the room. I wondered how their technology was capable of imaging in real time, as well as capturing a history of galactic evolution. They can pinpoint and observe any part of the Galaxy and beyond at specific time periods, although I do not know how far back in time this extends or how far out into the Universe – or even whether the display was real, or just realistic animation based on data.

RJ's overview of what this technology is capable of enabled me to see how it might be used to register places in the Galaxy where assistance is required, where survival is at stake. At the time when these weapons were exploded in Japan, extraterrestrials would have registered a change in the electromagnetic fields within our solar system. They have been able to capture that, or re-create it somehow, I don't know which, but I can see they have the capability to record such things on a phenomenal scale.

RJ now scanned my mind, drawing on my knowledge of language to find suitable terminology to express why he had shown me the far-reaching effects of nuclear warfare.

S. *He says, it seems the images will put "fire in my belly", terminology expressing a sense of purpose and commitment to have some influence on people's thinking, even though I am not a scientist. When we see something like this, we realise how fragile we are.*

Discussion

Mankind has recently developed a new generation of telescopes that can look into distant parts of our Galaxy using radio and gamma waves, x-rays and infrared photography. This enables scientists to view developments in the Galaxy that took place in the distant past however it could be some time before our data matches that which I describe in this experience, where the Greys have a database of the evolution of our Galaxy, and beyond. [35]

I describe how RJ showed a replay of the atomic bombing of Hiroshima, Japan, and warned against humanity continuing to develop destructive nuclear technology. A massive shock wave created by the explosion expanded outwards into space, thereby affecting the natural balance of the Galaxy even beyond our solar system. He warned that continued development of nuclear weapons might mean that a time could come when, *"Time could stop for you! There will be nothing left of you on the grid!"* A sobering statement.

In the latter part of this experience, which I have not outlined in the body of the chapter, I returned to a room with RJ and took part in a relaxed group situation between humans and Greys aimed at understanding each other at a deeper level. The situation was the reverse of what we were used to, now with humans leading the interaction instead of the Greys, describing their lives, families, interests, philosophies and so on, rather than structured around what the Greys wished to achieve.

From my experience, this indicated a new and defining development in their human contact programmes. Greys have a different mindset to humans. We are creative, spontaneous, individual but also fickle, whereas they are more standardised, with considerable structure to their lifestyle and the way they think, but with a holistic intelligence. They are raised and educated within frameworks and they can develop interests or areas of expertise, but in their society they don't appear to have the opportunity to develop as individually as we do. They express their individuality to us through humour, intelligence or knowledge. Humans devote a lot of time to talking about our emotions, problems, appearance, and relationships, whereas the Greys control their emotions and are more objective about them. They are all interconnected as parts of the whole whereas humans try hard to be individual, to stand out, and ego comes into play in many cases.

---

[35] Of course as an astrophysicist I wish I could play in that room, but that is not what the Greys deem efficient! This is amazing technology, but it is actually a relatively small step above what we do now, and we are headed in the direction of this technology, but, with the primary requirement that we would need to collect up all the data that it would take to make the display Suzy described.

As we prepared to leave, RJ made reference to a particular undersea base near Tahiti. We all wanted to know more about this base and were told it was constructed in the 1960s, and several species work at this base and others like it around the globe. Surprisingly, after what I had just seen, I did not register the significance of this at the time in relation to the many years of nuclear testing in the Pacific.

Robert Salas, author of *Faded Giant* (2005) and, *Unidentified – The UFO Phenomenon* (2014), was witness to a significant UFO incident that occurred at a Minuteman Missile Launch Control Centre in Montana, USA, on March 24, 1967, when a UFO appeared over the base and interfered with the function of the missile controls. Robert has spoken publicly about the 1967 missile shutdowns and nuclear issues since 1996.

In *Unidentified,* Robert states, "If each of us commits to the idea of the complete and total abolition of nuclear weapons, together we will have prevented nuclear war."

I would add we may just save ourselves from self-annihilation, and our galactic neighbours from the effects of our lack of sanctity of life.

Chapter 19

A Meeting at an Undersea Base: Disclosure of a Different Kind

1980, age 25 years

I watched on a w/screen as we slowly approached an illuminated opening in the side of an underwater rock face, feeling uncertain and excited simultaneously, as I had not been here before.

We passed out of the water and into a brightly lit tunnel, like a massive drainpipe, the craft moving slowly now as it emerged into an extensive hangar area. Other craft were here, along with machinery and vehicles like small hovercraft carrying humans and other species.

Our craft hovered near a high rock wall which showed signs of having been gouged by machinery. There were several humans onboard with me and we were directed to leave the craft over a platform connected to a moving gangway that ascended steeply up the side of the rock wall like an escalator. I estimated roughly a hundred humans and Greys were working around the hangar.

We entered a reception area, looking dishevelled and out-of-place in our night clothes. It looked more "human" here, with a series of rooms divided by glass windows, rather like an office block. A young human male, perhaps in his late twenties, ushered us into a spacious room and the Grey crew from the craft accompanied us. He did not use his arms to gesture with as most humans would do, but instead conveyed telepathic welcoming messages and directions.

The room was set up in familiar lecture theatre fashion with rows of ergonomically designed seats and we all silently settled into them, while the accompanying Greys stood in a group off to one side. Another young human male entered the room with a tall Grey and sat facing us at a console up the front. We waited.

I studied the dark-haired male. His appearance was essentially human but he could have been a product of genetics, a human/Grey mixture. He wore the same overalls without insignia as the other humans, but he had an air of confident calm authority about him. I "picked up" on his skilfully executed communications with the Greys, more advanced and practiced than many humans, perhaps with some of the Greys' mind control capabilities. Instinctively I felt he would only use these abilities with integrity and I could sense no negative emanations from him. He seemed relaxed, but with obvious deference to the tall Grey seated on his right.

This entity was one of the *wise ones*, an ancient version of the Grey species, and you cannot conceal anything from them. His skin draped in curves and folds over the contours of the skull and his eyes were dark and complex. These entities inspired a sense of awe and reverence in me on the occasions I have seen them.

We were all aware of humans and entities moving past windows in the corridor, and a script symbol appeared on the screen to help us focus. The human prepared us for the fact that following some background information, we were about to view future events, possibly within our lifetimes, which may be unsettling for us. He began with reference to atomic warfare during the Second World War, reminding us of the destruction it caused to our world. Many years of nuclear testing took place, particularly in the Pacific and parts of the US, and much damage occurred, surface, subterranean, sub-oceanic, and out into space. He conveyed images and information to our minds of damage not only to human life, but to all other forms of life on Earth as well.

S. Building on this, he said, "And you can all comprehend the damage to other realms of this planet that are not yet visible to, or generally understood by the masses."

This was a reference to the unseen energetic forces, creatures and entities that inhabit and share the environment of this planet with us, perhaps in other states of existence (currently invisible to most of us), but which have been glimpsed by some.

Through this mental exchange accompanied by the images, he assisted us to observe this unseen damage, the ongoing effect that atomic warfare and nuclear testing has had on the emotions, consciousness and health of humans and wildlife. He expanded this concept outwards from the microcosm to the macrocosm, to how the magnetic field of the planet itself had been effected. This damage progressed outwards like a shock-wave into the solar system, and it was both prior to, and after these events, that extraterrestrial races were again drawn to our planet. Much of this I understood already.

However he described how direct contact was made at this time with certain people within governments and military, but the negative willpower and mindset of the human race was such that atomic bombing took place regardless of the advice and offers of assistance from extraterrestrial groups. These same offers were presented again after the Second World War, and at this time certain individuals and groups accepted assistance because of the resulting devastation, and their desire it should never be repeated on our planet. States of both trust and mistrust have occurred mutually since. He anticipated a time in the future when the work that has been carried out between the two species, humans and extraterrestrials, can be revealed to the public. But this eventual disclosure was dependent on mankind's readiness and receptiveness.

It seemed strange to witness a young man who certainly appeared human in most respects, communicating this way about humans, but he did so with certainty. He proposed that in the future there will be much confusion and speculation as the realisation emerges that extraterrestrial races are actually here. Sightings of their craft will increase, but more significantly, members of the public will begin to encounter not only the craft, but also glimpses of the occupants. This is a planned agenda, eventually creating a turning point whereby mankind will no longer be able to explain away all anomalous lights or objects in the sky. Other incidents and events will occur which will trigger human consciousness (he did not elaborate on these events). True logic will eventually prevail and people will begin to accept the reality of extraterrestrial visitation.

However he warned us of the long and gruelling process required to raise human understanding and awareness to a sufficient level where the masses could cope with such a significant leap in their existence. Too many humans lead narrow day-to-day lives and do not have the mental, emotional, or psychological capacity as yet, to deal with exposure to extraterrestrial visitors.

Scenes appeared on the screen, similar to those we had been shown before, concerning the degradation of our environment and the current and future projected state of the planet, but he was attempting to shed a new light on it, cast a new perspective on something previously covered. Just as information has been introduced to groups such as ours over a long period of time by the Greys, enabling us to understand their technology, perspectives, and ideas foreign to our day-to-day lives, he said the same must be applied to the general public concerning future open contact. However with the general public, it must proceed at a much slower pace and over a considerably longer period of time. He stated the programmes we are taking part in are, in effect, accelerated mini-versions of what needs to be achieved worldwide in the future, and members of our group will eventually speak publicly about our contact experiences as part of this slow exposure.

More futuristic images appeared, causing a ripple of murmurs of surprise and intrigue as we watched ourselves on-screen talking to groups, writing, filming, or working in technology and science. We would all in some way, familiarise people with the reality of "visitors to our planet", putting it in its most simple and non-threatening form, as a part of the disclosure process. Our ultimate goals may be the same, but the ways in which we will carry out our tasks are many and varied. The human provided a continuing stream of information to accompany the images. He warned there will be groups and individuals who will latch onto the idea of an extraterrestrial presence and will seek to create a fear-factor around it, and much of our work in the future will be around defusing that fear.

The images ceased and were replaced by the script symbol, allowing us to refocus as he drew our attention to the planning taking place on our planet relating to future disclosure. He revealed there are many brave people, particularly older people in positions of authority on this planet, who have had knowledge of the extraterrestrial presence for many years. The public has suspected this, viewing such people as either deceitful or ineffectual where disclosure is concerned. He stressed that many of these people have been under great pressure, weighing up the myriad of factors relative to the profound effect disclosure would have on the populace of this planet, in every facet of our lives. They may want disclosure to take place, however they understand from ongoing communications with the extraterrestrials, the importance of adequate preparation and timing. Many of these people have a greater commitment to future disclosure than the public will ever know about or understand, and they are preparing the way for open communication between species.

He reminded us that when we returned home from this visit, only a residue of memory would remain in our consciousness as a sense of commitment, a word central to many of these sessions. We may also have a vague idea of something we need to do in the future, but for the meantime it must remain just that. If we were to consciously remember everything we have been told and shown, we would probably never reach our intended goals. Instead, we would likely take control of our destiny in an intellectual sense and try to make things happen, whereas they prefer to assist us in gradually unfolding our future roles.

The ancient Grey now took over, presenting in a markedly different manner to the human, reaching out to us, impressing ideas upon us. These thoughts and emotions touched us deeply, engendering an intense state of concentration. He described how in the years to come, we would hear a great deal about the endangered state of our planet and we would watch as it deteriorated. The perspectives and mental images he conveyed of the misery mankind is creating for itself evoked feelings of extreme sorrow in us all. By now, most of us were quietly weeping.

The wise one asked us to reach inside ourselves, taking that feeling of sorrow to the deepest places in our consciousness, where it would become the firm foundation of commitment to our tasks. He reiterated what the male had expressed, that the human race is capable of great compassion and intelligence, but many people on our planet have only developed narrow, superficial spheres of thought and emotions, stunted by greed and selfishness. Until that level of awareness is expanded, becoming more discerning and spiritual, then in many ways, our planet and civilisation would continue on a downward spiral.

Overlaying this, he discussed the psychological structure of the way humans think and react when perceiving new information. This was very enlightening, as he analysed the human processes involved in examining, and eventually either accepting or discounting information that has the potential to threaten human society and civilisation. Any plans by the visitors to reveal themselves openly to mankind must work within the parameters of that human thought structure, and constantly changing levels of understanding across billions of people.

He stated that in the future, there will be wild speculation, enthrallment, blame, fear, and a multitude of theories pertaining to the idea of contact with extraterrestrials. We are not to get caught up in this hype, but we should strive to work independently or with like-minded people, many of whom will be brought to us one way or another by the Greys and the spiritual hierarchy (UGB) of our planet.

Powerful negative dogmas and theories will arise about contact with the visitors, and conversely, there will be pro-alien cults and organisations, some of which may ultimately be equally as damaging to the prospect of our acceptance of an extraterrestrial presence.

The opposing psychological states of both fear and ego will be behind mankind's reluctance to accept the prospect that we are not alone in the Universe.

The tall Grey released us from the intense state of focus and immediately the air was literally filled with questions from many of the group members. Even though the human and Grey had gone to considerable effort to elaborate on *why* the process of disclosure needs to be slow and steady, many members of the group were still demanding to know why disclosure cannot happen sooner, why it cannot happen now!

I sat quietly, observed and listened. From somewhere within the strands of thought-exchanges I discerned a separate, private analytical process occurring and realised I had tapped into a conversation being carried out between the Greys and the human concerning those members of the group demanding disclosure now. I realised this gathering was not just an informative lecture – it was also another of their tests for the humans in this group!

My eavesdropping confirmed that those who continued to express questions and demand answers, which had already been explained at length, would be shifted into another programme. They had revealed they would likely fail at their future tasks due to lack of patience, and they had shown a lack of vital comprehension of timing and readiness, required to carry them through.

The human up the front was now looking directly at me because of course, he knew I had "overheard", and he communicated privately to me that I was correct:

> *S. He conveys, "Now you understand why it* (disclosure) *has to take so long; why it has to be handled so carefully. Even amongst those of you who have had thirty or more years of contact, there are still those who don't comprehend the difficulties. Imagine what it is like with the general populace."*

The screen went blank and the human and Grey communicated with only five of us now, the rest excluded. They reiterated we must be patient with the drawn-out process of disclosure of the alien presence. There will be times when we will feel frustration, lack of movement, and uncertainty about our tasks, but above all we must trust it will unfold. They warned us the Greys will be much-maligned in the future. There will be suspicion, rumour and speculation about them, and they wanted us to be aware of this too.

The lecture was complete and to lighten the mood, we were ushered along the corridor to a glass-enclosed viewing deck high above the vast hangar. One of the Greys told us this particular base was in the Pacific Ocean. Below us, species worked together with mutual understanding and acceptance, and it was overwhelming to consider how big this preparatory process is that has been going on behind the scenes for so many years.

We were directed back to the moving walkway leading to the craft. Out of curiosity, I asked one of the Grey crew how it is that the seawater does not pour in through the tunnel entrance. He replied there is an energy field in place across the entrance which prevents water from entering, but the craft can pass through it. [36] Unfortunately my knowledge of science did not extend to understanding this concept.

Discussion

As is often described by contactees, experiencers, and abductees alike, our group lecture again included mention of the Second World War atomic bombing of two Japanese cities by the Allies. Clearly the visitors have grave concerns about our development of nuclear weapons and our lack of spiritual and environmental awareness of the ongoing damage they create, reverberating beyond our planet. [37]

This visit was to a Pacific undersea base, and it follows mention in the previous chapter of an undersea base near Tahiti, French

---

[36] I was fascinated by the remark that the entrance to the undersea base is protected by an energy field (force field) which the craft passes through. The hydrostatic pressure on an underwater opening is enormous as submariners know, so this is another technology trick I am curious about.

[37] Here it was interesting to me that there was no real apocalyptic vision of the future mentioned at this time (pole change, destruction of land mass, collapse of living ecology, disastrous climate change etc.) I found these remarks re-assuring; the Greys recognize that we are not yet on an optimal path to enhance our development and join a wider civilization but they also have not tried to manipulate their chosen few by resorting to and emphasizing fear.

Polynesia, also in the Pacific Ocean. Significantly, the human male who spoke to our group outlined the damage done to the Earth through nuclear testing, much of which actually took place in French Polynesia, so it is not surprising that extraterrestrials would create an undersea base there to monitor this.

After the Second World War, the United States, along with their French and British allies, frequently tested nuclear weapons in the Pacific region. Mururoa Atoll was the site of extensive nuclear testing by France between 1966 and 1996. France eventually abandoned nuclear testing in the atmosphere and moved testing underground in the midst of intense world pressure. New Zealand has a Nuclear Free Policy and led the way in anti-nuclear protests in the Pacific, being involved in ongoing protests from the mid-1960s when France first began testing nuclear weapons in French Polynesia.

Between 1945 and 1992, the United States conducted around 1045 nuclear tests as part of the nuclear arms race, including 216 atmospheric, underwater and *space tests.* Many of these tests took place at the Nevada test site, and the Pacific Proving Grounds in the Marshall Islands and off Kiribati, as well as other tests within the United States (see 'Resources' for YouTube time lapse video link.)

The reality of undersea or underground UFO bases is by no means far-fetched. As a UFO sighting investigator I know that people have reported sightings of UFOs entering and leaving the ground, oceans and lakes for many years, and we have had such sightings in New Zealand.

Many of the humans I have observed in these bases were involved in becoming familiar with alien technology and craft under the guidance of these entities, and there is often a human in the chain of command. I have never witnessed or experienced the negative and sometimes traumatic incidents described by some abductees who report being taken to underground military installations. However I acknowledge there may be other covert negative groups on both sides, human and alien, which may not have benevolent agendas or our best interests at heart.

As mentioned, the Greys assess our responses to these lecture situations in order to profile the humans present, relative to the programmes best suited to them. However in this case, the humans self-selected their fate by not being willing to accept the parameters of the programme. Freewill? Freedom of thought? Perhaps not entirely, but there is always cause and effect to consider, and the greater good.

We were warned of a future time when the reality of the extraterrestrial presence would be examined, resulting in chaotic thinking, discrimination, both negative and positive theories, and the emergence of cults – all stemming from a combination of man's arrogance or fear. [38] For some years now, I have seen evidence of this phase beginning. The media worldwide has struggled with the question of UFOs, as have the military, governments, religions, and science, based on varying agendas, perspectives, cover-ups or dogmas. The man-in-the-street still largely doesn't know what to believe about UFOs, and there are human agendas to maintain control over sectors of the population through belief systems and fear-mongering.

While many in the UFO research community worldwide seek immediate disclosure, I maintain this process must be slow and well-prepared. This experience took place back in 1980, and we have still not attained full disclosure of what governments and the military worldwide may know about the UFO presence.

In the future, if greater numbers of experiencers/abductees from all walks of life and parts of the globe were to come forward with their testimonies, would this in itself tip the balance and influence public acceptance? Add to this the ongoing discoveries of Earth-like planets, and the growing number of astrophysicists, astronomers and scientists now publicly stating their belief that life exists elsewhere in our galaxy, in the universe.

The human male indicated some people in high places have taken great personal risk in order to develop an appropriate timeline to disclosure. Some experiencers/abductees have suggested that an amnesty for those involved in covert military contact with extraterrestrial groups might hasten disclosure, but the question is: what is the nature of those military/alien alliances?

Many within the UFO field insist mankind is ready for disclosure, but are we all ready, are enough of us ready? Considering the environmental and societal disasters, wars and human suffering evident in our world today, I have my doubts.

In relation to this, the ancient Grey discussed the human psychological process of examining new information, particularly that

---

[38] I had not imagined the issue of emergence of cults till now. I have undertaken to address issues of the impact of disclosure on religion, but had not concerned myself about cults that would inevitably fill a void left by diminished traditional religion.

which might pose a threat, and how this process can be an encumbrance to mankind rather than an avenue to enlightenment. This is evident today, possibly more so than at any other time in our history. Consider the way we are addressing issues of climate change, use of fossil fuels, and global food distribution – a great deal of talking yet little in the way of results beneficial to civilisation. This same attitude is evident in the proliferation of conspiracy theories surrounding the UFO topic, perceptions of "good" and "bad" aliens, and the like. Would immediate disclosure of governmental/military knowledge necessarily circumvent negative human traits?

I believe we must collectively undergo a spiritual awakening, an elevation of awareness and self-responsibility, reaching a majority tipping point before we can cope with open contact with aliens.

We have not yet become a planetary civilisation. In an ideal world, a planetary civilisation may be structured something like this: global cooperation and cessation of wars; sharing of resources, food, technology and medical supplies; cooperative environmental clean-up programmes; international programmes to protect species and habitat etc. But instead we are divided, at war, degrading our environment, resources and food, and technology is often seen as a source of revenue rather than advancement. Scientists struggle to secure funding for humanitarian projects outside of the large controlling corporations and military/industrial complexes.

We are trying to run before we can walk, attempting to become an interplanetary civilisation, with forays out into our solar system before we have cleaned up our own back yard, and all of this makes us a threat to other life-forms in the galaxy. Acceptance of a "friendly" alien presence requires that first we must recognise the sanctity of life on our own planet (including all species), or we may perpetuate our warlike tendencies in space.

There is a vast difference between disclosure in the sense of governments and militaries divulging what they know about UFOs and extraterrestrials, and disclosure in the sense of a growing global awareness of the alien presence through a variety of means. The former may rely upon human nature and control, while the latter is a process that may be largely driven by the aliens themselves, over which we ultimately have limited domain.

Their assessment of timing and our readiness may prevail.

Chapter 20

Merging: Soul-insertion

During the eighth month of pregnancy with my first child, I awoke in the early hours of the morning with the extraordinary feeling that my entire body was filled with light and joy. I felt as if I was floating! But within minutes of waking, the feelings faded away. I retained memory of being in a room with a blue ball of light and a group of Grey children during that night.

1983, age 28 years

I was crying, heavily pregnant, dressed in my nightgown with bare feet. Two big-eyed mixed species entities accompanied me along the corridor, one on each side, tenderly supporting me with their arms looped through mine. They conveyed calmness, but concern, because I had been ill throughout the pregnancy and my doctor had told me there was a possibility the placenta was failing. I could feel their love for me and my unborn child.

I had met these entities before and they were part of a medical team working this night. We entered a small warm room with walls that sloped inwards slightly to a circular domed ceiling, with a variety of circles set in the ceiling above a shelf-bed. The assistants helped me up onto the shelf-bed.

Soon a senior Grey entered the room and having greeted me, he conversed with me about the baby, matter-of-factly telling me it would be a boy. He wished to bring someone along shortly who would merge with me, become part of me temporarily. I wasn't too sure about this at all.

He was concerned about my upset state and did not want to give me too much information at that point and risk unsettling me further, knowing I was exhausted. I cried again and the Grey placed his hand just above my forehead, calming, causing me to feel slightly dizzy, like when you have had a glass of wine on an empty stomach. He told me his explanation would be brief and possibly a little confusing for me, but assured me all would be fine and after this, they would begin the procedure.

Continuing to hold his hand over my face, he told me they had brought me onboard this time in my present human consciousness, that is, without the full memory of certain aspects of previous visits here, which I would normally recall the moment I come onboard. They had embedded memories in my subconscious sometime in the past, and he now wished to bring those memories fully back into my mind before they continued with the procedure, so I would understand it. Instantly, he evoked a multitude of pictures in my mind of particular visits onboard craft when I was a young child.

S. He's reminding me of something, and he says, "This is what you've been doing sometimes when you come here." He's showing pictures in my mind of me as a child, playing with a blue ball of light! And I'm beginning to understand what's happening! The ball of light is going to be my son!

He gently revealed why I was here on this occasion: I have a living baby within me, but it requires a soul, a consciousness to inhabit its body. The blue ball of light would be brought to the room shortly and allowed to enter the body with assistance from the senior Grey. The soul may then leave and re-enter that body at any time, but the procedure was vital for this particular soul as it entered the body it will inhabit, to feel that existence for the very first time.

I felt calm now. The Grey removed his hand from my forehead and it was as if our minds were humming on the same note, creating a reverberating feeling of oneness. The assistants rested their hands on my forearms and there was a moment of quiet stillness and expectation as we waited.

Soon three short Greys entered the room with a bunch of different-species children, accompanied by the blue ball of light. I lifted my head, turning to one side so I could see them all, as these children had played and associated with the blue ball too and they knew it well. The Grey explained they would continue to relate to both the soul and the human child as he grew into adulthood. The child/adult would not consciously realise this until a later time in life, but the group would play a part in guiding him in the future. The room was abuzz with excited streams of thought between them all about witnessing this event.

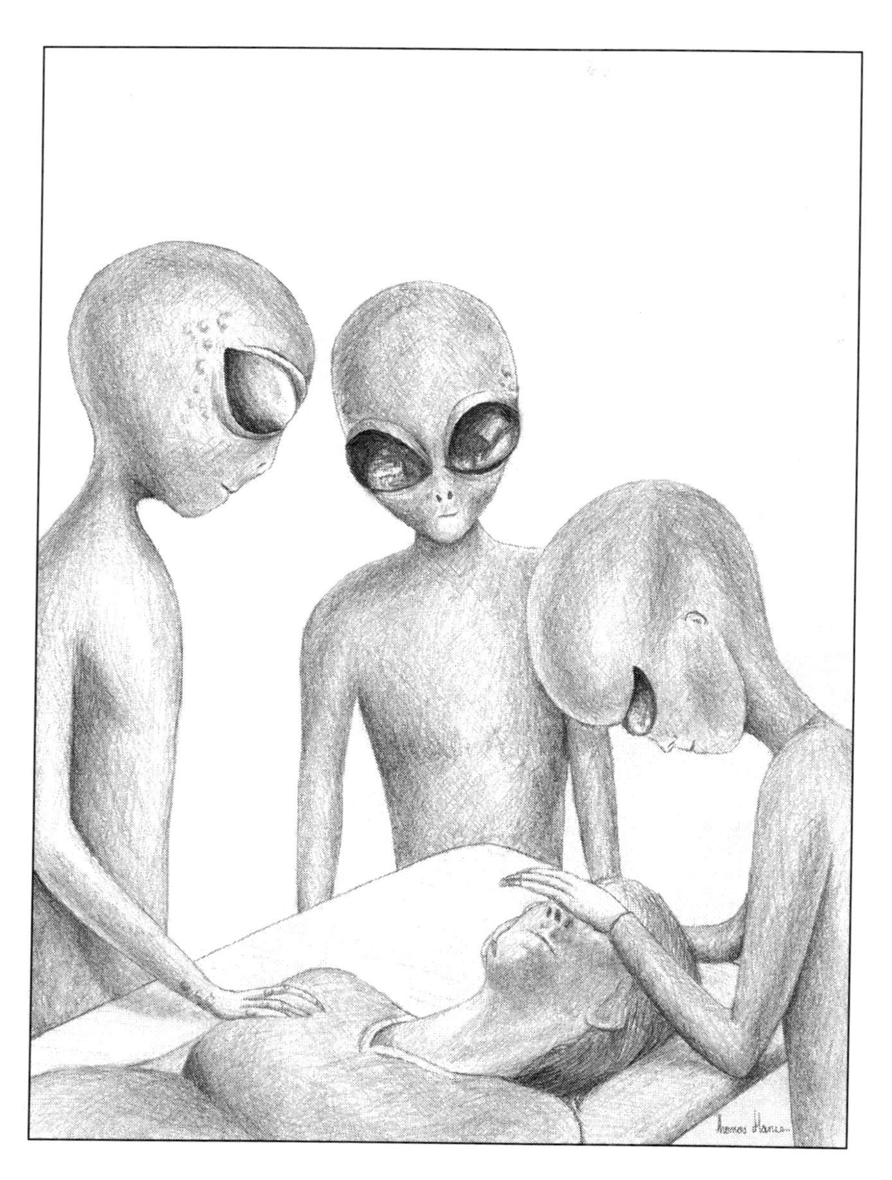

Calming

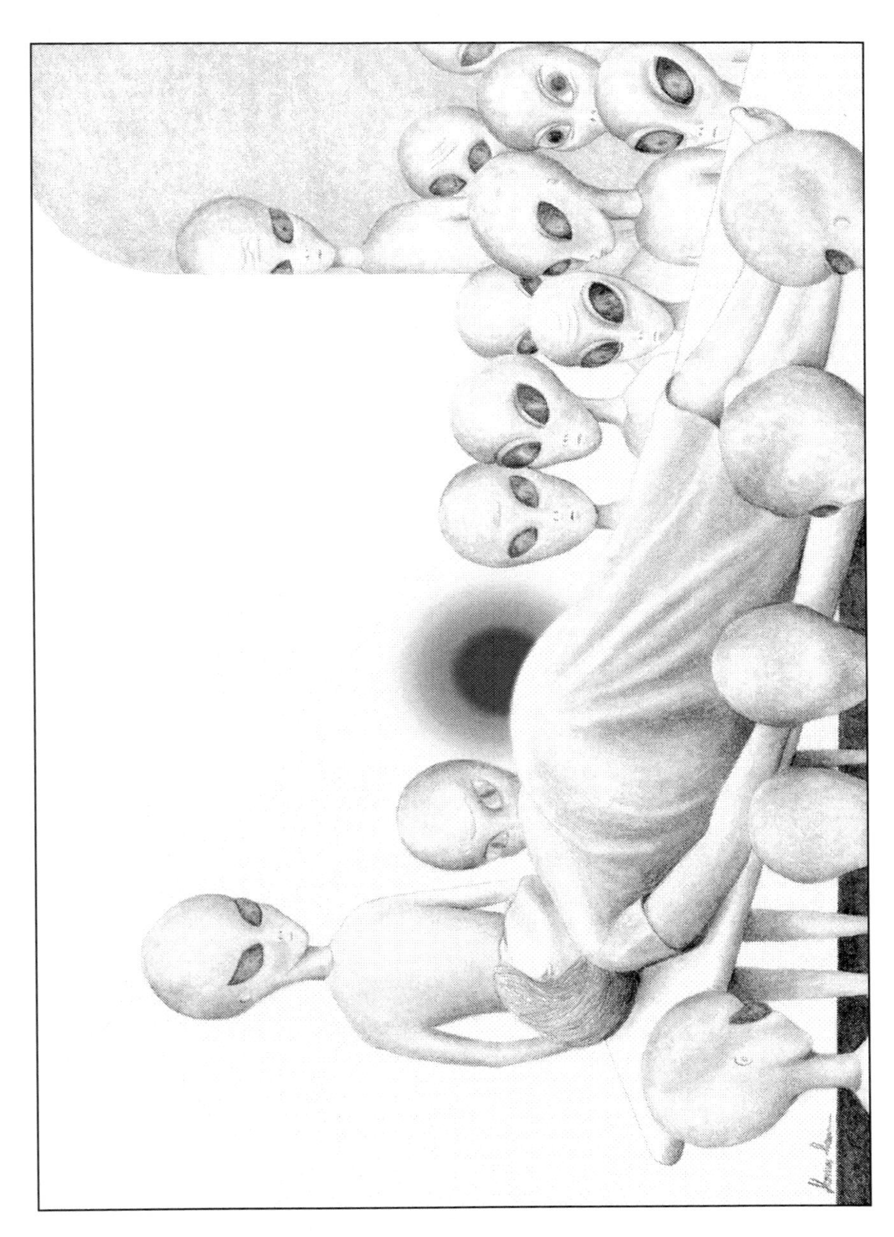

Merging: Soul-insertion

The Grey began calming my emotions again, explaining he needed to slow down all my metabolic functions to enable the blue soul to enter my body, and equally as important, to allow my body to fully acclimatise to the intense energy of this soul. My heart rate and breathing began to slow, and I felt cold, almost in a paralysed state. The whole atmosphere became intensely still and quiet as he asked the children to control their thoughts and movements.

Slowly the soul-insertion began, with the blue ball entering my body and the foetus of my child to be, infusing me with light.

S. *I can see the blue ball moving slowly towards my stomach. It's just disappeared into me! I feel as if I'm full of light! Like I'm floating! I can't make my body or my mind work properly, but I feel so elated!*

I tried to convey this to the Grey but he had already read my thoughts, and replied that the sensation was caused by the enhancements they had made with this soul, and the dual soul factor. These enhancements are what make this soul different from many others, requiring a specific procedure when the soul combination merges with the two human physical bodies, baby and mother. If they had not lowered the rate of my metabolism during the procedure it would have caused considerable shock to my system.

Slowly, he brought my metabolism back to normal and my body warmed up. I felt considerably better emotionally and physically and certainly did not feel as if there was anything strange within me, but the feeling of light and joy continued. All the children now released a deluge of well-wishing thoughts to me, but it was over-whelming and I could only smile at them as they were ushered from the room.

I'd been worrying about whether the baby would be born safely and in good health and the Grey assured me all would be well, apart from some human complications through which the baby's birth would be delayed somewhat, but he gave no explanation for this (my son was born two weeks late, by Caesarean section due to complications with a breech birth).

The Grey explained this child, who he referred to as a "complex system", would be accompanied throughout his life by "watchers", terminology he used as the best way for me to understand this concept. From the mental impressions I received from him, I gathered these watchers would be a group made up of Greys, souls and humans who have volunteered to perform this duty, along with the use of specific Grey technology.

He will be watched and observed and in many ways, protected, but they cannot prevent all human incidents that may occur in his life and he will experience ups-and-downs like anyone else. They do not see this level of protection as interference, because they perceive this as a joint project, agreed upon by the soul before entering this life.

The senior Grey added I will sometimes be aware of these watchers as balls of light, while at other times they will present as unusual human beings who cross our path, but who we will know by their energy fields, are not fully human. The child's energy would be like a magnet to many earthly creatures and non-human entities in other states of existence. He emphasised they have invested a great deal of time and education in me and in this future child, and many others like us.

I asked what it is this child has to do in his life and he answered by raising his hand and projecting an image into the air: a man stood talking to a large group of people and I assumed he was my child, but grown up. The audience before him displayed a mixture of anger, fear, confusion, and scepticism, but also an underlying and overwhelming desire for hope. They needed something to hold on to, something to give them reason to carry on in life and I became tearful as the effect of this image swept over me. The man stood talking to them, his demeanour conveying integrity as he calmed the group and allayed their fears.

Abruptly, the Grey said, "Enough." He lowered his hand and the image vanished, but I had seen sufficient to answer my question.

He stated there are thousands of children presently being born in the world like this child-to-be, part of an extensive agenda to create positive changes towards our very survival.

The procedure over, he wished me well and left the room.

Discussion

As a mother, I have often pondered, at what point does the soul enter the body of a new human life? Is it soon after the baby is conceived? Or does the physical body continue to grow until the soul enters it at some point later in the pregnancy? Does it enter and leave the body at will? And once the soul enters the body for the first time, does it endow it with consciousness, with "mind", from this point?

The merging or soul-insertion experience answered these questions, for me at least, although circumstances may vary between people, souls, and their purposes. It seems in this case, the soul entered the baby's body by arrangement at eight months gestation.

I learnt some humans within these programmes are provided with watchers, a protective structure that includes technology as a kind of surveillance system, and I have caught glimpses of these technological watchers. I recall an occasion when I was driving alone one night in a remote area, when I glimpsed a metallic-looking sphere around the size of a baseball, travelling alongside the car at speed. Over the years I have learned these watchers are tuned to human brainwaves and thoughts, like an alert system, observing and recording. They have replaced most implants and are generally not visible to humans.

The senior Grey mentioned this child's energy field would be like a magnet to other non-human entities and earthly creatures. This has certainly been the case, as throughout his life my son has shared my affinity for animals and creatures, often experiencing telepathy with them as I have. One such occasion occurred when my son was at university in another city. He rang me one evening to say he would be coming home for a few days and as this was unexpected, I asked him why, but he simply said he would like to help me out. I was grateful for this kind thought because my husband was away.

He arrived home the next day, and within a few hours our beloved dog Nisha collapsed, and we rushed her to a veterinary clinic. She required surgery for a perforated bowel and thus her health quickly deteriorated until we made the difficult decision to put her to sleep.

Later, I commented to my son how lucky it was he had come home when he did and he replied he had done this because he knew something was wrong, and that it had to do with Nisha. Despite my own love of animals, I had no inkling of this situation, perhaps because the message needed to go to my son so that he would be there to support and assist me.

The merging procedure was one of the most profound emotional and physical experiences I have undergone onboard craft. The feeling of every cell in my body being infused with light as the soul of my son entered my body, and his, for the first time, will stay with me throughout my life, and perhaps forever.

Chapter 21

Inter-species Psychology: Developing Fourth Intellect Children

A strange incident occurred one night in November, 1983, seven weeks after my first son was born. I awoke suddenly during the night and sat bolt-upright in bed. A clearly defined, pale blue shaft of light shone through the sheer curtain of the floor-to-ceiling window, onto my son's bassinet and the surrounding floor.

For a split second, I observed my baby son. He lay transfixed, staring into the beam of light with eyes alert, face animated, arms freed from his bedding and waving in the air.

One would think the normal reaction of a new mother would be to leap out of bed, pick up her baby, retreat to a safe place and yell loudly to wake her husband to look out the window and see what was causing this blue light. So what did I do? I have no memory of doing anything except sitting up in bed. On waking the next morning I remembered the pale blue light and leapt out of bed in a panic to check on my son, peacefully sleeping.

1983, age 28 years

R. Where are you? And what is happening?

S. I'm carrying my son down a corridor.

We entered a spacious room on a craft, white and sterile-looking, although the air was vibrant and alive with thoughts! My baby son and I had come to this room on one previous occasion since his birth and I can best describe it as a psychology centre where the developing psyche, awareness and inter-relationships of newborn babies of several species, including humans, are studied in a group situation.

Seven white rectangular tables were spaced around the room, their surfaces soft and warm with raised padded edges. Each table stood on an attractive pedestal with several intricately beautiful arms.

Thirteen other women had already arrived, cuddling their newborn babies and looking around in expectation, and the Grey assistants directed two of us to each table. The woman at my table was perhaps in her mid-thirties, and I wondered if I had been paired with her because she was an experienced mother, whereas this was my first child. She was a solid woman with a chubby face, short dark hair and a striped nightgown, while her baby girl was dressed in a pale pink stretch-and-grow suit, with a mop of black silky hair.

An unusually large group of around thirty five Greys were also in the room gathered around each of the tables, conveying a multitude of excited conversations and comments to each other as the human babies were placed on the tables before them. I felt a rather inflated first-mother's pride as I looked down at my son, knowing he was a nice-looking baby because his head was perfectly shaped due to a caesarean birth, while some of the other babies' skulls were still misshapen from the natural birth process.

More Greys entered the room, each carrying one or two Grey or mixed species babies (including those with human genes), placing five or six of them gently on each table alongside the human babies. All seven tables now had a crowd of entities and mothers around them, keenly watching as the babies began to notice each other and react.

My son and the other little girl kicked their legs while the alien babies lay relatively still, lacking vigour, but alert nevertheless. I knew they were thinking, observing. They soon all became aware of each other, feeling each other's presence, becoming excited and the kicks and hand movements increased.

The Grey staff began communicating with the human children, attracting their attention with their minds, leaning over the babies and making lots of eye contact, touching them, putting the palms of their hands over their foreheads and eyes. They were "listening" to the thoughts of my son and the little girl, with reciprocal communication going on, on some level. I couldn't hear him thinking, but they seemed to be able to!

This group and others like it enabled first communications between human and extraterrestrial babies, but it also provided the opportunity for the human babies to bond with the Grey adults who would become their mentors. The Greys were examining these processes occurring between the children, studying comparisons between how the pure-blood Grey babies, the mixed species, the human/Greys, and the human children reacted and related to each other. Their aim was to raise the human babies' telepathic and observational awareness, and their sensitivity to forms of energy. As well, the Greys would slowly increase their brain function by teaching them mind skills and psychic perceptions from post-birth. The Greys' powerful thought processes can affect the function of the human brain and mind, which must work in synergy, in cooperation with them.

The senior Grey in charge outlined their aim to develop powerful early memory in these children so that by the time they are toddlers and reach school age, their memory will be exceptional. It will be important they have this memory capacity for future activities and tasks in their education on the craft.

He now asked us all to turn the children over onto their stomachs for a short time so they could observe any changes in the children's interactions when they were distracted by this altered physical position. I was worried about this because I felt my son was too young to have developed appropriate muscles for lying on his stomach, but the Greys seemed unperturbed. The human babies objected loudly, while the rest did not seem to be fazed by it.

Once the children had settled again, the senior Grey asked the mothers to leave the room with some of the staff to have our physical status monitored. We all filed out of the room, along the corridor and into an area with rows of cubicles without doors, each equipped with only a shelf-bed and screen. The male Grey attending to me activated the bed's scanning technology and immediately data began appearing on the screen. He expressed concern because he sensed I was developing a breast infection, and he also wanted to check on tissue healing associated with the caesarean procedure. A circular scanner concealed in the wall revealed the abdomen was fine, but there was a blockage in my breast tissue. In characteristic blunt fashion, the technician told me I would soon not be able to feed my son and this was something they would not fix, but he gave me advice. (When my son was ten weeks old, three weeks after this event, I was hospitalised with a breast infection and the doctor recommended I bottle-feed).

I chatted telepathically to the dark-haired lady as we returned to the psychology room, as telepathy had become a universal language for us. Upon entering the room we saw the babies were still alert, and while we were absent they had also had a health check. The large beds were capable of monitoring their well-being and metabolic functions in a non-invasive way by isolating and identifying each baby's individual signature energy.

The senior Grey told us these meetings, which included the mothers, would take place regularly while our babies were very young and dependent, and they wanted us to observe and understand this interactive process. In this way too, the Greys could continue to monitor our health. As the babies grow older and settle into interaction with the Grey and other species babies, they would be brought onboard craft without their mothers. At this point, a further selection process will take place in the group, isolating those babies most adept at interaction.

Most of the mothers in the room had been involved with the Greys themselves since pre-birth, but the remainder had not. The latter had agreed in the soul-state to bear these children, with their partners/husbands being the ones involved with the Greys. In these cases the mother will be brought onboard only while the baby is young, but will not remember these occasions, and once the child is a toddler, the mother's role in these sessions will cease and the father will become involved in them.

The sessions were also like a psychology lesson for the staff studying these human babies, a new process which could not be based on the data the Greys gathered when the parents were little, as these children have a different psyche, genes, and potential. All of them are "end-point children", with dual souls.

This regular opportunity for the human babies to interact and initiate communication with alien babies was the preparatory stage for their future education onboard craft. By the time they are up on their feet and toddling, they must be proficient in communicating telepathically with a variety of species.

However test situations will occur to select children from this group and others like it, because they intend to fast-track the education of those selected children. The remaining children will be reassigned to further education that is still in line with their soul agreements in terms of spiritual learning or other life tasks.

The senior Grey explained that once final selections have been made, this group will become a priority with a significant three-fold education:

1. the Greys will continue to have discussions with the children's souls concerning their life-purpose
2. they will have an education as human children adapting to extraterrestrial technology and knowledge
3. they will have an education as the Grey component of the dual soul identity

These three elements will create the "Fourth Intellect" children - the combined intellect resulting from the three forms of education and the three psyches working in harmony, creating an expanded human consciousness. Each child in this group will be prepared for a particular role on our planet, and their task will be to blend the three educations together as their purpose begins to unfold.

I watched the Greys clustered around the tables, leaning over the human babies.

> *S. They love these babies! They are so tender and loving with them, touching them with reverence. They love them because they have worked so hard to achieve them. The human children are like a curiosity to them.*

We mothers were encouraged to leave our tables and wander around the room; to communicate with all the babies, noting their differences according to species.

> *S. Their eyes! I just love looking at their eyes ... the variety of shapes and sizes ...*

The eyes of these alien babies seemed to consume their faces, diminishing all other features with their mysterious depth and character. In a blue eye you may see bright violet shimmers and flashes of aqua, with filaments moving within the clear tissue. Sometimes the pupil and iris turned and looked at you, but the entire eye didn't turn, giving the impression of an eye within an eye. Upon closer examination, stark black eyes became intriguing dark gelatinous domes, with fleeting colours moving within them. The eyelids varied too – pale flesh-coloured or relatively clear and shiny. Some eyelids met in the middle, or slipped down over the top of the eye, extending to the bottom and back up again.

Many of the babies wore no clothing at all, revealing spotty bodies, smudged with pearly cream and muted charcoal patches on a variety of fawn and grey backgrounds. Others wore a cover consisting of squares of fabric joined together and slipped over their heads and arms, with their feet poking out the bottom like delicate rat's feet. The human babies seemed doll-like by comparison and perhaps the Greys were fascinated by this.

"Whispers" became obvious to me after several minutes – fleeting snatches of telepathy from these babies, registered not in words or imprints of language, but through the senses. A little bit of anxiety from this child, a good measure of curiosity from another.

The Greys were equally absorbed by this gathering of babies, as they too intermingled and circulated around the tables.

All too soon the session drew to a close, and as we reluctantly returned to our tables to pick up our babies, the senior Grey suddenly began verbalising! A stream of "crystalline" sounds came from his mouth, delicate tinkling tones resonating in the air as he thanked us for our participation. [39] We all became tearful, not wishing to leave, and he soothed our emotions, placing us in a state of limited awareness, but assuring us we would not drop our babies.

Discussion

On a number of other occasions I have recalled being in rooms with alien babies, pale and spindly-limbed, with large bright blue or dark eyes. They were unusually quiet and still by human standards. On one occasion I was told by the Grey present that three of these children were actually mine, or at least produced by my genetic material. These kinds of vivid memories of "alien babies" are shared by both experiencers and abductees alike however the circumstances, emotions and reactions these visits elicit may differ between these groups or individuals. Many who have been introduced to babies and told they are their children, feel revulsion and anger, while others are fascinated by the tiny babies or toddlers, and feel maternal or paternal instincts towards them. Some people report seeing their "off-spring" on many occasions as the children grow older.

Recent neurological research into brain plasticity indicates that talking to a baby from an early age develops a greater capacity for language later on. In a similar sense, perhaps the Greys use this knowledge too; in their early communications and developmental goals with the babies they foster a high level of telepathic aptitude, memory, and awareness of species-specific nuances.

---

[39] I am fascinated by these vocal sounds Suzy describes were made by the senior Grey, and have an idea about them. Since aliens would not commonly use vocal sound, but rather telepathy, they are probably not well practiced. The sounds described previously as "crystalline" and here as "tinkling", are evidently not based on our tonal system with heavy reliance on octaves and musical thirds and fifths. Instead they would logically be based upon fractal mathematics, which imply a wider frequency range and more sounds at more extreme frequencies (higher and lower frequencies than associated with human voice or music) and less confined to our tonal system of thirds and fifths.

One of the most striking things I recall about the psychology room is that it was incredibly quiet. Normally you would expect some of the newborns to be crying, needing to be changed or fed, but instead, they were focused and animated, making only the occasional gurgling sound, only crying when some of them were briefly placed on their stomachs. The Greys' modes of telepathy include infusions of colour, imagery, unusual energies and feelings so that we understand their communication in a much more complete and holistic way than human language. Most human babies would be intrigued by this composite package and would learn to welcome it, hence the mothers were encouraged to support these methods and use telepathy too whenever possible.

The senior Grey mentioned they would foster the development of exceptional memory in these children. It is interesting that by the age of eighteen months my son could speak competently with an extensive vocabulary and was able to memorise his picture books and "read" them to friends and family, managing to turn the pages at just the right time, thus giving the impression he really was reading. By age two to three he could complete a variety of complex puzzles, jig-saw puzzles and brain teaser games that some adults had trouble calculating and piecing together. He learnt to read (properly) at an early age, follow lengthy instructions, and recalled conversations, names, places, song lyrics and events with ease, exhibiting exceptional memory. His achievements throughout his school years were exemplary and in his final year at High School he became Head Boy and was awarded Dux. Following this he attained three university degrees. He exhibited psychic abilities from an early age including pre-cognition, communication with spirit, and described past lives – traits seen in many children being born today.

There are millions of brilliant young people who achieve similar educationally or in other areas, who give me hope for the future of our planet. Humankind is capable of high intelligence, creativity, ingenuity and achievement, and this has been evident for thousands of years, but it is the specific mix created by a combination of high intelligence, genetics, the dual soul, and psychic abilities, which characterises these end-point children (the last of four generations).

The emotional bonds that had already formed amongst all the children, between the entities and the children, and between the mothers as well, were very strong and I can still feel the depth of emotion. We were all young mothers in this together. Momentarily, when it was time for us to leave, I felt as if my life on Earth no longer mattered; it felt distant and uninteresting by comparison and I could sense from the others that they shared my thoughts. We could have just walked away from it with our children and stayed there together. As the Grey vocalised his song/language of thanks, he became aware of this underlying human bond forming between us and that is when he sought to calm us down, reminding us we had to lead our chosen lives and return to our families, and so he blacked us out (induced an altered state of awareness) in preparation for leaving.

These children represent a first generation in the Grey programmes where the Grey and human psyche/identity, the dual soul, is fully melded, whereas my generation has had some difficulties with this, a struggle, experimental, sometimes not fully combined. This new generation is distinct, balanced and centred.

There is an intense, long-standing bond between the Greys and these souls, these children, a sense of "fathomless-ness" to the depth of their association.

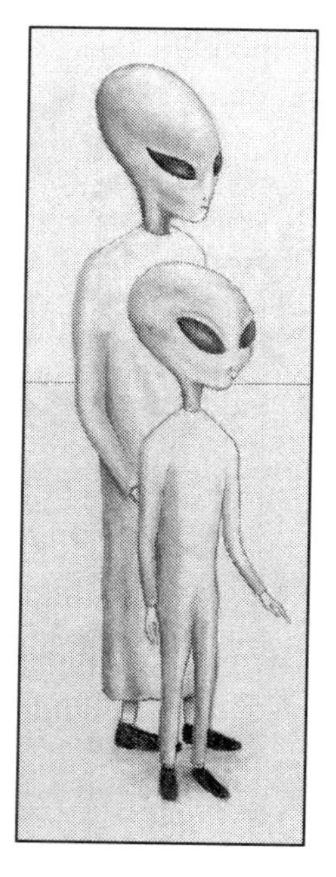

"Cone-head" and Small Grey Carers

Chapter 22

Seeding Planets

1987, age 32 years

A mixed-species Grey scientist, a geneticist I had met on other occasions, took me to a room in the genetic research area of the craft. We had engaged in intense conversations over the years and he always welcomed my questions, challenging me and provoking me into lateral thinking. His openness allowed me the freedom to argue and banter with him without feeling daunted by the Greys' greater knowledge base, and a wide-ranging conversation took place between us on this occasion. He wanted me to understand that the Greys are not just conducting research with our planet and race – their research is far-reaching. They, and the species they are linked to, are master geneticists in comparison to humans.

Rows of tall, white columnar pedestals were spaced evenly across the room, each around eighty to one hundred centimetres in height. Large clear glass cylinders stood on top of each pedestal, in which foetus-like bodies of a variety of species or creatures were suspended in fluid. The scientist explained the pedestals contained complex monitoring equipment to ensure the fluid around each different foetus was maintained at the right temperature, with appropriate "ingredients", and tubes extended from inside the white pedestal into the cylinders and attached to the bodies.

The scientist stated many humans involved in their scientific research have provided genetic material and some of this is used to create new species or enhance existing ones, but only if the souls of the donors give consent. However I queried their use of human genetic material to create species that many humans would consider to be "Frankenstein-ish". He responded that these new species containing human genes were not being created for our planet, but would be taken elsewhere. Again, I questioned the wisdom and morality of this, considering the human genes "belong" to Earth. Was this akin to playing God?

He countered this, challenging my perspective by focusing on the other genetic origins of the particular foetus we were observing. Those genes came from elsewhere, so, why shouldn't the newly-created species be dispersed throughout other suitable planets?

Their genetic research also aims to correct genetic faults within species, and he used the example of how human genes may contain predispositions towards certain diseases, conditions, or inherited traits. These same kinds of weaknesses or faults occur in the genes of other species. The Greys are working to create, not perfect life forms, but mixed species with genetic modifications that enable them to survive well on certain planets. Similarly, they aim to create a better quality of life for some individual species through genetic modifications, according to their home environment. All of these foetuses were being produced to survive on planets in certain locations in the galaxy and in particular, in climates or environments the Greys have already studied in detail in preparation for seeding those planets with new life.

We walked slowly from one cylinder to the next, examining the features of each foetus. Some clearly had Grey characteristics, while others were distinctly different in every way. One in particular caught my eye and I was curious about it, but at the same time, taken aback by its appearance. The head was overly large with an elongated skull and enormous eye sockets however, the body was small and fragile-looking. This seemed incongruous and I wondered how big the species would grow and how the torso would support this large skull. The Grey was amused by my naïve thoughts, reminding me I have had children and should know that the human foetus has a large head and small body initially, but eventually the human form becomes proportioned over time!

He stressed this research is universal in nature and humans are not "special". I queried whether this was interference, and what gave them the right to create species, or even consider that a species might need improving. He politely invited me to consider how humans have degraded our own planet and species, with the effects of chemicals, drugs, poor nutrition and environmental pollution causing changes to our physical bodies, emotions, hormones, brains – the list went on!

S. *He says, "Come on! Think! You can do better than this!" He's sort of telling me off. "There are other species that have created problems in their evolution and we are assisting them. We don't just improve the species – we help to improve the state of the planet as well."*

The scientist explained the Greys are one of a number of species involved in visiting planets where civilisations need assistance. They are able to aid what he referred to as the "two systems", the planet itself, which they see as a living entity that can be healed and modified, as well as the species that inhabit that planet. They are not just helping humans, but other creatures on our planet as well, and he made an aside comment that resonated with me: *that many humans fail to realise the value of their companion species*. Extinction of species can be through human-created causes, such as loss of habitat and toxic pollution, or it may be a natural course of evolution, where the demise of some species is replaced with newly evolving ones.

We moved on along the rows of glass cylinders and stopped in front of another one. A new revelation struck me as I stared at the creature and recognised a genetic input possibly from a familiar animal. It resembled an ox! They were not just developing mixtures of what many humans would consider high-intelligence species, but they were incorporating Earth's animal species in the mix as well!

When this realisation occurred, the scientist immediately began a different form of communication with me, as if to address any wild speculation or assumptions on my part – a kind of instant filtering effect through my mind. I can liken it to using a sieve when cooking: you pour something into it and some of the material will remain in the sieve, while the rest will pass through and down the plughole. He quickly force-fed a great deal of information through my mind concerning their wider genetic programmes and the way they are seeding or assisting other planetary systems. I consciously registered what I have the capacity to understand, and what was beyond me sank into my subconscious. Finally, he told me what I had understood was sufficient at this point. It was quite an experience.

He commented humans must eventually evolve past our belief that we are superior to other species on our planet. The Greys and their associates recognise the soul-status of other (non-human) creatures and they are aware the soul-source can choose a life in any form, including an animal, if the learning gained from that incarnation is useful or evolutionary.

The new species they create are life forms in which souls can choose to incarnate, providing experiences and opportunities for spiritual and soul development in an ever-expanding universe. These comments opened new questions in my mind around how these newly-created life-forms become "available" to soul-sources in the

Field of Consciousness, and how the Greys and other extraterrestrial species may facilitate this.

The scientist also sought to expand my thinking by discussing their vast gene-bank, and how this relates to human survival and that of other earthly species. My understanding up to this point had largely related to their contact with our own planet, but the Grey told me their programmes not only extend throughout the galaxy, but even into other dimensions and states of existence. We humans are only at the very initial stages of even considering life could exist elsewhere, let alone in another parallel or other-dimensional reality. He stressed it is imperative to understand their advanced level of research ensures species survival, particularly on planets with civilisations tending towards retrograde. No matter what humans may do in the future to our planet and civilisation, the Greys have already selected, collected and studied human and other genetic material in order to ensure the continuation of our Earth's species. They can accomplish this either through genetic reproduction, intervention/alteration, or by introducing genetically engineered human/mixed species life-forms to other planets if need be.

He expressed concern about our potentially destructive course of development and outlined future situations on our planet which will cause many human's lives to implode:

- Widespread chaos will eventually cause people to become insular and concerned only with their day-by-day survival. This will create what he referred to as a "dead stage" on the planet, as focus becomes confined and self-centred, rather than global.
- Many people will stop looking outwards for a period of time; they will not want to even think about space or what species could be out there.
- The human psyche will experience global despondency and people will be at a loss to know where to go (even physically/geographically), or where to turn for assistance and guidance.

However, their hope is that this will be followed by a slow upswing of recovery and forward momentum again. Things will start to recover and there will be a deeper examination of the possibility of life elsewhere. There may also be scrutiny of those who state they have already had contact with extraterrestrials, and we must be prepared for this. He explained I need to continue to live my life up until that point without worrying unduly about the future.

S. *When an examination of the concept of extraterrestrials visiting our planet occurs, there will need to be people who have this greater understanding of what these extraterrestrial groups have sought to achieve.*

The Grey outlined how in my later life I would become a "conscious observer", taking an increasing interest in current affairs and spending more time each day following what is taking place in other parts of the world. They will monitor a variety of human perceptions and perspectives through humans like me, and he reminded me the Greys have taught many humans to analyse using a variety of energetic senses to read between the lines of what leaders, politicians and so-called experts are saying. We will need to become aware of "overlaying agendas, humans against humans, humans harming humans" – and I understood only too well it was a different kind of human "survival" he was describing now, with an accompanying sense of deep sadness from him.

His stream of telepathy fell silent momentarily and I became aware of a spark of light in the air between us, which had emerged from his forehead.

S. *It's moving towards my head and I'm stepping aside. He says, "No, don't step aside! Stay right where you are!" And it's going into my left temple!*

He stated this super-ball of their consciousness will assist me in knowing how to contribute at this future crucial phase in our evolution, describing it as a little bit of them speaking through me.

Discussion

I have memories of seeing life-forms growing in clear tubes on several occasions on craft.

The Greys consider the Earth as a living entity, a complex evolving system that contributes to maintaining the conditions necessary for the continuance life. The Plant and Animal Kingdoms play an integral part in maintaining the balance necessary for our survival. We are interdependent. This view is reminiscent of the *Gaia Theory* as formulated by scientist James Lovelock in the 1970s.

The Grey scientist emphasised a point they have reiterated continually throughout my contacts with them: that many humans fail to realise the value of our companion species on the planet and their part in our survival through balance in the ecosystem.

Over the years there has been widespread discussion in the UFO community worldwide, speculating that present-day humans are in fact the result of genetic intervention by extraterrestrial species in the distant past. Although details in this experience do not specifically point to this concerning our planet, there is mounting historical evidence to this effect, and ancient artefacts suggest this may be the case. We are still struggling to comprehend how many of Earth's megalithic monuments, ancient pyramids and stone cities could be constructed without advanced knowledge of engineering, stonework, physics, metallurgy and cosmology. All of this could point to alien intervention in our past, or to advanced human civilisations that destroyed themselves in repeated cycles throughout history, having to start the process of attaining knowledge and technological know-how again and again.

It is clear the Greys and other species are involved in collecting genetic material from an unknown number of planets and dimensions, providing a gene-bank for the creation of both new and genetically enhanced or improved species. These may be introduced to planets which have already been extensively studied, or introduced into locations in other dimensions. [40] They have already ensured our genetic survival by creating a gene-bank of Earth's life-forms.

The Grey scientist/geneticist pointed out that the creation of new species offers opportunities for souls to experience new lives in our universe and beyond. This brings to mind my description in Chapter 9 *Soul Origin*, where the Field of Consciousness offered my soul-source two lives, one of which was a life as an intelligent sponge-like form on a newly developing planet. Our own genetic research has advanced in recent years, and future moral questions relating to creating new life-forms may require a reassessment or upgrade of our understanding of the soul.

The Grey warned of a time of "humans, harming humans" on a near-global scale, adding that experiencers would need to become more analytical about whom we associate with. I believe we are now in an important period of time where people who have experienced contact (no matter what category they may label themselves by

[40] It has also been noticed within the biology community that there have occasionally been apparent giant leaps in human evolution, but a connection to alien intervention is never made because such is not considered acceptable as science and is not amenable to experiment or collection of relevant data.

(abductee, contactee, experiencer etc), need to link up and support each other. [41] The way we perceive and convey information is often different from others and this key difference will become increasingly relevant and crucial in the future, potentially providing alternative and positive avenues of thinking between us during what may be a time of global despondency.

Information provided by this Grey scientist covered the general theme of their concern for species survival and specifically predicts a time in the future when our planet will undergo an intense time of chaos, where our very survival may be in question. This contact experience occurred in 1987, and now in 2016, one only needs to read the newspaper, watch the news on television, or search the Internet to find daily horrendous indications that what the Grey scientist metaphorically, yet prophetically referred to as a "dead stage" on our planet, has already begun.

---

[41] It will also be useful for persons with related anomalous experiences (e.g. remote viewing, channelling, seeing ghosts, para-psychology, etc.) to inform each other to the wider reach of science to explain all these phenomena in scientific terms, since acceptance by the wider science community at university level is important to this development of our species, and because of the difficult times to come as some segments of our population will be deposed and threatened. At the same time we are aware that many people in our civilization are being given special gifts to prepare our civilization for these difficult times. This book will be a key component.

Chapter 23

Passing through the Planet

In 1987, I retained detailed memory of learning to fly a small scout craft, with recall of technology and extraordinary "people".

1987, age 32 years.

RJ and I stood in the hangar waiting for a group that he said would be taking me on an instructional flight experience.

Five human-like people entered the hangar area from the interior of the large craft, all of them at least 180-195 cm tall, with uniform angular physiques. At only 163 cm, I felt daunted by their stature: slim-bodied and long-limbed, with pale flawless skin. Three males were blonde haired, while a fourth male and a female had mid-brown hair, hers gathered in a roll at the base of her neck. Unlike the humans I had seen on the craft who generally wore navy overalls, they were dressed in fawn tight-fitting jumpsuits. They had an air of self-assurance and refinement about them, and the overall image was immensely striking as they strode towards us. RJ informed me these humanoids were part of an association of species and civilisations working together along with the Greys, and they seemed like advanced models of humans to me.

RJ and the group rapidly exchanged information that was difficult for me to follow at first, as the frequency of their telepathy was different from what I was used to with the Greys, akin to listening to a foreign accent. After a brief conversation they invited me to go with them and it was evidently a foregone conclusion that I would. Leaving RJ, we walked towards a disc-shaped craft, bulbous in the middle and supported on a separate tripod, which apparently the craft had lowered onto. The brown-haired male, who seemed to be in charge so I will refer to him as "the leader", explained they would assess how adept I was at using instruction the Greys had given me on operating consciousness-enabled technology, to interface with their similar technology. I wondered why they had selected me and he immediately told me it is a standard procedure they carry out periodically with a lot of humans. They related to me in a polite, but slightly distant manner.

As we approached the craft a series of small steps automatically elevated from the ramp, and as I looked behind me they closed down again, rather like the flaps on an aircraft's wing. The interior cabin was circular, some 4.5 to 6 metres wide, with adequate headroom and a ceiling that arched into a shallow dome. Panels, screens and w/screens were regularly spaced around the perimeter and a single console extended to the centre of the craft from the wall. Behind this console were two pedestal seats, with a further three in a row closer to the wall. A raised screen was embedded in the console, with a smaller screen, two touch-pads and a lever set in a slot – everything a non-descript beige colour.

One of the blonde males left the craft, the ramp closing behind him, and the leader asked me to sit on the right-hand seat behind the console, with the female seated on my left. The remaining two blond males were busy monitoring screens behind us and the leader stood in front of me to the right of a w/screen. I gathered all these positions had significance in the operation of the craft. The female, who I had gleaned was a scientist, piloted the craft, which was now making a humming noise indicating movement. I tried to reconcile in my mind that "people" were operating a craft as advanced as this and I felt a bit inadequate. I didn't even know for sure whether they were fully or partially human, humans from our future, or a separate humanoid race altogether, and I did not feel confident enough to ask.

After what seemed only minutes, the leader informed me we had reached another place on our planet that I was not familiar with, and he would expose the w/screen soon. He was aware I was nervous and suggested I should relax and enjoy the change of routine. It was obvious all communication would continue to be telepathic.

The w/screen opened revealing a fantastic vista, a hilly region entirely ablaze with spectacular autumn coloured trees, brilliant in red, orange and gold hues, the likes of which we do not have in New Zealand. And it was daylight! The craft hovered above pylons carrying power lines over the hills, appearing in a horizontal line across the w/screen. The group smiled, showing pleasure at my surprise and I felt a little bit of warmth developing between us.

Flight instructions began with the leader requesting my focused attention while he explained and demonstrated, and then I would be expected to emulate what he had done. I must learn two modes of flight (thought and manual), and an oscillation movement necessary for the stability of this small craft. While the craft is in a hovering position it maintains a slight swinging, bobbing motion, which he imaged within my mind as like a pendulum, or a buoy bobbing in the water. His instructions would assist me in mastering the "wobble" (sometimes referred to by UFO sighting witnesses as the "falling leaf" movement.) I should take note that the exterior w/screen view was stabilised (he did not explain how), but the degree of oscillation could be viewed diagrammatically on the large console screen. The smaller screen showed a stand-out (3-D) representation of the craft in relation to surrounding topography.

He explained this oscillation is the result of the craft, or its energy field when hovering, being aligned to a natural regular movement or wave fluctuation of energy, the source of which I did not understand at this point. When using thought-mode to fly the craft, the pilot does not have to create the oscillation, as this is a built-in process involving the craft's computer consciousness and technology combined.

So the first mode involved movement of the craft using thought, by energetically connecting to the consciousness of the craft and all its systems, and the leader demonstrated for me. It is interesting that he connected to the craft's consciousness by thought alone, whereas I was used to connecting via a touch-pad. By looking at the w/screen, I saw we moved forward smoothly and came to a stop, and he said the oscillation was now occurring, but I felt no movement; it was almost as if we were "going with the swings", or the interior capsule or environment of the craft was compensating in some way.

The second mode of movement involved manual operation of the craft using the lever I had noticed, set in the console. The manual method is designed specifically to be used at certain times, or in particular locations. My instructor supported this statement by placing images in my mind of adverse weather conditions, electrical storms, movements or currents in the atmosphere, electromagnetic field anomalies, and places where earth energies merge or emerge. He did not dwell on these explanations as I was unlikely to encounter these circumstances during this session, and the focus was simply on teaching me to use the two hovering modes of the craft's technology.

He indicated the small lever embedded in the centre of a cross (+) shape on the console and told me that when the pilot engages this lever, it bypasses the mind/telepathic communication with the craft. Flying the craft and creating the oscillation then become a manual operation, switching from mental to physical mode. The lever flips up and can be moved in four directions, as well as a rotational movement in the centre of this, which enables the pilot to move in any diagonal direction, including ascent and descent. However these more refined movements were not going to be part of my instruction today. I felt confident the manual mode might be easier for me because it is aligned to what I'm used to in my daily life, like driving a car.

The leader responded laconically, "We'll wait and see."

He operated the lever, explaining it had a "light touch", and I observed as he moved the craft forward and used the lever to oscillate it. He now drew my attention to the diagrams on the screen in front of the scientist, with white regularly spaced markers down each side of it and a stable horizontal red line across the middle. Superimposed over this was a floating blue line that tilted, indicating the degree of oscillation, and he demonstrated the manual mode a few times while I watched the diagram on the screen.

S. ... and the more I look at this manual mode, the more I think I should be able to do it. It looks quite easy.

The male asked me to connect to the craft's consciousness by placing my hand on a small pad, thereby opening a channel of communication between my thoughts and energy, and that of the craft and its technology. For a split second I felt an electric tingle radiate across the palm of my hand as it read my electric field. I felt my sensory awareness had immediately expanded, or become a part of the craft's biology, and I noted an immediate drop in body temperature accompanying this energy shift, to the extent that I shivered for a second or two. There was also a slight difference in how their system felt in comparison to the Greys', but still becoming part of a bigger "mind" associated with the craft.

He instructed me to practice the thought-mode first, giving me a running commentary and encouragement, with us both keeping an eye on the outside view on the w/screen, and the horizontal lines on the console screen, as I mentally expressed the active intent to move the craft forward. Having accomplished this, he instructed me to bring the craft to a stop and move into the oscillation mode using telepathic instruction.

S. The blue line is moving too much! The scientist says, "Modify! Modify!"

Panic! There is no human verbal terminology that can equate to the thought-instructions, which are about telepathic intent expressed in energy, aligning with and influencing natural universal fluctuations or waves. The craft becomes part of a wave flow of energy and the extent (distance), or duration of the craft's oscillation (the length or height of the wave pattern) can be altered by the intensity of the thought patterns or telepathy. In this case I needed to dampen down the intensity. I practiced moving, hovering, and oscillating a number of times, until I felt confident in the process.

The leader asked me to disconnect from the touchpad and I immediately began to feel warmer. I now used the manual mode, but this proved to be more difficult than I had anticipated and my first attempt again resulted in excessive oscillation of the craft, with the blue line tilting dramatically on the screen in front of me. This was embarrassing and the group was amused by it, but told me I could have destabilised the craft without their intervention. The leader had warned me earlier that the lever had a light touch, but I wasn't prepared for the effect of taking the lever too far and I think he let me do that to make a point. I resorted to slow forward momentum for a few seconds while I gathered my wits before a second attempt, and we continued practicing until I had mastered this mode as well. He asked me if I was a perfectionist and I replied that I probably was! He was amused again at my expense, but I liked his sense of humour.

Having been used to driving a car, I was surprised the manual procedure was more difficult and came less naturally to me than instructing the craft by thought. He explained how telepathic interaction with the craft is not reliant upon initial neurological messages to muscles, tendons, ligaments and so on, which were required by the manual method of flight. Therefore shared consciousness between craft and operator was an instantaneous and more reliable way of flying it, by-passing physical interferences, fallibilities and constraints. He told me I (ie. humans) would utilise this kind of knowledge and conscious technology more in the future.

The session had been pretty intense and just as I was getting used to it all, the instructor announced their intention to return me directly to my home rather than to the Greys' larger craft, due to time restrictions. I was enjoying myself immensely and perhaps had not noticed the passage of time, but he commented a "surprise" still lay in store for me.

S. *He says that in effect, we'll be going right through the planet! And the moment he announces this I'm struck by a terrible anxiety and uncertainty – like a bomb has dropped in my stomach! It is about the last thing I was expecting to hear! There's an immediate feeling of fear and trepidation!*

He assured me I would be quite safe and that I should not dwell on the ghastly images he was aware were now arising in my mind, of molten lava and incineration, because the experience would be nothing like that at all. Sensing my discomfort, he sent a spurt of information and imagery to me illustrating how a change in the status of the craft and everything in it would take place. There would be a "shift", a temporary phase of movement from one place to another, like moving outside the current existence, place and time, then running alongside it in some shortened parallel reality or dimension, before moving back in again. During that shortened space of time, in that altered reality, *in effect*, we would pass through the planet from point A to point B.

All of us were now seated. The instructor's explanation had not entirely quelled my fears and the irrational thought crossed my mind that I wasn't wearing a seat belt. We would ascend out into the atmosphere at speed, where some seconds of preparation were necessary before the transitional "jump".

S. *He says simply, "Watch", and I'm absolutely astounded at what I'm seeing on the w/screen! I'm overwhelmed by it!*

First landform, and then ocean and cloudbanks receded into the distance. A breathtakingly beautiful vista of planet Earth such as I will never forget, filled the w/screen. We hung momentarily in the higher reaches of the atmosphere, or beyond, I am not sure which, but from where the curvature of the Earth could be seen. The instructor warned me I may see changes on and through the w/screen and that normally they would close it if humans are afraid, but he sensed my curiosity too and decided I should watch some of the changes taking place. The scientist's screen on the console now showed a stand-out (3-D) image with a representation of the craft in the centre of it, with series of lines moving around it, rather like the low-pressure lines on a meteorological map.

S. *So we're going in! ... accelerating down towards the earth ... and I'm feeling a bit sick!*

The landmass came closer again, but within seconds, the view transformed until familiar aspects of landforms and ocean were no longer identifiable, spiralling clockwise into a cone-like form, leaving me uncertain as to whether this was just the effect of the w/screen, the craft spinning wildly, or an image of some dark tunnel or vortex ahead of the craft.

We plunged into darkness, with just a few lights flickering over the w/screen like static, accompanied by a soft, but high-pitched humming/whining sound. I dared not move. The flickers transformed to random short bursts of coloured vertical strips, changing position and height, and the whining increased in volume.

The leader indicated the procedure was nearly over, and suddenly the whining sound was replaced by an unpleasant noise, brief but distinct and disconcerting, like the deceleration of a screaming motor, quickly descending into a grinding sound. He explained this was part of the effect of travelling *through* the Earth; the effect of this jump from one place to another.

As the sound faded away, the w/screen cleared ... and there was a night sky! It was a tremendous relief to be safe and still in one piece, and I sensed the instructor was monitoring my emotional and mental reactions, and tried to compose myself. In that very moment, I felt the crew envelop me with expressions of pleasure in sharing the experience with me.

It seemed as if the craft had simply reappeared out of a hole in the air, popped into existence above the sea. The whole process had taken minutes and we were now in the southern hemisphere again, at a low altitude, and I could see distant lights scattered along a coastline which we were moving towards at speed.

My last memory was of getting into bed in my silent house.

Discussion

Suzy:

I retained extensive conscious memories of most parts of this experience, which I have spoken about at conferences since 1997.

Over the ensuing years, I have come across a handful of other experiencers from around the world who have given corroborative, but limited accounts of being taught to operate small craft as well.

I will note that my memories of alighting from the craft afterwards involved an unusual process, but with too much detail to include in this chapter, so I have focused on the flight experience itself.

Despite the speed at which we travelled, and the nature of a shift into a parallel course or state of existence, and back again, I came to no physical harm.

RJ commented these humans were part of an association of species working with the Greys, but the people themselves made no mention of their origins to me, and nor did I ask, given the intensity of extreme focus on the tasks during my short time with them. Like the Greys, they offered no names, and nor did I; there just seemed to be a mutual knowing in relation to each other.

I have included this experience with human-like beings in the book to illustrate the wide range of off-world races or species that are involved in working with our planet, and with this species of the Greys. It challenges stereotypes, generalisations and negative theories held by some people about the Greys and inaccurate speculation that all their agendas are negative.

This occasion was just one of a number of times I have had contact with this human-like group. I also have recollection of them showing me their planet, either in reality or in a virtual environment where I was shown their peaceful society, abodes, modes of travel, landscape, and flora, which I may write about in the future. Once again, I am not alone in experiencing viewing another planet. As impossible as these memories may seem to some, they are shared by thousands of contactees, abductees and experiencers worldwide. Fellow New Zealand experiencer, Alec Newald, has written a book entitled *Coevolution*, about his ten day visit to an alien civilisation.

My view of Earth from an ultra-high altitude is a sight I will always remember, engendering in me an intense love of our planet. At that altitude, one only sees the natural universal beauty of our globe, and all unpleasant thoughts of war, degradation of the environment and the like occurring on the surface below, recede from one's thoughts, as the planet takes on a fresh new image.

I can only imagine how astronauts and cosmonauts feel after viewing our tiny fragile planet from out in space, hanging in "the void". Many of them experience the *overview effect*, a term coined in 1987 by Frank White to express the shift in awareness felt upon viewing our planet as a tiny ball, engendering a desire to protect Earth.

Perhaps by allowing me to see something similar, the "surprise", these humanoids intended a deeper, more meaningful objective for me than just a straightforward flight instruction session.

Dr. Schild:

This is the most amazing thing I have ever read. I envy you your experience Suzy. I suspect, but cannot know, that the "falling leaf" movement of the craft occurs because the craft is trying to ride on (respond to) a consciousness wave having a spiralling form. In that situation the craft is activating anti-gravity, but the intensity of the wave is locally oscillating, most probably at the frequency of human consciousness, near 72 cycles per minute, or approximately one cycle per second. But if the craft is moved forward or backward by a small amount, comparable to the radius in metres of the spacecraft, it would find a location in the consciousness (gravity related) field which is not oscillating in this mode.

The description of flying through the planet is also fascinating. Many experiencers have reported seeing craft burrow through oceans and lakes, and also rock faces. In my view this involves the same manipulation of the phase information of the material as walking through walls, windows, and doors. Adopting the view that the craft is able to analyse the quantum field of matter, it must also be able to manipulate the quantum state of its own matter, and pass through the spaces between electrons and nuclei of atoms. Recall that experiencers often report that when a UFO is observed shooting away at high speed, an energetic precursor beam is often seen shooting in that direction moments before the UFO departs. This precursor beam might combine functions of analyzing the forward gravitational fields, and also re-arranging the quantum description of the matter.

Recalling Suzy's description that flying through the Earth's interior produced images of a dark tunnel-like cone or vortex on the w/screen, suggests again a process dominated by spiralling waves related to consciousness.

And I was particularly interested in Suzy's account that the experience suddenly changed to a blackness accompanied by a high-pitched whining sound. I would expect the nature of the quantum description of the UFO's environment to change when passing through the iron core of the earth, because the magnetic properties of iron would, working through Maxwell's equations describing the relativistic quantum field theory, introduce additional physics that changed the experience.

And the UFO is revealed to be an amazing bio-feedback machine.

Chapter 24

The Box-shaped Craft

1988, age 33 years

R. Where are you?

S. I'm in my bedroom and there's a small Grey here. He's by himself this time.

The Grey invited me to go with him, telling me there would be something different about this evening's activities. Immediately upon expressing my intent to accompany him, we rose off the floor and floated through the floor-to-ceiling window next to the bed. A beam of light extended down, encompassing our bodies and drawing us up over the neighbour's roof and through an opening underneath a hat-shaped craft, steely-charcoal in the nightlight.

Three Greys and seven other people dressed in nightwear were already onboard and seated together. The lead Grey informed us we were travelling to a destination not far away, where we would be required to disembark from this small craft. Through the w/screen, I could see we had already descended low above a moonlit forested area, with sizable pale clearings visible amongst darker areas of trees.

The four Greys' minds were abuzz with rapid communications now, excited about something. The craft hovered just a few feet above the ground, a ramp lowered and we disembarked with one of the crew. It was cold outside with sharp pine needles underfoot, and we stood scanning the sky, wondering what we should be looking for. The crew member perceived the exact moment when we all spotted something, and told us this approaching craft would seem surprising to us all.

S. There's an orange light coming down, out over the sea ... getting closer now. I can see a row of lights around the middle now! Oh! It's like a flying shoe box! He says, "Well, we told you it was something different."

I asked him, "But how does this thing fly?" He responded that I should know the answer to this and fired a simple abrupt statement at me: "The human mind only sees a flying box which doesn't appear to be aerodynamic, but we do not use your out-dated technology."

The rectangular prism-shaped craft approached quickly, hovering above us – and it was big – about the size of two or three small houses combined. The crew member advised us we would be transferred onto it shortly to attend a lecture. Each of us had been selected for specific reasons, and he added that we were fortunate because the Grey who would deliver this lecture did not usually have much direct contact with humans, having a position in their society that we would refer to as a "sage".

The smaller craft moved off, hovering further away, and the Grey began supervising the transfer by standing us in position in a tight group. A wide beam of energy, causing the air to vibrate and shimmer, descended around us, lifting all eight humans at once. Out beyond the beam, the small craft moved in closer again to pick up the remaining Grey. We passed through the opening, momentarily startled by the exceptionally bright interior.

As we were ushered into a corridor, an unexpected yet awesome incident unfolded, bringing us to a sharp halt. A group of four tall light-beings manifested before us, infused with light and yet outlined with bands of dark. Silhouettes of limbs, heads and torsos shimmered luminously, dazzlingly. The initial reaction of some of the group, who had not previously witnessed entities transforming, was to huddle together like a bunch of frightened sheep.

Upon sensing this adverse reaction the four entities immediately imparted feelings of peace and calm, telling the group not to be afraid and instantly making us feel more comfortable in their presence. As our heart-rates returned to normal, they asked us to observe. Each form now intermittently displayed the features of different genetic origins of species, transitioning, overlaying each figure. But yet another unexpected change took place as the figures materialised like old-fashioned film negatives, semi-transparent and ghost-like.

S. They say, "It's okay. It's us! We have these other forms too." They can project and take on different forms, create forms for other dimensions and utilise them for a variety of purposes. Sometimes they appear in a form they simply want us to see.

The Grey accompanying us explained they had expected some of us to be shocked, but we had been selected to witness this transformation because it was time for us in particular, given the programmes we are part of, to better understand the other-dimensional nature of the Greys (and other species) and their ability to utilise and transmute a range of energies to occupy, albeit in a ghostly way, two different life-forms at the same time. These concepts of energy transformation would be developed in the lecture we were about to attend and for some of us, in activities at a later date. This information was less surprising to those in our group with dual soul identities, who had personally experienced the transformation from the human form to that of a Grey.

The figures simultaneously filtered back to their recognisable Grey or mixed species physiques, and one of them gestured with his arm, inviting us to move along to a room where three other groups of eight people were already waiting for us to join them.

We were asked to quieten and compose ourselves and after a little shuffling and throat-clearing, the groups became still and attentive. The lead Grey prepared us for the fact an entity would shortly come from the right-hand side of the room, and it would look markedly different also. We were to remain calm.

Soon a short entity clothed in a floor-length garment entered the room, moving with a slow dignified gait, and I suspected the coat concealed a body or form that might shock or repulse humans. The most intriguing aspects of his appearance were the deep folds of skin on his neck, face and hands, layers and layers of folds and deep grooves, and I wondered how that delicate neck could support his large head. He moved to the front of the room and turned to face us. There was total silence, not even verbal exclamations, as we all struggled to remain telepathically polite, but to no avail because he was "reading" us all and everyone knew it. It was quite ironic really, the whole group frantically trying to quieten their thoughts and reactions, but he was able to simply look at us and assimilate everything about us in a short space of time. He remained totally still, and we sat equally still as he got to know us.

With riveting clarity, a sudden telepathic stream issued from the entity:

S. *He says, "Okay. This is going to be rapid and you need to be brain-wise, focus-wise, awareness-wise. Please prepare yourselves now for that". And we're all doing that, rising up a level, and then rising up another.*

Ancient Grey

The lecture would be delivered in quick-time, but *mental*, *psychological*, *psychic*, or *intellectual* are not quite adequate words to describe the category of awareness necessary to connect with this particular ancient entity. It seemed on this occasion, our focus must be increased tenfold.

Now holographic images hung in the air around us and we realised the lecture was to do with plants; it was amazing, like being in a jungle! He said he didn't tell us the subject to begin with because, "You humans immediately start drawing on what you already know. We don't want that. This is *our* awareness. Don't go to *your* awareness! It's not relevant at all. Just clear your minds and allow this information to come in."

Images of different species of Earth's trees and plants manifested, now with coloured energy fields flaring around them. Some members of the group recognised vegetables and I could hear someone thinking, *oh, yes, food!* The Grey immediately registered their thoughts had strayed from energy to food!

S. He says, "Keep that thought right out. It's not about eating the plants. We're talking about the plants remaining, and continuously providing you with sustenance at an energetic level."

The plants remain, continuously providing us with *sustenance* at an energetic level! The concept was exciting! Intense interaction now relayed backwards and forwards between minds on this subject, with the Grey delving into our thoughts, registering questions, drawing perceptions out and pushing information in. We were all part of every interaction, every level of inquiry and explanation. He was capable of addressing multiple questions, thoughts and impressions at once. It was fascinating!

The ancient Grey explained a specific aspect of plants' energy fields which can be *absorbed.* This is a level of energy humans have not discovered yet, which can be extracted from the plant's energy field, transmuted with the mind through our energy field and absorbed by us, leaving the plant to continue growing. The result is an energetic aspect of substances we need in our bodies, like an imprint or frequency. He stressed it is only temporary sustenance which may be necessary in times of need and this knowledge will be valuable in the future, enabling those who understand the concept to survive longer periods of time between ingesting normal foods.

The Grey performed a *telepathic spray*, simultaneously placing an information capsule in each person's consciousness containing details about how this energy is actually obtained. Many in the group wanted to know why this information must remain in our subconscious for the time being, when it could be put to good use on the planet now in countries suffering starvation and crop failure. However he insisted the human race was not yet ready to accept this information, nor responsible enough to use the information with integrity and "right application". An unfolding process of scientific discoveries must take place first in order to lead mankind towards acceptance of these advanced concepts of energy.

S. He says, "Let's do number one, and in time we'll release number two, then number three. There's much more to this than a simple idea of getting sustenance from plants. More is to come."

He stated that in the distant future, humans will likely move towards the opposite of how we function now, not just eating food, but absorbing some food and ingesting energies as well. As we gain a broader understanding of energy, the human form may also become significantly different.

I wondered why the Greys had chosen to pass this information on to members of our group in particular, and he picked up on my thoughts, responding that some of us may even need to use this skill in our lifetime when there is a time of great hardship, in which case it would be released into our minds.

This revelation disturbed us, as did his next, although I had heard this warning before: as the issue of contact with extraterrestrials is examined more deeply by the public, people who have had contact already may be scrutinised for their knowledge of, and association with these species. He emphasised this with holographic projections of futuristic images.

Likewise, people who claim to have had contact with extraterrestrials, but who are not telling the truth, will eventually be exposed and suffer for this. He added that it is sad but true, that human nature is sometimes attracted to opportunities for ego gratification or exploitation.

Our group did not wish this sort of thing to happen to anybody, whether they are dishonest, or not. He responded that during times of change there may be casualties.

S. *He says, "Remember that you are a cog in a wheel. Don't be concerned, just focus on the big picture."*

Sensing our despondency and wishing to leave us in a more balanced emotional state, he began a calming process, not placating or humouring us, but rather caring for us with his mind. Visions of beauty replaced those of potential dilemma or difficult predicaments, and panoramas of nature, wind in the trees, snowy mountains, and glistening lakes emanated from his mind all around us.

"Just remember this and hold it in your minds." He slowly moved away through the doorway. The entities remaining gave us a little time to gather our thoughts. We were subdued; nobody spoke to anyone else, the only interplay between us having taken place when the ancient one interacted with us all.

Discussion

I first spoke publicly of my memories of the box-craft experience at the New Zealand UFO Symposium, in 1997.

When I recalled this event the morning after it occurred, I was sure I must have remembered the shape of the craft incorrectly and certainly felt it could never fly successfully. But within weeks of the event, I received a serendipitous phone call from my friend Harvey Cooke, who mentioned a new book he had read recently entitled, *Beyond My Wildest Dream – diary of a UFO abductee,* by Kim Carlsberg (US), and loaned the book to me.

On page 10, Kim stated, "... but I did want to present all the different types of spacecraft I have encountered. They are included as thumbnail sketches throughout the book."

I quickly flicked through the pages and was thrilled to find a drawing of a craft on page 145, which is virtually identical to the rectangular box-shaped craft I travelled in, even down to the row of lights around the middle. I am constantly amazed at the corroborative evidence that has inevitably turned up when I have doubted the accuracy of my memories. Since then I have come across numerous descriptions of box-shaped craft from witnesses worldwide, including box-craft sightings reported to UFOCUS NZ in New Zealand.

I have ascertained the smaller craft initially set us down in a pine forest south west of where I was living at the time. The area had been clear-felled, leaving a lot of debris, dry branches, and areas of ground covered with pine needles. Some years later while travelling on the country road through this area, I recognised the shape of a hilly outcrop I had seen in the moonlight and realised I could roughly pinpoint the spot where we had landed to await the box-craft. The area had been replanted with pines after lying fallow for some time.

In this experience I was once again made aware of a time of future chaos on our planet, and a time when people who have experienced contact may face intense scrutiny, as man's preconceived theories of our origins, religious beliefs and limited concepts of the wider universe are challenged, threatened or shattered. [42]

Information about sustenance absorbed from plant energy was deposited in our subconscious minds, with the expectation that in the years to come, we may pass this knowledge on to younger people experiencing contact. Again we see preparations for the future, and people from various programmes being drawn together to share knowledge and support each other.

I consulted with a New Zealand neuroscientist regarding absorbing energy from plants as a form of sustenance.
He stated: "I am still thinking about the plant hypothesis, but I will give you my first thoughts: contrary to providing further building blocks to synthesise glucose, I think an "energy field" that is emanating from the plant's surface could replenish sources like NADH and NADPH, which represent important redox systems in the body. These substances are important for the energy metabolism in the body and provide the basics for cell proliferation (for example, myocyte (heart) regeneration is crucially dependent on the concentration of NADPH). But I do not know how electron transfer could happen through the atmosphere and also through the human skin to get access to the organs."

A recent scientific body of research proves that plants communicate with each other, contributing complex interactions within the ecosystem. They can even tell the difference between various humans and ascertain the nature of their intentions. Plants support each other, sensing when one nearby is injured or diseased. They release complex chemistries for a variety of reasons, including

---

[42] I have myself wondered why the aliens have held back revealing themselves and their benevolent purpose, and this report provides a possible answer; they are afraid for the safety of the participants in their experimental programme to improve the human condition.

specifically targeting groups of insects to assist with their processes (eg. pollination).

Although man has utilised the healing properties of plants for centuries, we understand little about the energy they produce. I am intrigued by the process of harnessing this energy form as sustenance, as outlined by the Grey, but for now it remains a mystery. I have noticed however, that plants, their energy and their importance to humans, have featured in many of the Greys' lectures over the years.

The group of Greys that initially manifested in light-being form stated they manifest these forms in other dimensions, or sometimes appear in a form they simply want us to see. This statement may corroborate descriptions from experiencers and abductees of *screen memories*, where they recall seeing a clown figure, spider, deer, or other familiar form, which they may later realise or discover through regressive hypnosis, was a Grey or another species. Their appearance in this form also shatters the simplistic perception promoted by some people that light-beings are "good", but Greys are "bad".

The ancient entity projected captivating holographic images of nature in order to calm our emotions. Recent medical research indicates human physiology and mood are affected by images of natural beauty, activating the insula part of the brain associated with emotional stability and love. Less tranquil images trigger the anterior temporal area of the brain, governing anger and depression. Clearly our human brain function and psyche are well-understood by alien species, to our benefit.

There were several aspects of this experience which showed an underlying intention by the Greys to observe human reactions to certain situations:

- They displayed an element of excitement and anticipation while waiting to see our reaction to the box-shaped craft.
- Once onboard the box-craft we were immediately confronted with a small group of light-beings: Greys presenting themselves to us in an alternative form, which they stated they can utilise in other dimensions, and they had expected us to be shocked by it. [43]

[43] By the words "other dimensions", I surmise they were referring to higher dimensionality in the String Theory sense, rather than a state of existence from another star system in our Einstein 4-D space manifold, but with such radically different physical parameters such as temperature, density or strong magnetic field.

- The lecture was conducted by an ancient Grey whose persona could be summed up as being extremely intense. There were no limitations to him being able to communicate with humans and in fact, any limitations were on our part. Telepathy is universal in nature, but we had to attune to his high energy until we attained a sufficient telepathic match with him.
- The ancient Grey revealed how they can access and transmute a level of energy from plants, as yet unknown to man, which could provide a temporary form of sustenance for humans. [44] Although fascinating, most of us found this difficult to comprehend and perhaps this is one of the reasons why he encapsulated the information and embedded it in our subconscious minds (which we unsuccessfully attempted to unlock through regression). Our reactions were monitored by other Greys present and it was as if they were seeing how far humans could stretch their acceptance of unusual data.
- And once again, we were confronted with possible future difficulties for those who experience, or claim to have experienced contact.

I suspect this total experience, a combination of surprises, shocks and revelations, was also somewhat of a psychological test, providing the Greys with data to be used within their programmes and in future contacts with members of the group.

---

[44] I assume here the process may work something like this: the plant energy does not actually change the elemental composition of the living being, but rather returns the carbon, nitrogen, and oxygen into plant compounds with a higher chemical energy state so that there is more carbohydrate available to again power human biological activity. In that case the nutrition would be in raising the level of chemical energy in the human.

Chapter 25

3-D Scans and an Unexpected Reminder

1989, age 34 years; my son, age 5 years

(Refer to Chapter 7, Reality Checks, see Circles in the Mud)

Three Greys floated my son and me from our home, moving us in an upright position past shrubs and letter-boxes, down a short road and over shallow water and into a waiting craft standing on three legs in the mudflats. I felt a bit woozy, but my son regained full consciousness quickly and was soon smiling and laughing with the Greys, standing there in his blue and white pyjamas. They were amused by his instant animation, how he switched from a relaxed state to full-on talkativeness and excited anticipation.

This was a relatively bare craft not usually used for transporting people and while some of them have a moulded plastic look about their interior, this was more metallic-looking in structure. They had already picked up another woman with shoulder-length black hair, who sat at the far end of the seat. Once underway I began to feel more alert. Eventually the pilot opened the w/screen and I saw we were entering an opening in the bottom of a larger craft.

The three of us exited down a ramp and ascended a walkway into a corridor, where Greys and around fifty humans dressed in charcoal-grey pants and navy tops were all busily occupied. I had not seen humans dressed like this on craft before and I noted most of them were young.

A human I had seen before approached us, directing my son off down a corridor. The human and a Grey took us to a room with twenty-four consoles and screens spaced in four rows of six. Other humans dressed in their night attire were seated at each console and we quietly slipped into our seats as the human and Grey moved up front.

> *S.* *We are going to use these computers that make the images stand out from the screen so they look "real".*

Tonight's activity was two-fold: a continuation of becoming familiar with this technology, and further developing brain/mind abilities without overwhelming us.

The Grey explained we would examine what we might call "medical information" on this occasion. As we connected to the technology, differing miniature human silhouettes appeared suspended in mid-air between us and the screens (3-D), each with flaring, flowing colours emanating outwards from the form.

We rotated the images, viewing them from every angle, and the Grey asked us to isolate areas of the energy fields where there were anomalies, and to consider which organs or areas of the body may be affected by this. Although some of us had done this kind of exercise before, most felt unqualified to do this, but he stated we must not limit our abilities simply because we believe we don't have the right human (medical) training to do this.

> *S. He tells us to put aside any medical knowledge. It is obsolete and we don't actually need to know any of it. "If you know where organs are positioned in the body, where the head is and where the feet are" ... he's being a bit facetious! ... "then you can do this task."*

The Grey told us they intended to divide this group after tonight's activity, and they were looking for those of us who have natural healing tendencies using intuitive perception and analysis, to receive further instruction in these areas.

The group was deep in concentration now, adjusting and examining the images to identify areas where the colours faded out, or where the field looked as if it had collapsed or caved-in. I could magnify certain areas to the extent that it felt as if I was actually inside the projection, moving through layer upon layer of the brilliant field, combining consciousness in the process.

After we had spent some time experimenting, the Grey extended our focus, introducing a new concept to us. He projected a person's silhouette from his mind as a hologram, accompanied with a dialogue, and our attention was captured as we viewed the projection of an *inner* energy field.

He commented most humans are unaware that the human electric field emanates both ways, not just outwards as we have always imagined, but *inside* the body as well. If the interaction between these two fields is interrupted in some way, it can cause ill-health. In the future, humans will have a fuller understanding of energies and the space between molecules, allowing us to disintegrate and re-form our bodies as the Greys do, or pass through solid objects. He gave instructions on how to alter the frequency of the technology in order to see this illustrated on our individual images, turning the form and slicing through it, revealing the inner field.

S. *So we've got a very different picture of the human silhouette without the external emanation to distract us. It's all internal! It reminds me of coloured coral, or seaweed waving! The Northern Lights* (aurora borealis) *flowing within the body! He says that until humans understand this inner energy field, we will not be able to truly self-heal.*

The human contributed now, commenting that when people meditate, they focus on the inner self and so without realising, they are actually positively affecting this inner field. An understanding of the interaction and balance between the inner and outer fields was crucial in understanding illness and self-healing. We readjusted the images in order to see how the inner and outer fields interfaced on or near the surface of the body.

At this point someone asked, "Are these images of real people?" The human replied that they image (scan) people who have been brought onboard for healing, so they can utilise the images in these sessions. Using the "MTM" method, he placed capsules of further in-depth information in our minds, potentially to be revealed in the future at a time of awakening, when there will be a furthering of knowledge, a flow-on effect, because their aim is to upgrade and educate humans on all levels. I was surprised it was the human who used the telepathic spray method this time, and I also noted he was totally aligned with the Greys' philosophies.

The Grey refocused us on our images, asking us to use this new knowledge to ascertain where there were blockages in both inner and outer energy fields affecting the physical body, instructing us not to use our visual capacities alone, but rather in combination with our intuitive senses.

Using these capacities changed the process of analysis from relying on visual cues, to realizing a blockage in the energy may affect a part of the body elsewhere, or the emotions. Eventually I ascertained that interruptions and weaknesses in the flow of energy in my image might indicate a kidney problem, and as soon as the thought crossed my mind, the image on the screen changed, indicating my every thought was being monitored.

The screen now showed a woman lying on a shelf-bed, as if asleep. The image automatically rotated to a view of the back of her body with organs revealed, showing a red dot over the left kidney indicating I was correct. Looking around, I could tell by the expressions on people's faces whether they had been successful or not, and we continued for some time examining other images in the same way.

Just as the session finished I registered a telepathic request for me to proceed to a side room, and I immediately felt unsettled by this. Two entities joined me in the room and gently reminded me of something I had agreed to before entering this life, but which I had since forgotten: my marriage was destined to last only a certain length of time, and that time was now approaching.

The union had achieved a genetic purpose with both of my sons, and they discussed a preparatory process leading to closure of the marriage, placing a timeframe in my mind and assuring me I would be assisted through this process.

They reminded me I would eventually have a second marriage, and that I had already met this person as a soul presented to me by the Grandfather when I was a young child. The focus of this second relationship, for me, would be on achieving a personal task, while *their* main focus with this new relationship would concern the well-being of my sons.

S. *And on some level I knew my marital relationship was heading that way, and they are soothing my sadness because it is difficult to think about another relationship when you are still in one. They are reminding my soul intelligence why this has to happen, and that I will not be able to complete a task if I remain in this marriage.*

Through this reminder, they paved the way for significant changes to take place in my life.

Discussion

I recognise there was a change in direction in my life around the time of this experience, with regard to natural healing. I joined magnetic and spiritual healing groups in the early nineties, and began focusing on meditation and natural therapies, rather than relying solely on conventional medical health methods.

This chapter is actually a much shortened version of the full experience, where we gained skills in diagnosing human health problems using our consciousness linked to technology, enabling us to consciously "enter" the moving images to closely examine the body, energies, and emotions. I described this as a "complex task". The (3-D) images we worked with were like holographic vision of peoples' electrical fields and bore a passing resemblance to a combination of Kirlian photography (electro-photography) and fMRI scans, but there the resemblance ended.

Before completing the regression, the therapist asked me if I felt the humans who were onboard the craft on this occasion were military personnel. I made the following statements:

"They are like a police force, but not actually a police force. I understand they are trained and integrated right across societies worldwide, indicative of a behind-the-scenes preparation for when the public becomes more aware of the extraterrestrial presence, or a specific form of disclosure occurs. It is interesting they were mostly young adults in their twenties and early thirties. This was a Grey craft, but there was a joint project taking place although these humans are not part of the Grey programmes which I and many other humans are involved in. They are part of a preparatory structure, a framework, so that when contact becomes more open and accepted by mankind in the future, these people will assist with a transition process and there will be this immediate organisational structure in place, more readily accepted by humans. It is a societal framework upon which contact can rest. The timeframe for this is rather like a piece of elastic – it can expand and contract, constantly adjusting according to the ups and downs of the whole awareness process of humans. It is a spiral process rather than a linear process, which may take many years."

I believe "a societal framework upon which contact can rest" are significant words. Many people are pushing for governments and militaries worldwide to divulge what they know about extraterrestrial visitation, but perhaps they will never divulge this to us. Instead, bearing in mind there may be any number of human groups working with any number of alien visitors, it would seem that some groups at least, are putting a structure in place to assist mankind when we do finally acknowledge the alien presence. Many of us have considered the instant and potentially devastating ramifications to our civilisation if disclosure takes place before we are ready. It makes sense that when the time of global disclosure comes, in whatever way it may manifest, a structure will be needed to deal with those ramifications, since it will be such a major global shift that not everyone, or every societal group or organisation, will be able to make that leap easily.

Another interesting description not included in the body of the chapter is the method the Greys used to return us to our home. As mentioned, the small craft was not usually used for transporting people and therefore was not equipped with a light-beam. [45]

At first the crew considered landing in the harbour again and floating us several hundred metres to our home, however there were time constraints to consider. After some discussion, they decided to hover near our house and levitate us down into our home, one after the other, using the power of their minds. There were two Greys onboard, plus the pilot, so one Grey floated down ahead of us. Going first before my son, I stood on the edge of an opening in the side of the craft and the crew asked me to step out into the air. As I did so, I felt pressure on my torso, as if my chest and back were caught between two magnets and in this way, the two Greys levitated us down, through a glass door and into our home.

---

[45] We also see that the Greys have to operate their agenda and programmes within the limitations of their equipment. In this section we see that they had to use a sub-optimum transporter craft not equipped with the transporter light beam.

Chapter 26

A Glimpse of Cosmic Culture

1989, age 34 years

I felt a bit dazed as I stood in our hallway with one of my sons and three Greys. The lead Grey conveyed we were about to depart, and I lurched out of a state of relaxation when I realised we would be leaving my younger son alone in the house on this occasion. I began an indignant dialogue with the Grey concerning this:

"I'm not going. I'm not leaving my son in case he wakes up and there's nobody here."

"He will not wake."

"But he might and he'd be terrified!"

"We will ensure he does not wake."

"No, I'm not going."

"One will remain."

"What do you mean?"

"We have put him in a state from which he will not wake, but if it will make your mind easier, one will stay".

"Okay."

S. *I'm a bit surprised! I'm quite happy with that and it's as if I forget about that quite quickly! I feel rejuvenated! I feel quite keen!* [46]

I later retained clear memory of this conversation, and the delay frustrated the trio as they were running to a schedule. With his

---

[46] It was interesting to me that the Grey negotiated with Suzy to leave her second son guarded by a Grey in the house. This is in contrast with accounts by US experiencer Jim Sparks, who recounts dreading his abduction experiences and being forced to learn Grey writing and logic in lessons marked with unpleasant coercion. That was happening during the same human time frame, 1989, that Suzy assigns to her more loving and negotiated experience.

superior mind control, the lead Grey had the choice of overriding my wishes however, he chose not to, instead treating me as an equal with respect for a mother's concern. But I also picked up further significant remarks between the Greys, which they had obviously not anticipated I could discern:

"She is conscious."

"... aware and can understand."

"She is ready to retain more."

We moved towards the wall and I was momentarily deprived of vision, a brief state of blackness as we passed through it. [47] Once outside the house, a defined beam of bluish-white light descended, which we stepped into one-by-one. First came the floating, disorienting feeling. [48] We ascended in a line, silently, peacefully, living beads on a string of light, with the flat bottom of the beam rising beneath the last Grey. I looked up and saw my son's feet dangling limply out of his pyjama legs.

Anticipation welled up inside me as we passed through the entrance, and the lead Grey indicated we would travel to a larger craft high in the Earth's atmosphere.

---

[47] Suzy describes a momentary "blackness" when passing through a wall of her home. I presume that in the process, the molecules of her physical body are a part of the quantum description of her body, and that the beam reads and adjusts the quantum wave of body and of the wall to pass her molecules through the spaces between the wall molecules. The fact that she describes an experience of "blackness" means that her consciousness process is still operating during the process, and I understand that her consciousness is achieved by the brain's continuous 16 Hz (beta rhythm) refresh process, and that her experience of "blackness" is actually a statement that the brain process is functioning normally but that the visual stimulation of the eyes has been interrupted in the experience.

[48] Here we have some fascinating details about the anti-gravity transport involved in the contact experience, and it is because Suzy has such a long history of contacts that she can focus on a typical event and describe it as familiar. When being transported to the first craft in a beam, she describes how initially the levitation process was "disorienting". Astronauts report how it is disorienting to be in orbit around the Earth; the experience is disorienting, because human consciousness uses reference to up and down as a constant reference for spatial orientation, so the experience of being in an anti-gravity beam is described by Suzy as being "disorienting."

Time passed with just the quiet hum of the craft's technology, and eventually a ramp unfolded leading down into a hangar. Two short Greys approached to fetch my son and he greeted them with familiarity, bright-eyed and enlivened.

The lead Grey escorted me into an area with corridors like rounded white tunnels with flattened floors, and I realised we must be in the Greys' private living area of the craft. He directed me through an entranceway into a large room and I sensed something, a door that seemed to close up behind us, although I did not see it happen. Seven other humans were already present and he invited us to experience a cultural aspect of their species, one that is shared by other extraterrestrial species as well, which he described as "a glimpse of our own future". He would explain the purpose of showing this to us later on, but at present they just wished to observe our reactions and possible participation. This sounded intriguing and nobody declined the offer.

The Grey made the captivating statement we were about to be surrounded by "pure thought" and asked us to move towards the centre of the room. He described how they could create a space beyond a space; make a given space appear larger than the area in which it is contained. I had witnessed this aspect on a number of occasions, where for example, small craft sometimes seem much bigger once you are inside them. He asked us to mentally prepare ourselves for a change in our surroundings and he would continue to convey information to us about the process as it unfolded.

The room suddenly became infused with a strange bright white light, appearing to extend the walls outwards away from us, creating a vast space. All the while, his thought-voice continued, describing how we were now inside "intelligence", a vast "mind", within which they can return to the source, or state of original energy, simply through thought.

The walls, floor and ceiling of the room were no longer visible causing me to feel as if I was floating, and if I had not been able to still feel the soft floor under my feet, I could easily have believed I was suspended in midair. The humans around me had taken on a silvery-white look, illuminated by the brightness. Now out of the light came a number of other different entities and forms to join the Greys: luminous, drifting silently, gracefully standing before us.

The thought-voice continued in my mind:

S. *"You will learn how we "enjoy". We are about to show you our recreation, our relief. We too need time away from our duties and work. We have created this space where we can release our responsibilities, the pressures of the intense work we undertake. This mode of pleasure or relaxation is very different from yours. Humans look externally for relaxation, whereas we create it with our minds."* [49] *He expresses concern that it may be overwhelming for some of us. They will involve us in the activation of the process so we understand this "atmosphere" that is specifically theirs. They are curious to see if we have the ability to participate.*

Our concentration stepped up a level with the feeling of being hyper-alert, waiting for something to happen. My heart thumped in my chest and my breathing quickened as I tried to be aware of both the entities in front of me and the total space around us, wondering what would happen next and from which direction.

Slowly, the form of the entities began to take on an indistinct smudgy appearance, their outlines beginning to waver and shimmer, until their facial features were no longer visible. Vibrant colours began to emanate from the figures, at first like little tongues of flame, but quickly engulfing their entire bodies with kaleidoscopes of blazing intensity. The entities began choosing partners in this energetic dance of the mind, mentally and spiritually joining with each other, merging their energy fields, becoming effervescent, swirling and exploding their colours like fireworks.

The Grey's over-riding thought-voice explained how they can control their energy fields and transform them with their minds.

S. *I'm turning around, looking! The colours are all around us, around our bodies, spiralling around our arms and legs.* [50]

---

[49] This may well be the first documented account of a version of extraterrestrial sexual liaisons, created through consciousness.

[50] During the beginning of the "dance" experience Suzy describes a spiralling wave, both as a wave around her arms and legs, and later as spirals of light. I believe that the quantum description of consciousness involves spiralling quantum wave (technically these are off-diagonal terms in the matrix description of the quantum wave). Thus from the description, I infer that spiralling waves are pure consciousness manifestations.

It's beautiful! I feel like all the worries I've had, all the pain, suffering and stress, is lifting off. Oh! I can't believe that ... they've disappeared!

By now the entities' physical and energetic bodies were completely disintegrating into a vivid mist, rising high above us in the boundless space, and were now forming patterns, designs, and shapes in the air.

S. ... but they are still here, their consciousness, their thoughts are still with us. I can feel the Grey smiling, saying, "Well, you didn't know I could do that!" They are above us now, spiralling, swirling. I feel freedom, absolute elation ... I have never felt like this before!

In this way, the entities impressed their personal sense of pleasure and recreational relief upon us, allowing us to feel their ecstasy and joy, inviting us to expand our energy fields and see what we could do with them. I mentally sent a stream of purple energy to their combined consciousness and received encouragement from them as they transformed it visually into stunning, intricate, shifting shapes and patterns intertwined with their own. The thought-voice asked each of us to visualise an object we would like to see manifested, and we watched transfixed as our thoughts were transmuted into a giant lotus flower, a honeybee, a pencil, and other random objects, suspended or moving fluidly and realistically in the air. [51]

The exercise now took on a new phase.

S. There is sound coming now! They say, "You didn't know this either ... you thought we had no sound (with this experience), *but we have only maintained silence for your focus. The sound is not melodious, as you know it. To us, "music" is motion* (energy?) *in a form that is "musical"."*

Our consciousness resounded with celestial music, registered in waves of varying depths, lengths, and complex layered combinations. No earthly music, regardless how majestic or beautiful, could compare

---

[51] I liked Suzy's invention of the term "thought-voice", which describes beautifully how information as quantum holograms gets projected into her mind, and then she interprets it in human words of her own voice to herself. This suggests to me that there is a language implied in the quantum hologram that is the same for all species on all planets. They don't have to go to Earth school to learn 300 languages to communicate with humans. They never seem to make language errors. This justifies the concepts of Noam Chomsky, of profound primitives in all human language.

to this wave-movement of energy transformed into sound – "motion in a form that is musical".

S. *Two of our group are crying ... not through sadness but because their joy is overwhelming. This is foreign to us... we are not a species that feels such an intensity of joy ... we drag ourselves down. They cannot understand our mental and emotional heaviness when we have such beauty around us* (on our planet). *They need this* (relaxation) *as constant travellers, far from home. It is a rejuvenation process ... food for the soul.*

For some time we remained in a state of ecstasy, transfixed in every sense by the power of consciousness, transformed and manifested in sound and visual beauty.

Slowly now, their combined creations disintegrated back to the form of ribbons of light, and then a colourful mist, sinking down, separating, and re-forming into the familiar bodies of Greys and other species.

Once again, we were just two groups of living entities, sharing the same consciousness in a room of strange light.

S. *... they are saying to each of us, "This is the recreation of our cultures. We can create a joyous reality and it frees us."*

The Grey explained the reason for showing us their form of recreation, was threefold:

1. To observe our reaction to it, and our ability to comprehend and participate.
2. To illustrate the fact they are not really so different to us; they also aspire to uplift and rejuvenate the soul through recreation and pleasure. [52]
3. And most importantly, to reinforce the fact that consciousness is the source of all creation. Our physical form is but a manifestation of consciousness, and can be transmuted. In

---

[52] This chapter also reinforces something that Suzy mentioned previously. We are coming to understand that the visiting Greys are not so much visiting our planet as vacation from their own planet, but rather more establishing an outpost (like our International Space Station) where they work for a long period to undertake a complex mission involving generations of human lives, perhaps a hundred years. Thus they offer us glimpses of their entire life experience, including their eating and food preparation as previously described.

this case, their consciousness also interacted with the "intelligent light" of the room.

He remarked that in the future humans will understand that form is energy; thought is energy and movement; thought, form and energy are consciousness manifested, and all can return again to the pure consciousness of the Source.

Future humans will be able to manifest in various forms just as the Greys can.

The room was quiet again and he directed our attention to the walls, which were now moving towards us, returning the room to its former dimensions. The outline of a doorway appeared on the wall near us and I realised there was no actual door across the opening as I had previously thought and the light simply "stopped" in the doorway, contained, and did not emanate outwards from the room. The Greys are able to create an end-point to light, manipulate it, programme it, and infuse it with intelligence. Faint shapes of figures were visible moving in the corridor beyond the light, like looking through a giant drop of water.

We were given time to re-orient ourselves, to digest this phenomenal experience in a few moments of silence, several in the group with tears of joy still wet on their cheeks. Each of us was lost in thought, contemplating how different human life would be if we could attain such fulfilling happiness so easily and completely.

They invited us to leave the room and as we passed through the doorway, I had the strange sense of walking out of bright fluid light into a dimmer, drier environment in the corridor. We made our way back to the departure area and I saw my son running towards us down an adjoining corridor, happy and animated. I realised I had not thanked the Grey for this opportunity of experiencing their recreational consciousness room, but before I could even convey the thought to him, he told me my thanks had already registered with them all the very instant the thought occurred in my mind.

Discussion

Strange as it may seem considering the nature of this experience, in my day-to-day life prior to this contact, I was afraid of the thought I may be having contact with extraterrestrials. However my clear conscious memory of the conversation with the lead Grey, which took place in my home prior to this experience, resulted in a major turning point in my fearful perspectives. I realised a state of mutual respect and concern existed between us, and I was surprised by the Grey's compliance to my request not to leave my younger son alone. I also pondered on my astonishing sense of trust in these entities and my willing cooperation in leaving the house, which was rather shocking for me to acknowledge as a careful and protective mother.

My interception of the private conversation between the three Greys was a pivotal point for me too, with them commenting the time was now right for me to consciously remember greater detail of future contacts, which I would understand and utilise in the future. These conscious memories eventually became a basis for research and deeper investigation, for speeches, and later, for further focus through regression. These pure memories are the foundation and the quintessential substance of this book, which is part of my life tasks. [53]

The experience indicates some humans have been selected to take part in activities that expose them to aspects of the Greys' culture and lifestyle, perhaps as a way of expanding our awareness, or to gauge human acceptance or reactions to it, with a view to future open contact and interaction with the human race. The Grey also reinforced we were glimpsing mankind's own future.

I wonder too, whether all the humans present had dual souls, and whether the Greys were allowing the Grey identities of those souls to experience profound human emotions through this experience, or alternatively, to assist the humans to reach the intensity of feeling expressed by the entities, through the consciousness of the Grey identity.

Another possibility, which Dr. Schild has pointed out and which crossed my mind when reflecting on this experience, is that this may be the first documented account of a version of alien sexual liaisons, manifested purely through consciousness, a spiritual interface in which humans were encouraged to participate. I described the effect of this extreme immersion in pure thought and sentience as

---

[53] It is also interesting that the Greys have been programming Suzy with a lifetime of experience of understanding their experience of life, and have told her that she will describe her experiences at a later time in her life, as she now does with this book. Presumably our civilization was not ready for such revelations till now.

“overwhelming joy” and “rejuvenation”, although even these words are inadequate.

The music that accompanied the manifestation of energy in various colours and forms created a strange but beautiful “cosmic ‘disco”. I described wave-movement of energy transformed into sound; motion in a form that is musical.

We know that some classical music, particularly Baroque, can induce a relaxed alpha brainwave state. This complex layered form of classical music is reminiscent of the multi-layered waves of energy we registered as music in the “intelligent light” room, where the Greys’ joy and relaxed recreational state also manifested through consciousness as sound.

Revelations and new beginnings emerged from this experience; a momentous change took place, a mighty shift in my human understanding of these entities and our ongoing contacts.

In my day-to-day life, the human mind wasn’t afraid anymore and I registered a strong sense of kinship with them.

Chapter 27

Children of the Mind: Using the Brain like a USB

1990, age 35 years; my son, age 7 years

The bright light accentuated my son's silvery-blonde hair and suntanned skin against his pale blue summer pyjamas. He enthusiastically dragged on my left arm with both hands, leaning backwards to try to make me walk faster. Eager to reach the end of the corridor where a familiar Grey waited outside a doorway for us, he skipped on ahead of me, a streak of colour and movement in otherwise bland surroundings.

In our society this Grey's profession would be an eclectic combination of perhaps a neurologist, a psychologist, IT expert, and sociologist. My son had an "appointment" with him tonight and was keen to show me an aspect of what he had been learning from the Grey instructors. They had brought me onboard as well on this occasion to observe his activities, as this was part of the parenting process for these children, to understand their abilities. They had included me in my son's training sessions previously and I had attended lectures with other parents of this group of children to understand our roles in the unfolding of their future commitments.

The stark difference between their facial expressions belied the interaction actually taking place. Although the Grey instructor's lack of expression depicted what we would consider a deadpan face, telepathically, he related to my son in a joyful and humorous manner. My son, by physical contrast, grinned broadly, eyes bright and facially expressive as he communicated at speed, occasionally turning and including me in the conversation telepathically. Even at the young age of seven years he was more skilled in these communications than I am – a familiar second language to him.

After greeting his mentor, my son ran into the room and climbed up on an unusual chair and the Grey directed me to sit nearby. More similar seats and apparatus were positioned around the room and I was surprised we were the only parent and child present on this occasion, as there was usually a group of eight to ten children and their parents.

His chair was wide and shallow, made of the same intelligent material as the shelf-beds. A narrow telescopic stand extended vertically from the back of it, upon which sat a dark screen around ninety centimetres wide and sixty five centimetres high, resembling thin smoky glass or shiny plastic. It was positioned just above and behind my son's head and I was curious why it wasn't on a console in front of him, but I figured there must be a reason for this.

The two excluded me from their telepathic exchange so I surmised they were discussing the activity, and clearly it was important I had no foreknowledge of what they were planning. My son grinned as if he was party to a secret, behaving in a relaxed manner on an equal footing with the instructor, yet he would not have behaved in this familiar manner towards a human adult or teacher.

The Grey explained he would begin a transfer of images into my son's mind, and he in turn would then process this information in some way. I nodded and waited, assuming I would not have access to this exchange either.

S. *My son has become very focused and clinical for a seven-year-old. I can tell there's an information transfer going on because I've done that a lot of times ... they're very still ... the whole atmosphere in the room has changed.*

Now my son's demeanour was starkly different, as if all his energy had suddenly poured into his mind or brain, with his arms at his sides and hands resting in his lap. A slight tension was apparent in his body and his head tilted backwards a little, with eyes wide and attentive, fixed on the Grey's. It was electrifying, as if they both emanated such intense energy as to affect everything around them, remaining in this state for ten or fifteen seconds as the transfer was completed.

My son then connected to their computer by placing his forearms on rubbery pads, but the Grey explained to me my son would not just simply instruct the technology to function this time – there was more to it than that.

R. *What's happening?*

S. *Oh! I'm astounded! All these things are appearing on the screen – there are script and images and some kinds of designs – a whole range of images appearing one after another in a blur!*

Hundreds of images flashed across the screen and I realised my son was transferring the data from the information transfer, onto the computer directly from his brain! A few more seconds passed, and the instructor confirmed my son had completed the transfer without mistakes and congratulated him. They conversed for a short time, and taking my son's small hand in his long slender fingers, he thanked him for his participation. It was overwhelming to witness the sense of closeness, mutual love and respect between them.

Turning to me, the Grey outlined the fuller test procedure that had actually taken place using a mathematical kind of format. Using the information transfer, he had first placed sets, or groups of images in my son's mind covering a wide range of topics: photographic-type nature images, complex designs, matrices, maps, and script, etc. with each subject set containing numerous images. Some of this material was already familiar to my son as it was human or earthly in context, such as a set of images of waterfalls, but the rest was unfamiliar, specifically Grey or cosmic material. He had transferred the data to my son's mind with the subject sets in a particular order. In turn, the images contained in each set were in a specific order as well.

The Grey had then given instructions to my son, requiring him to make specific changes to the order of the sets, and to the order of the images within each set as well. My son was then required to mentally re-sequence this large quantity of material accordingly and transfer (upload) it onto the computer in its new format, without any omissions or mistakes.

The images appeared on the screen behind my son so as not to influence his concentration and confidence. The Grey did not need to visually check for mistakes because he could telepathically register my son's output to the computer, therefore, the screen was used on this occasion solely for my benefit.

However, he explained they also use the screens when training groups of human children in these skills. An instructor will select a child from the group and convey a set of images to their mind, and all the other children are allowed to telepathically register this transfer of data. The instructor then asks the child to transfer the images to the computer and the other children watch the screen as the child completes this, checking the child has not omitted anything and that the images are in the correct order. At the same time as they are watching the screen, the children are also registering the child's output telepathically. Over time, they become more adept at using just the mind to double-check for accuracy and so the screen is eventually phased out, replacing their reliance on sight, with the mind. He commented humans rely on their visual acuity far more than the Greys, and that human children respond well to these constructive competitive games amongst their peers.

I asked why the children were learning this technique and he described how thousands of these children have learned to use particular aspects of their advanced computer technology for specific purposes, and in this case, learning a new mind/brain/consciousness methodology involving imprints and frequencies. They have trained them to use the brain like a storage system (similar to the way we now use a USB, or memory stick), from which they can upload imagery or information onto computers onboard craft, or into another trained receptive mind. Although ordinary humans can hold images in their mind, we cannot mentally convey those images in their entirety to anyone else because the images are constructed solely within our memory or consciousness. However these children can, using their soul connection, and knowledge of energy frequencies and telepathy.

He explained my son can deal with a large volume of images and information however, he does not necessarily need to have viewed each of the images himself, nor does he need to consciously recall all the detail unless he wants to. The information can be likened to a bubble which can be passed on or transferred, and my son has learned to recognise an energetic pulse from each image. In other words, each set, and each image within the set, has a complex frequency or blueprint which my son must absorb. The (energetic) frequency is then converted into imagery when transferred to the organic computer.

For example, if we were able to look at say, a sunflower, in the way the Greys do, we would perceive frequencies, a blueprint of that flower that we could convey to their conscious computer, and it in turn would produce an image of the sunflower on the screen.

In the future these trained children will have the ability to convey large volumes of information into each other's minds, but more importantly, remotely over great distances, using these processes. The information will be transferred as frequencies, which like-brained minds can mentally view as imagery, like the organic computer. However these skills will only rise to their day-to-day conscious minds if events or circumstances in their lives require it.

The process is similar to the one I have learned from the Greys, of inserting a thought-seed or information package into someone's mind, however this new process involves information and data packaged differently. The children will learn to access the information if they so wish or their mind/brain can simply be used as a carrier, or storage system. Another significant difference is that they can add to, and alter the information/data as required, and resend. This may become a requirement or necessary course of action as they link up with each other in the future.

I thought the Grey's final comment was intriguing: in the future, in my son's lifetime, there will potentially come a time when information between these humans will need to be conveyed in no other way than with the mind, because it will not be safe to convey it in electronic, audio, or written form. He has been trained to be able to identify other people like him, and to be able to exchange information with them through this method without having to use forms of communication that may be under surveillance.

I wondered – what is our world coming to? What are these children going to have to do one day? This ability was astounding, but to me as a parent, almost shocking as well. The Grey assured me there was no need to fear, but it is an essential safeguard they are providing for these children.

He added that when many of these children are adults, there will come a time when people's rational thinking will be overcome by uncertainty and confusion. At present the children have no conscious memories of their onboard experiences and the learning that has taken place in these programmes. However, during and after this time of chaos the Greys will progressively awaken them, unlocking these memories and abilities. It is at this time that the parents of these children will use their knowledge and understanding of contact to assist them, as they will need to quickly assimilate this hitherto hidden aspect of their lives.

Seeking to reassure me further, the Grey explained how the parents fit into this future scenario. They must always work hard to maintain close emotional bonds with their children. We must recognise that the onboard education of this generation of children is more complex and far in advance of what we as parents have been taught. Once they have been awakened, their skills will set them apart from us. Consequently, the Greys have high expectations of their values and morals, which their parents have played a part in establishing (along with the Greys), and they trust the children will never abuse these specialised abilities, but will use them wisely and intelligently for the benefit of mankind. They consider these children to be pure of heart and intent and they have been constantly screened to ensure this.

The instructor stated our two generations have, in a sense, become part of the Greys' "super-consciousness", which he likened to having their genes vibrating in us, and we sense this other part of us at times, outside of our humanness.

I asked why there were no other children and parents here on this occasion, and he stated they had selected my son for increased training because they recognised his potential to achieve highly. Already, at the age of seven, he could absorb and convey large amounts of re-sequenced information, and his early advanced analytical skills were recognised by the Greys as being akin to their own.

The future implications of this were obvious to me, but although I understand their programmes, in the human world, he is still my son.

Discussion

Suzy:

This experience indicates the Greys have possibly been developing a "hive mind" between these children, similar to their own social and communication structures; a different way of communicating whereby they can recognise each other in the future and exchange information. These children are not easily "programmed" by our limited education systems, although they still succeed to a high level within them.

It is interesting that during recent times (2013-2014), a number of countries, including New Zealand, Australia, Britain and the US, have introduced new national security laws, increasing surveillance of citizens' communications through electronic means, purportedly to protect us. This may be the case in some situations however humans have proved time and again that we are a species that cannot be trusted. Misuse of power and technology, or human error resulting in false accusations, are a near-certainty.

The Grey spoke of this ability they have provided these children with as an essential safeguard, adding that "there will be a time when people's rational thinking will be overcome by uncertainty and confusion." Perhaps our future freedom and safety will depend increasingly on our ability to train and broaden the capabilities of the mind.

Dr. Schild:

This chapter is for me an amazing corroboration of what I had understood about the Quantum Hologram (QH) formulation of information processing in the alien technology, but also by the entire universe at all levels. The chapter shows to me that the Dr. Edgar Mitchell QH underlies all information processing in the universe, and Suzy has been very successful in describing it in simple human terms.

Suzy reports, "There are script and images and some kinds of designs – a whole range of images appearing one after another in a blur!" Here her son is repeating back information previously transmitted by the Grey, and in particular, it was near the 16 Hz rate of human beta frequency, meaning that the images passed in almost a blur.

The essential detail of the mental sharing process as QH is explained by the alien Grey to Suzy with this sentence: "The information will be transferred as "frequencies" which "like-brained minds" can mentally view as imagery." This tells me that the information is transferred as 2 or 3 dimensional QH, which are frequency and phase patterns that can be transferred in an instant, and it is key that "like-brained" is mentioned because the participants are in agreement about how to encode and decode these into complete images, patterns, matrices, etc.

The point is made earlier that these patterns cannot be exchanged so far by ordinary humans, because their soul connection and personal history is required for humans to store and process the QH data from holographic frequency and phase patterns to images, patterns, data, etc. The fact that the alien Greys can do it in a universal way, so that trained human children can do it telepathically, means that there are some universal hologram patterns that can be decoded to complete images or data without reference to personal history and memory. The Greys and trained children can telepathically transfer more complete data sets because they are trained to respond to the universal holograms.

For those seeking a fuller description of the QH as a complete process in nature describing information packaged in its frequency/phase information, see the article, *The Quantum Hologram and the Nature of Consciousness,* by Edgar Mitchell and Robert Staretz in Journal of Cosmology, Volume 14, April-June 2011, section XII. http://journalofcosmology.com/Consciousness149.html

This information is repeated and confirmed in the two sentences immediately preceding the sunflower analogy: "The information can be likened to a bubble which can be passed on or transferred, and my son has learned to recognise an "energetic pulse" from each image. In other words, each set and each image within the set has a complex frequency or blueprint, which my son must absorb. The energetic frequency is then "converted" into imagery when transferred to the organic computer."

I read in this the fact that the QH has energy, which is sometimes referred to as a bit of the quantum zero point field (QZPF) and is sometimes called dark energy. And then we learn from Suzy that the ordinary brain function of interpreting the QH energetic packet can also be done by their "organic" computer.

Chapter 28

Experiencing the Dual Soul

Here I describe two memories of meetings onboard craft to discuss the roles of the dual soul, including the implementation of tasks and support systems. Shifts occur between both the physical forms, and the intellects of the Grey and human identities, as well as shifts in time – observing the past and present, and accessing the future.

Part One
A programme assessment meeting for the Grey identity
1991, age 36 years

I stepped out of a light elevator and was met by a tall Grey wearing a long robe. A sudden moment of confusion struck me because I no longer felt as if I had a human body and looking down at myself I could see one physical form ethereally super-imposed over another. The human body, dressed in nightwear, stood still in the corridor while the form of a Grey shimmered backwards and forwards, in and out of the body, hesitantly. The tall Grey also stood perfectly still, watching with amusement because he knew exactly what was happening.

S. *It's as if I've got two minds thinking at once. One mind is "Suzy", a human, and I'm thinking, "Have I got another body?" And the other mind* (Grey intellect) *already knows I've got another body or form!*

He asked me to choose, commenting that some Grey identities opt to stay in the human "robe" (body) but still operate with the Grey mind, but I chose to present as a Grey, stepping out of the human body. I now looked through large cricket-like eyes, my limbs spindly and light. It took a few seconds to get used to the over-sized head and shorter body, with a different balance point.

In the Grey physical form and consciousness, with increased clarity of thought, I was now fully aware I had come onboard to take part in an important meeting that included one of the ancient Greys. We proceeded to a room where three others were already waiting.

Now began a meeting of minds where my (Grey) input into the dual soul was to be reassessed. Such meetings occur regularly to ensure the goals fit with the pace of events and awareness unfolding in the human life of "Suzy". I was now thinking as a Grey.

Discussion began with how the human awareness of Suzy could be positively assisted by the Grey identity; to what extent it could and should be affected in order to implement the next phase. One of the senior Greys projected holographic images of places and people, thus preparing and informing me of certain events to come in the life of the human. As he conveyed this, on another level, I (the Grey identity) was sensing and experiencing layers of information from which I could sample a number of aspects of these future events, and not just visually. I heard particular human voices, snippets of conversation, and perceived human feelings and emotions. It was all conveyed to me rapidly, so that in a short space of time I had assimilated considerable relevant data about coming events in the human's (Suzy's) life.

The group emphasised the next phase would be a difficult and crucial one needing a much tighter blending of the two identities. Some of the human's life-events I observed were traumatic, involving illness and turmoil, but as the Grey identity, I felt no sense of surprise or shock; I viewed the events with an analytical and objective intellect, however the human side of me may have had an entirely different emotional reaction to this future life.

The amount of time the human (Suzy) spends onboard craft would be stepped up now as she will need to become more aware of negative influences. The Grey identity will gain new insights about humans, and the human side will experience increasing psychic awareness in the next period of time in her life.

But I foresaw pain and sadness in these inevitable personal events, as I momentarily accessed my human counterpart's emotional awareness to experience a depth of feelings normally foreign to Greys.

On a global scale, the group concurred that the human race was fast moving towards difficult times, which would evoke a human emotion best expressed as "trepidation". The ancient Grey commented that much human suffering is self-created and unnecessary, and future humans will eventually evolve to a higher consciousness where such pain and sorrow will be eliminated.

After the disturbing details they had outlined, it was difficult for me to contemplate returning to combine with the human form.

Discussion

Part One is a brief example of one of the three strands of education mentioned in previous chapters (Grey identity, human, and soul), involving an up-date for the Grey identity on how it can assist the human and the "whole persona" over the coming years.

As predicted in the meeting, major changes took place in my life during the 1990s after this contact occurred, both positive and negative, including the end of my first marriage.

Conversely, my new-found contact with people in the New Zealand UFO field resulted in important lasting friendships and supportive links. My old friend Harvey Cooke and I set up the *Bay of Plenty Abductee Support Network*. I qualified as a grief counsellor. But notably, I made the psychological and emotional transformation from abductee to experiencer, gaining a whole new perspective on the contacts taking place in my life and my children's lives.

Again, as foreseen by the group, on a global scale the 1990s were a time of wars: the invasion of Kuwait, the Persian Gulf, Kosovo and Bosnian Wars, civil war in Rwanda and Afghanistan, and conflict in other parts of Eastern Europe, Africa and the Middle East. I am aware the Greys study human emotional, societal, political, and intellectual reactions to tragedies and significant events, through humans they are in contact with.

The Grey identity was pre-warned of major personal events in my life which would provide ample opportunities for its constructive input and guidance.

Part Two
Resolving a conflict of interest within the dual soul
2011, age 55 years

I had been taken to an underground base, hollowed out of rock, with offices and spacious areas, and upon arrival, a human picked me up on an open vehicle like a small hovercraft. As yet, I had no idea what the meeting I was being escorted to would be about. The vehicle quietly whirred along and eventually we came to a halt outside a set of open doors where a familiar tall Grey was waiting for me, an assistant to a senior Grey I call "the Grandfather".

I quickly shifted from the human consciousness and moved out of the body as a mixed species Grey, leaving the human body standing outside the doorway.

My intellect was different now and I realised I had actually called the meeting! There was a dire need to discuss issues, largely from a Grey perspective. We entered the room where the Grandfather was waiting and I immediately felt my mind speeding up. Directly, he commented he already knew the dual soul was out of sync: the Grey identity held a differing perspective to the human on a particular issue and wished to resolve it quickly, while the human side was hanging back. This had created a conflict of interest within the dual soul, and the human was not able to move forward on this issue, feeling considerable discomfort about what action was best to resolve it.

The Grandfather had observed this dilemma and realised that how the two identities conjointly dealt with the issue could have future relevance and ramifications for other dual soul combinations too. He saw the need to physically bring the human (Suzy) here to address both human and Grey identities/intelligences together, to facilitate a process of analysis between them.

He began by conferring with the Grey identity, which had already made a clinical, objective assessment of the situation and was able to discuss how the human side (Suzy) was functioning, including how to deal with a problem relating to progress on this book.

The Grandfather then addressed the human intellect or mind (Suzy), which the group could still access through consciousness, despite the fact the physical human body was "switched off". His main focus was on the central issue raised by the Grey identity: counter-productive influence from an associate that was affecting my incentive to complete the book. He stated that establishing associations and sharing expertise with others is often mutually beneficial however, if that association becomes difficult or negative for the human (the experiencer), then they must step back from it in order to achieve desired goals.

I'd had concerns over breaches of confidentiality and unauthorised use of my research/contact experience material. The main issue for me was maintaining my right to express the material myself and to decide when and how it should be released. I had come to a virtual standstill with progress on my book, with feelings of despondency. The Grey identity supported ceasing contact with the person concerned, but the human side had developed a friendship with the person and tried to resolve issues to maintain a civil relationship.

The Greys had brought me onboard on previous occasions to address the problem, but I had continued to waver with uncertainty between the two avenues of action. The Grandfather wished to move me forward again with clarity of position and perspective. He understood that I need to live in this world and relate to people as a human, but nevertheless, he had a clear expectation of me taking resolute action on this problem. The Greys have a clinical outlook but at the same time, they are respectful of the human psyche and way of doing things and so their intervention had been minimal until now.

The Grandfather stated that unless I acted decisively on this problem, and soon, I would not achieve what I had worked towards for many years – completing the book. He reminded me I am a cog in a larger wheel and if I stopped functioning, it would affect other cogs (people) around me who are all part of unfolding awareness in humanity. Time was short and I must keep moving forward.

Finally, the Grandfather put an information capsule in my mind, telling me it contained an image of a person, a male, with some details about him which I would not be able to access yet. There will be an instant recognition when I see his face, or hear his voice, and make contact with him. He will assist me with the book in some way, and this person will be one of "theirs" too, although he does not realise it yet.

R. And so are they communicating anything else to you?

S. No, nothing further. It's finished now.

Discussion

Suzy:

I describe meeting with the Grandfather, who has been part of my life since childhood. I do not know how old he is, but he has not appeared to age noticeably in around fifty years.

Although Part Two is of a more personal nature, I felt it important to include it in the book to illustrate how the combined dual souls function, and how the Greys assist the "whole persona" to problem-solve. My son's generation has blended the two identities more easily than my generation, which requires more assistance to achieve goals.

Part Two raises important issues for experiencers (and abductees/contactees). There are many reputable researchers worldwide who have helped to bring awareness of extraterrestrial contact to the public. However I believe increasing numbers of experiencers will go public about their contacts in the next few years, and it will be important that as many as possible release their own material, rather than necessarily allowing others to do this for them.

There are relevant issues to consider arising from Part Two:

- It raises important issues relating to "ownership", for want of a better word, of personal experiential material and accounts of interactions with non-human species, and regression transcripts. Experiencers have the right to expect confidentiality and integrity from researchers and regression therapists. This material relates to our lives, our very existence, and should not be viewed by some as available information to be used in speeches, articles and interviews, without our permission.
- Privacy and confidentiality are particularly vital if these personal accounts include references to other family members. The disturbance of an experiencer's family relationships through careless use of delicate or personal family information is no small matter.
- It is not easy for experiencers to go public with some of their information. They need time to be able to assimilate it, no matter how long that takes, without fear of exposure or pressure to release that information before a state of readiness is reached, which I believe is of paramount importance. A researcher once accused me of "clinging to my data", when in fact I was just not ready to release such information.
- I believe we have an innate and crucial understanding of "timing" on when and how information should be released. Kim Carlsberg, USA, expressed this timing issue clearly in her book, *Beyond My Wildest Dreams: diary of a UFO abductee*: "Perhaps people of contact have indeed "inherited knowledge of great importance" that can only be extracted at precisely the right timing. Given all the variables of a changing world, the determination of that timing may need to be realised instinctively, rather than by a designated date." Similarly, I stated in a regression pertaining to specific information, "Only a few will have this information and it will (is to) remain private until it can be released and it must be respected and handled with great care by (any) researchers (involved)." Most experiencers in particular, intuitively understand that material released too soon, or by the wrong person, will likely fall on deaf ears.

- Some support organisations set up purportedly to "assist" experiencers/abductees to understand their experiences and provide *them* with information, are misnomers, because in fact, they are largely dependent on acquiring data-bases of material and knowledge from the experiencers/abductees themselves in the first place. To the greatest extent possible, it is they who need to assist each other.
- There seems to be the attitude out there that many experiencers/abductees are not capable of expressing, analysing, presenting, or commenting on their own material. US abductee Sherry Wilde, author of *The Forgotten Promise, Rejoining our Cosmic Family,* summed up this attitude when she stated in a speech synopsis, "The Alien Abduction topic is one filled with lots of speculation and conjecture by the UFO investigators. Most of the analysis is being done by those who have never even had a contact experience themselves and can only form opinions based on what they hear and observe from the actual participant."
- In 1980, the Greys warned me of organised groups that could become cult-like, with leaders and followers. They stated that in the future, large "pro-alien" groups could be just as damaging to public acceptance of the subject as "anti-alien" groups (see Dr. Schild's footnote 38). There is always the danger they could be infiltrated by subversive elements, or mismanaged, thereby placing experiencers/abductees at risk. With the concerns the Greys have raised about societal chaos and surveillance of electronic and other communication systems, I have deep concerns about the confidentiality and security of large data-bases containing personal sensitive material about us, along with contact details etc.
- Information previously conveyed to humans by the Greys (or other species) as information capsules will begin to surface *en masse* in the coming years, and this information is best expressed by those who understand its complexity and meaning on various levels – the experiencers themselves. Many have been taught to impart this information energetically, emotionally, spiritually and vocally in a way that awakens others, including those who may not as yet have come to terms with, or realised their own contact history.

- It will be crucial in the future that the general public sees an increasing number of experiencers speaking for themselves, as this will have a significant impact on public awareness of the reality of these contacts and of the extraterrestrial presence.

I am sure experiencers/abductees reading this will recognise other important issues arising from this chapter: the relevance of timing, commitment, creating strong supportive networks of other like-minded experiencers/abductees, and appropriate like-minded people.

Reassessing personal relationships and being aware of their positive or negative effects upon us is essential.

Believe your path will unfold when you are ready, when the time is right, and with underlying guidance.

Do not allow others to force this process on your behalf.

There is a need for preparedness for the times ahead.

In 1990, the Greys outlined to me "three waves" of souls incarnating over recent decades for particular reasons. I have called the wave or group I am associated with "the communicators", although I also like to use this terminology inclusively and broadly to describe experiencers, abductees and contactees as one group. Communicators are being activated quickly now worldwide, and when more of them start communicating their experiences and understanding of extraterrestrial contact for themselves through a variety of means, it will facilitate an unlocking process in people who as yet, have no conscious memory of why they incarnated in this life. How the communicators present their knowledge and experiences to the public will be crucial.

This ongoing process of triggering human consciousness is part of our expansion of awareness, a microcosmic reflection of our expanding universe.

Dr. Schild:

I like Suzy's statement above. I myself feel that human consciousness and all consciousness are simply understood within the quantum relativistic field theory as aspects of our description of space-time, and this takes the form in the science community of "dark energy". You will also see it described as the "Vacuum Zero Point Energy" (VZPE). This produces an effective dilution of Einsteinian gravitation (that results from mass curving space-time as described mathematically in the General Relativity theory). And that reduction of gravity induces the accelerated expansion of space that the science establishment calls “secondary inflation”.

This brings us immediately to Suzy’s statement, which I consider *profoundly correct*, thus, I paraphrase Suzy’s statement, “This ongoing process … is a microcosmic reflection of our expanding universe” as in her paragraph above.

Consciousness enhances the VZPE and assists the accelerating expansion of our universe. Thus we, as sentient beings, are co-creators of the universe.

Chapter 29

The Test
Part One: An Alien Internet?

I awoke one morning with extensive recollection of activities onboard craft, more detail than I had ever retained previously. I felt as if my mind was stuffed with new and exciting information, and vivid recollection of specific technology.

1993, age 38 years
A moving capsule of light

I was with a group of sixteen humans, walking down a curved corridor. Several Greys accompanied us, listening to us converse in a mixture of spoken language and telepathy, and I recall joking with a tall thin man with a great sense of humour.

An unseen source of light created a moving capsule of illumination around us as we walked, leaving the otherwise unlit corridor behind and ahead of us dark. It was as if the walls or air were intelligent and knew we required light, or perhaps movement sensors initiated this strange light source. [54]

Preparation begins

The Greys led us into a large bright room, but still less intense than usual. I knew from previous occasions that the Greys often adjust the light to suit human comfort and eyesight during test situations involving visual focus.

---

[54] The light in the air that follows Suzy and others around in corridors is probably produced by a local (to the person) ionization of the gas molecules by some kind of infrared pumping by something in the walls you are passing by. In other words, light is being produced in the air around you, and only around you, and the activating mechanism would logically be the detection of your consciousness.

The room was set up with rows of pedestal tables and seats, and large semi-transparent screens stood vertically on the tables with small connection pads in front. The adjustable furniture was designed for human physical proportions, and I had been told on another occasion that the soft dark floor was a kind of insulation for humans.

Although a large room, it seemed busy and cramped with eighteen Greys already there, an atmosphere of anticipation, excitement and unity of purpose emanating from them.

We each had an individual console and a symbol of alien script, our personal logo, rotated as if floating just beyond the screen's surface. My personal symbol had the appearance of our letters "g" and "k" however certain lines ran alongside each other, rather than branching off. Each personal symbol, when viewed or accessed with consciousness, provided information about us: genetics, health, personality, abilities, strengths, background and so on. It carried our frequency in other words.

Once seated, a Grey partner joined each of us, entities we had worked with previously. There was an atmosphere of familiarity, even jocularity, as we conversed briefly with our companions while waiting for proceedings to begin.

Observers: the elders

Two Grey elders entered the room and stood behind a console on a small raised platform. One of them was what I refer to as a "new" tall Grey – a more recent derivative of the ancient Grey species, which has heavy lines and folds of skin on the face and body. However he had only inherited a lined forehead from his genetic background, but no doubt the intense intelligence and wisdom of the ancient lineage as well. There have been numerous mixes and adaptations made within the Grey species over time, however the ancient genetic blood line has also been maintained, like the root-stock of their evolving species. The second Grey was a mixture of this rootstock and another species characterised by the elongated skull.

These entities derived from the ancient bloodlines are sometimes present at occasions of some significance, sessions requiring specific assessment, or that have pivotal outcomes. Their complex intelligence is behind many of the programmes, and they plan and manifest these programmes rather than implement them. The presence of these intelligent beings is both daunting and awe-inspiring. They convey an intelligence that is expansive in a way we find difficult to comprehend, or can hope to match at this time in our evolution. From a human perspective, using our narrow perception and interpretation of body language, their physical demeanour conveys an air of authority and aloofness that belies their depth of wisdom and compassion.

They both wore floor-length cloaks with patterned borders around the neck and down the front, designating their particular echelon of authority. We were told they had come to preside over and observe the situation today, as this was the final test in a long series of eliminations. They began communicating to the other Greys present, multi-levelled streams of thought too complex for us to decipher in their entirety.

The knowledge transfer: information capsules

The two elders now communicated more basically to the humans about what was about to take place in this session. This was a test. We would each receive a different information transfer of equal complexity and volume, and then use this vast information to solve a problem.

The knowledge transfers would be larger than usual, taking around one and a half minutes (in our time) for our partners to complete, rather than split seconds. We turned and faced our Grey partners, entering a focused state of receptiveness. The transfers began and I cannot quantify the exact extent of the information, but I can liken it to volumes of encyclopaedia conveyed at lightning speed. A mild tingling sensation began in the centre of my forehead and images flashed somewhere in my vision – colours, shapes and symbols – until my eyes felt as if they were on overload.

An information storage tablet

With the transfers completed, the elders explained they would pose a problem to each of us and we would need to use information from the knowledge transfer, combined with data from an "information tablet" to assess the most logical solution or outcome.

Our challenge was to use a variety of intuitive, brain, mind, eye and energy functions the Greys had taught us. This included: speed in accessing and assessing volumes of data from both the transfer and external sources, creating holographic images, interpreting script, "depth-reading" script, use of new technology, and a range of other skills. Most of all, it tested our ability to process vast amounts of information in a short time frame, a factor that sets the extraterrestrial intelligence apart from our own.

We each received a tablet-like sheet which contained our individual tests, and my partner explained there was yet more data from separate sources available through this tablet. It was only relatively small, around twenty five centimetres long and twenty centimetres wide, and resembled a small smoky-grey x-ray sheet. He allowed me to hold it. The fine edges were tapered or bevelled and it was light and thin, only a couple of millimetres or so thick and flexible, with no visible source of power. I had worked at consoles with large touch/thought operated screens before, but I had never seen a miniature, paper-thin, portable version of them until now. As soon as he touched it, a number of coloured "boxes" appeared within its screen-like surface, as if by magic! The moment I laid eyes on the tablet I was fascinated by it. How were those images embedded in that material?

My tablet sheet had five boxes on it, small rectangles spaced randomly on the surface, each with vibrant colours and clarity. Wow! They were beautiful! You could "look into" the boxes and there were multiple layers of moving colours forming the images. [55] It was as if they were alive! Upon glancing up, I saw other people around me were also captivated by their information tablets. I noticed some had more or fewer boxes on them than mine, with large spaces where there were no boxes at all. Everyone's was different!

I examined the tiny boxes on my tablet. They portrayed: a small map of sorts which looked like a star chart with travel routes marked on it, an image of a planetary system, and three boxes each with a mixture of Grey script and diagrams. I was particularly fascinated by the box depicting a planetary system, tiny planets with coloured areas around them subtly moving and swelling like a tide, or as if they were alive and breathing!

My partner told me each of the images could be enlarged by touch so that they filled the entire surface of the tablet, however on this occasion we were going to insert the tablet into a slot on the console,

---

[55] I suspect that the technology Suzy witnessed in the tablets was 3-D technology, not the 2-D technology of our commercial devices. They would involve a much deeper quantum development of computing much closer to consciousness itself, and a giant leap for our civilization.

and instantly, the intriguing coloured boxes I had glimpsed were enlarged on the screen in front of me.

Our partners gave us final instructions on the problems to be solved, operational instructions relating to the layout now replicated on screen from the tablets, and instructions specific to the computers we were using. It was conveyed to us quickly with the expectation that this was sufficient, and we were given a few minutes to experiment with the new knowledge. We could now connect to sources of information not only stored on the tablet and computer, or through depth-reading, but elsewhere as well! We must piece things together in a logical way, like a giant research assignment, defining, looking for the best material to potentially solve the problem or create a best-scenario response. Our test solutions or outcomes were actually secondary to being able to demonstrate and utilise the skills the Greys had taught us. *This* would be the measure of our success from their perspective.

We connected to the touch-pads and this connection was maintained even if we removed our hands, and would not disconnect until we telepathically instructed the technology to do so. Now we could open information boxes either by thought or touch, enlarge or reduce an image, flick rapidly through pages of script material on screen, and access deeper levels of information by depth-reading abbreviated script.

The thought we could connect through pure consciousness to utilise a variety of other alien knowledge bases was astounding! This sophisticated, revolutionary technology was riveting and when I placed my hand on the touch-pad, I had an overwhelming sense of connecting to a vast network of information and knowledge, crossing time, space, and species.

"Rivers" through space

The test began. My particular task was to ascertain the most appropriate travel route from a specific location, to, and between three planetary bodies in a solar system, using the subtle interactions and flows of energies surrounding them.

I enlarged the box containing the three planets until it filled the screen. This was the image I wanted to go to first because it was so beautiful! Three floating planets, bright marbles suspended in the fluidity of space. I could rotate the image to view the planets from any perspective.

However this was a mistake, wasting valuable time! I quickly realised I needed to enlarge the star chart first and examine the visual information contained in it. There were the three planets again within the map, rotating, circling a strange sun. It was thrilling to use this technology, but I needed to settle down and concentrate in order to focus on the task. Next, by touching one of the script boxes, I was able to access considerable information pertaining to flows or "rivers" of energy through space, and the effect these flows have when they enter solar systems and interact with energies (magnetic fields) surrounding the revolving planetary bodies. [56]

I obtained this information in two ways: 1) by touch-flipping through many pages of script and diagrams on the screen, reading them in the high speed manner we had been taught, and 2) through mentally connecting with a symbol on the screen I could simultaneously access further and deeper sources of information (depth-reading), which passed through my mind like a stream of telepathy, supporting and extrapolating on what I was reading. I can liken it to reading a book, while listening to a speech at the same time, and absorbing both.

In a relatively short time, I felt I had an adequate understanding of the first stage of my task and needed to move on. I returned to touch my favourite box showing the three planets.

S. So I've got this picture in front of me and I can come in closer (zoom in) *to look at one of the planets.*

I viewed the three planets and the interplay of energy between them as the fields ebbed and flowed, reaching far out into their solar system, and on into space where they mingled with similar flows from elsewhere. Was this an animation, or real-time images captured by an extraterrestrial telescope or satellite? These thoughts prompted my partner to impart some helpful background information. This was not considered to be cheating or unfairly advantageous, but rather assisting me to understand their perspective on certain issues relating to my test problem, and in this case, its relevance to our own human space ventures.

---

[56] I believe that the energy fields shown to Suzy are fields of energy that are created by the mass particles as quantum fields, combined with life energy fields, that are important attributes of all life forms, particularly strongest in sentient beings.

While I worked, he explained the Greys use a variety of ways to travel through space and within solar systems. One such method is to utilise the natural ebbs and flows of energy in space, which they have studied in depth allowing them to navigate these celestial currents like rivers. It is therefore a benign method of travel, and these flows of energy can be traversed at speed with only minimal propulsion from the craft. He gave particular emphasis to this detail of not disturbing the energy fields, particularly within solar systems where there are civilisations or life-forms, as disturbances can affect all associated life there. By placing images in my mind he emphasised that humans cause unseen damage far beyond our own planet, by thundering out into space in our primitive spacecraft. We disturb the natural courses of these energy flows by cutting through them and causing turbulence, whereas moving with the flows as they do maintains natural harmony.

On a smaller scale, they utilise similar natural routes or tracks of energy within our planet's atmosphere, so as to cause the least energetic disturbance to Earth's inhabitants and life-forms. He commented that thousands of aircraft traverse our skies daily and we will eventually understand the harm this disturbance to natural energy fields is causing to life on Earth, affecting our health and nervous systems, as well as the pollution caused by fuel consumption.

Through his dialogue it became clear to me that our planet "communicates" with all life within our atmosphere, and with the wider cosmos, through its electromagnetic field.

I absorbed and recalled all of this while concentrating on the test.

The Grey script

It was getting more complex. I could now work simultaneously with: 1) information/diagrams in the script boxes on the screen, and 2) my understanding of the deeper levels of meaning contained within the script symbols, combined with 3) the information transfer material, and as well, 4) I could access other forms of information from a vast network beyond that contained in the computer.

Each of the script boxes portrayed on screen contained only a few symbols, but I knew they related to hundreds of pages of data. Even how the symbols are grouped together can indicate different meanings or levels of data. The script itself is energy based, with spiralling patterns and waves giving meaning, and is viewed with a combination of consciousness and visual perception, thus seeming to "radiate" information. A descending and ascending spiral thought/energy process describes the progression into or out of, these deeper levels of understanding and information contained in a single symbol, or small group of script symbols. Reading "true" alien Grey script involves tapping into a greater consciousness. [57]

There was now a relaxed atmosphere in the room and it is an odd fact that I knew some of the Greys better than some of the humans. My partner gave me encouragement and there were some good-natured comments made at our expense about who was likely to complete their tests. Although we knew the purpose of the event was important to them, we did not feel pressure such as we might feel prior to a human exam. There was no stigma attached to failure here and we were aware that if we did not complete the test, we would simply be assigned to another appropriate group.

A visual hologram

I began speed-reading pages in my mind, like grabbing a deck of cards and flipping through them in a blur, looking for a particular page or subject and when I found it, I was able to place the information before me in a hologram.

S. *I can visualise if I need to ... place the information before me in a visual field. I can pull out a picture or a page from my mind and project it into the air in front of me, read it, look at it, and then just flip it away.*

I had slipped into a skill we had acquired from the Greys over many years, involving a progression from accessing levels of script through consciousness, to manifesting it in a visual holographic form using my connection to the conscious technology, and ocular or visual acumen combined. The visual hologram hung steady in the air in front of me, but with an accompanying regular fast pulse coming in waves, which I felt rather than saw.

Losing all awareness of everyone else around me for some time, I continued piecing things together in a logical way, a process of refinement and selection that would provide me with a solution to the problem. Eventually I glanced around and saw other people creating

---

[57] Wilhelm Reich emphasized how the quantum waves describing consciousness have a spiral form, and Native Americans in their sacred ceremony describe the consciousness waves in crystals as being ascending and descending spirals.

holographic images in front of them as well, about forty centimetres in front of their eyes.

Completing the test

My partner had shut himself off from me now, guarding his thoughts so as not to interfere in my final analysis. However, I could feel his mind close to me, like the vibration of a car engine quietly idling in the background.

Eventually the elders indicated we were to cease work. It was over. They examined the results on their console, before announcing that four of us had completed the test, the tall thin man, me, and two other people whom I did not know. The assistants removed the information tablets from the consoles and fortuitously, I was asked to take the tablets to another level on the craft to be cleared.

We all began moving towards the door and analytical thoughts continued to crisscross in the air as we spilled out into the corridor.

Discussion

It was not until 1999 that I first purchased a computer and used the Internet – six years after this contact experience in 1993, and two years after I first spoke publicly about the experience in 1997 at the International UFO Symposium in Auckland (speech recorded on video). In New Zealand in the 1990s, Internet use was largely restricted to academic institutions and it wasn't until 1995 that the Internet Society of New Zealand was officially formed to develop nationwide Internet. Therefore my knowledge of computers in my day-to-day life was zero at the time of this event.

By now most readers will have recognised some of the Greys' technology I describe, as being similar or more advanced versions of what we humans have now produced over recent years in our own technology.

Dr. Schild has commented that the larger console computer I used was likely a three-dimensional computer, organic and conscious, which as far as I am aware we have not been able to produce, and if we have developed it in secret, it is not available to the public as yet. The technology was operated by touch, now a common feature of our computer and Smartphone technology, and by thought, an aspect being developed for use with the disabled, and which military have been developing worldwide over the last decade or so.

Through linking to these conscious computers, our neural network and DNA becomes encoded in them, and all of this information is incorporated in, or can be accessed through our "personal logos".

I described "boxes" on the screen through which further information could be accessed. We now know similar boxes in current computer terminology as folders, programmes, or icons.

I believe the vast database accessible through this computer was undoubtedly an alien internet, enhanced by accompanying streams of consciousness and requiring specific mind abilities to access it.

The "information tablet" bears a remarkable resemblance to our iPads and Smartphones, although clearly a more advanced version – thin, flexible, 3-D, and with no obvious familiar source of power. I can imagine how advantageous this would be for use in schools, universities, and businesses if we could produce something similar, easily rolled up and transportable, lightweight, and relatively bullet-proof. In fact, while editing this chapter in 2013, I came across a newspaper article describing the development of a prototype flexible tablet computer. However unlike the alien model I used, the prototype cannot store much information, but the concept-similarity is notable and perhaps our computers of the future will look and feel like sheets of paper or plastic too.

My description of being able to rotate the planets on the screen to view them from various perspectives, and enlarge and reduce their size, is strikingly similar to *Google Earth* (2004).

None of these technologies were available back in 1993.

My Grey partner expressed concern about the way our aircraft and spacecraft cut through natural flows of energy in our atmosphere and in space. New technological developments in high-speed photography have now captured never-before-seen shock waves and turbulence from explosions, impacts, high-speed projectiles, and supersonic aircraft, illustrating the extensive damage that is caused by these energy waves, confirming what the Grey told me. In particular, I think about the "unseen damage" caused by nuclear explosions, as mentioned in previous chapters.

The Greys' concern for our well-being is reflected in the way they travel within our Earth's atmosphere, following energy flows, possibly magnetic grids, or ley lines. Retired New Zealand airline pilot, the late Captain Bruce Cathie, wrote several books on his theory of the existence of a world harmonic energy grid, proving this by advanced mathematics and suggesting it is directly associated with UFO activity, along with many other scientific puzzles, such as locations of sacred sites and monuments. Captain Cathie has recounted how when he first publicised his research, he was visited in New Zealand by members of the American CIA, who did not wish this information to become public, but who confirmed his theories. His initial book on the subject of energy grids was subsequently removed from bookstores in the USA. Captain Cathie persevered with his research and published several further books.

The idea that harmonious or disharmonious energetic (magnetic field) relationships between celestial bodies can affect our well-being is also reflected in the study of astrology. Astrology consists of a number of belief systems which hold that there is a relationship between astronomical phenomena, movements and relative positions, and that this has an influence on human affairs and the natural world. Scientists now know that solar activity directly affects our planet and all life on it, as well as some of our technology. It may be that a new understanding of ancient astrology will arise, based on our mutual relationship with the cosmos. I anticipate that in the future, we will better understand the information given to me by the Greys concerning the influential relationship between the macrocosm and the microcosm.

Astro-meteorology, long-range weather forecasting using astrology (the effects of the position and interaction of celestial bodies) is another subject considered to be pseudo science, but which may also prove to have foundations in fact, based on the Greys' information, and be of use to humanity in anticipating and planning for severe weather events. Recent medical research (2014) for example, theorises that solar flares may cause strokes and other health problems in humans.

Almost everything associated with the Greys' culture is multi-levelled or multi-dimensional in nature, ranging from their telepathic communications to their genetic diversity and technology. So too are their scripts. I have seen two versions of scripts: one is a kind of alien alphabet incorporating dots, dashes, geometric shapes and hieroglyphic-like symbols, as well as symbols that vaguely resemble some of our earthly alphabets or language symbols (such as my personal logo symbol). It is possible some of the script symbols described by abductees/experiencers, and also some military witnesses and whistleblowers, may be a kind of bridging or intermediary script, allowing large numbers of humans to learn how to read and understand alien data. Many people also describe seeing symbols on the exterior of craft.

However the second more complex and I believe, "true" alien script I describe using in this test experience, is impossible to replicate in simple written or symbolic form given its 3-dimensional nature involving consciousness.

Accessing this script, which I refer to as "depth-reading", involves a process taught to us whereby using consciousness, we can view a script symbol or specifically configured group of symbols, and instantaneously access many further deeper levels of data. In this way, drawing extensive information from a small condensed sample of script is rather like examining an abbreviated (truncated) language, which, when expanded to its original ancient form may contain deeper meaning than its contemporary or simplified version.

Acquiring this deeper meaning from script can also involve registering accompanying sensory input, like sound, smell, or emotions, derived from the consciousness aspect.

Using this version of script could really be better described as "complex knowledge acquisition".

Visual Hologram

Chapter 30

The Test
Part Two: A Light Elevator

The light elevator: a teleporter

I lagged behind with the pile of information tablets as the combined group proceeded down the curved corridor. My partner gave me instructions as he moved away: I was to head left, go down two floors of the craft and present the tablets at a console to be cleared, and he provided me with an appropriate symbol to use in the elevator.

A vertical tube, which I had nick-named the "light elevator" as a child, stood at the end of the corridor, enclosing a glistening column of light. A curved moulded "foot" seamlessly joined the tube to the floor and ceiling at each level. Circular, and around a meter and a half in diameter, it was constructed from a transparent material with the appearance of glass or Perspex. I have used three models of this light elevator over the years: this version with curved moulded attachments, one which passes directly through the various floors of the craft like a giant drinking straw, and a much larger rectangular elevator which could transport around twenty occupants or other equipment (like a service elevator). A section of the elevator tube slides to one side, allowing entry/exit, and a panel of lights with oscillating script symbols is sometimes positioned on a wall beside it.

Unlike our sources of light which radiate outwards, this light remains contained and active within the column, and does not spill out of the opening or shine through the transparent tube.

Bright bluish-white light, with random flashes of brilliant electric blue, streams fluidly upwards and downwards simultaneously within the column, resembling flowing "liquid light". [58]

The structure emitted a soft humming sound. I thought-instructed the door to slide open and stepped into the column, immediately enveloped in soft liquid light like velvet on my skin. I love this! It is like floating upright, suspended in intelligent sentient light.

By merely thinking the symbol I had been given, the elevator transported me to the appropriate level and after a split second of blackness, the door slid back and I stepped out into a small reception area. I presented the pile of tablets to a female Grey seated behind a console and without any communication she inserted them into a slot one at a time. As each tablet popped back out I saw the vibrant images and script symbols had been erased, leaving the tablet dull and inanimate.

A five-function screen

A large rectangular w/screen was positioned on the wall behind her, on or through which I was able to see a striking scene.

> S. *I ask her, "What's that through the window?" She won't discuss this with me.... and now she has touched something* (on the console) *and it* (the w/screen) *disappears.*

But the female was unwilling to discuss what I had observed because it was not part of my programme, as they tend to keep activities compartmentalised and specific. However she was willing to tell me about the technology behind this particular model of w/screen, commenting I may have seen them before but not realised their function can alter according to circumstances. She outlined the five functions: 1) a wall, 2) a window (on an interior or exterior wall of the craft), 3) a screen for communications with entities in other areas of the craft or between craft, 4) a screen to enable surveillance of

---

[58] The light elevator is almost certainly an anti-gravity device. Our modern science is now closing in on this technology, and it involves magneto-electric influence on gravity. Suzy's observation and recollection demonstrate that the device was under thought control, including the password symbol she focused her mind on, and this function of the brain is addressed most completely by Dr. Edgar Mitchell and Robert Staretz in the article, *The Quantum Hologram and the Nature of Consciousness,* see page 233 for link.

areas of the craft, and significantly, 5) what she referred to as "an information storage facility". [59]

A mammoth archive or database could be accessed through this screen as well as on their computers, both on this craft and between others. (What we nowadays may call the internet and cloud computing).

The dome: a synthetic environment

However before the w/screen converted to a wall, I glimpsed a strange and unexpected scene which captured my curiosity. What I didn't know of course, was which function I was viewing the scene with – on a screen, or through an internal window.

A large dome made from a clear glass-like material, some fifteen metres in diameter and three to four metres high stood within an expansive white-walled area, and Greys and humans were walking together or seated amongst lush vegetation inside it. The area was pleasantly landscaped with a pathway meandering through plants of various heights and species. The light contained within the dome was different to the harsh light of the area it sat in, more golden and not so hard on the eyes. This light also remained distinctly contained within the dome and did not emanate into the surrounding space, which was empty, with no personnel present and only a panel with flashing lights to the left of a door. The dome resembled one of those glass-domed Christmas ornaments that you pick up and shake, with a little scene and snowflakes inside it.

I asked the female about the dome and she replied, "That's where humans need to go when you are here with us for a long time." Why there were Greys present though, I do not know.

---

[59] The 5-function window sounds like an application of what we call liquid crystal technology, but of course I am speculating here. We have had this technology for 20 years for displays in consumer products like wrist watches. The display has black letters and numbers created by digital manipulation of the electric fields that produce the effects of transparency or opaqueness. A development of this technology could produce the 5 functions observed and beautifully described by Suzy.

Light Elevator, Five Function Screen and Dome

Blue-eyed Entity

A human-alien entity: a transgenic? A hybrid?

At that moment I sensed movement behind me and an intense presence or emanation of energy. Turning around, I was confronted by an intriguing entity walking through an entranceway. He was standing side-on, a little shorter than me, wearing black tight-fitting footwear and a white thigh-length coat similar to what a doctor in a hospital might wear.

I was instantly transfixed by his appearance and I cannot even select an appropriate word to describe him. Part human? Half Grey? Although he had some human characteristics, including sparse wispy white hair, his physical form was more that of a Grey. While his face was quite youthful, he walked slightly bent with a slow gait, giving an aged appearance to his physique. His hands were delicate, with three fingers and a long thumb wrapped around a small pile of tablets.

I was familiar with mixed-species entities however this adult human-alien was unlike any I had seen before. Curiosity riveted me to the spot and I felt an overwhelming desire to communicate with him, or strangely, even just to be noticed by him. While these thoughts were running through my mind I momentarily forgot that he would have perceived them.

S. He's turning and looking at me. Oh! He's got strange eyes like a cat! They're bright blue!

His eyes were captivating, with large sockets like the Greys, but instead of black eye colouring, he had white sclera (white of the eye) like a human, with bright blue irises and cat-like black slit pupils. But there the similarity to cats' eyes ended, because his blue irises were also slit vertically, while the pupil was slit horizontally across the narrow iris, giving them a more reptilian resemblance. The effect was compelling, not only because of the remarkable appearance of his eyes, but because an overwhelmingly intense power and intelligence emanated from them.

For a few seconds the entity held my gaze, rapidly accessing my mind and scrutinising why I was in this area of the craft. He addressed the female Grey, reminding her I should have been sent back up in the elevator by now. While he conversed with the female, I attempted to take part in the communication, however he was able to take hold of my mind in a way that kept my thought processes at bay and prevented me from interfering in their discourse. It seemed it was not my place to comment. When their exchange was over I ventured to ask him if he could tell me something about himself.

S. *He says, "No, it's not the time. I know who you are. We will meet again in the future and work together, but not this day". I ask him if he has some advice to offer me ... something that might help me in the future. He has conveyed the word, "Corroboration!" And he just turns and walks away through an archway, and he's gone.*

The intensity of his highly developed intellect and energy seemed to still linger in the room after he had left. He would seem to us more "alien" than human, but the human qualities were still recognisable along with the Grey attributes. Many experiencers report having seen mixed-species hybrid or transgenic entities onboard craft, as I have, but I sensed I was not supposed to have seen this "model" of mixed-species yet, but I can speculate they may be a part of our planet's future.

I was left standing quite still, staring at the place where he had disappeared, in awe of this unexpected yet opportune meeting.

The female Grey cut in on my thoughts, reminding me it was time for me to go. I entered the column of light again and returned to the other level where the corridor was quiet and empty now. I perceived a message from my Grey test partner, calling to me, "What are you doing? We're waiting."

Discussion

Suzy:

Although I have travelled in light elevators on other occasions, I retained detailed memory of this particular one. Some years later in 2006, while preparing for a conference speech, I searched the internet to see if I could find reference to such an elevator by other experiencers. The true meaning of that word of advice given to me by the entity, *corroboration*, became an exciting reality when I found a watercolour painting entitled, *Liquid Light'*, by US graphic artist "Jeff", completed in 1998, depicting a column of light virtually identical to my "light elevator". I later learnt Jeff has also worked voluntarily as an artist for MUFON (Mutual UFO Network) in the USA, assisting experiencers by accurately recording some of their memories and observations in visual (artistic) form.

I immediately emailed Jeff to introduce myself and ask him if his painting depicted an actual contact experience or not, and telling him I had seen something similar. I was careful not to divulge too much detail, but directed him to a drawing of the light elevator on my website.

Within hours I received a reply from Jeff confirming his experience onboard a craft in July 1997, just four years after my own experience. Jeff had checked out the drawing on my website and replied:

Suzy

Yes, the light tube looks very, very similar! Did you notice a panel anywhere near the tube that contained a waveform of oscillating alien symbols as well as blinking red lights? I felt as if this lit panel, with a wave of symbols, somehow monitored the light tube's functionality.

Jeff

Jeff and I communicated further about our memories of using this extraordinary piece of alien technology. We could identically describe its specific features, even down to the fact the light felt like velvet on the skin, and seeing oscillating lights and symbols on a nearby panel. But we also held other similar perceptions and memories, such as the fact the Greys have a distinct sense of humour, and that we each have had regular contact with a familiar entity.

Suzy

You have described the liquid light tube EXACTLY the way that I remember it ... both in appearance and in sensation!

I have found that some of the Greys seem to have a sense of humour. I see the same Grey/Mantis hybrid all of the time. One night, as I passed him on "the ship", he looked at me and communicated, "I see that they have you working thirdsies tonight" ("thirdsies" being "third shift" ... or an overnight shift at a place of employment). I thought, "Why you smart ass!" ... and as I thought that, he stopped and seemed to laugh at me!

Jeff

Also in 2006, while in Australia, I spoke to a support group for abductees/experiencers and a mother and daughter approached me afterwards. The young woman, who I will call "Ann", had also experienced contact since early childhood. During the course of our conversation, Ann produced a folder of drawings of some of the technology and entities she had observed in those encounters and I immediately recognised one of the drawings as being similar to the light elevator and asked her what she could tell me about it. Ann recounted how on a number of occasions, she had travelled in a column of bright sparkling light contained within a tube, and she had named this technology "the teleporter", describing how upon entering the tube of light she was instantly transported elsewhere, using thought to instruct. The column of light emitted a soft hum and was attached to the floor and ceiling with a curved foot or surround, and the light was extraordinarily soft.

I now had two other corroborative accounts of this phenomenal technology from clear conscious recall and from experiencers in two different countries. It is enormously gratifying to know that others have travelled in a light elevator and are able to describe it in the same way as me – an advanced form of elevator that suspends and transports you instantaneously in conscious light.

Other corroborative evidence of technology I observed during this experience had already emerged in 2003, when I spoke at the Hidden Truths Conference in Perth, Australia, where the late Dr. Roger Leir, author of *The Aliens and the Scalpel,* was also a guest speaker. Roger was a researcher and surgeon, known for removing alleged alien implants from abductees/experiencers.

The evening before my speech, Roger and I were dining at a restaurant when he related a surprising anecdotal account to me. In short, he described how he had been told by a former officer in the US military that at some time in his career he, along with other military personnel, had entered what he alleged was an alien craft, which was sitting on the tarmac at a US Air Force Base. At first, absolutely nothing was visible to the naked eye as the officer looked out at the tarmac, and he was informed the craft employed invisibility technology.

The officer and group of personnel approached the craft, flanked by staff that knew the exact position of it and were able to instruct him when to step up onto "invisible" steps, which he could feel under his feet. They entered the craft, which he alleged contained advanced technology and in particular, the officer described looking back out at the tarmac through a rectangular window. He was informed the window could also instantly become a wall and perform several other functions, totalling five altogether.

I was astonished by the synchronicity of this anecdotal, but nevertheless corroborative account, as Roger had no idea my speech the next day would include details about the "five function screen" I had observed in 1993. He gave me permission to include the account in my speech (recorded on video with Roger sitting in the front row of the audience).

One function of the screen, which allows the user to see and converse with another user in the craft, over distance between craft, or between locations of craft and bases, bears a striking resemblance to today's teleconferencing technologies and computer programmes such as Skype.

In Part One of this test experience, I described how my Grey partner pushed the information tablet into a slot in the computer console, allowing me to view and utilise all the data it contained on the larger computer and screen (using it as a USB). The flexible information tablet seemed similar to an advanced version of the tablets we have today, but with vastly more functionality than the models we now use in our daily lives.

Over the years I have read claims and theories that some of today's technology originated from back-engineered retrieved alien craft, or was provided by agreement with extraterrestrial races. The Internet and fibre optics are among those technologies mentioned. I cannot substantiate those claims – I can only present my own experiences, which certainly point to the fact that either we are developing technology along the same lines as the Greys, or we have indeed obtained some extraterrestrial knowhow.

For some years afterwards I pondered the personal significance and application of that simple word *corroboration*, which the entity gave to me. It was not until I set up the UFOCUS NZ Research Network in 2000 to investigate UFO sightings in New Zealand, and later when I began writing this book that the full implication of the word and the invaluable advice behind it, became clear to me. It was a major turning point for me, because seeking corroborative evidence relating to my experiences engendered confidence at a time when abductees/experiencers were being subjected to derision by the media and public in general. Later, it gave me courage to approach Dr. Schild to ask him to examine my accounts and descriptions from a scientific perspective.

Through this word of advice, I realised the importance of valuing all accounts of contact shared by the three major groups that have evolved in this area – contactees, abductees and experiencers. Corroborative evidence can and should help bind us together, along with the common factor of having experienced contact, of being “communicators”, regardless of whether our experiences are described as positive or negative.

I believe much of our future technology will be thought/brainwave operated, and we are already moving in this direction. However nanotechnology, implants, wearable technology (glasses, jewellery, headsets etc), and even technology incorporated in fabric fibres may also be involved, possibly linking us to health-regulating technology, and instant access to collective databases.

Dr. Schild:

Suzy describes three kinds of light involved with the alien technology, and not related to ordinary electromagnetic radiation. The alien kinds are confined to 3-D space, whereas ordinary electromagnetic radiation shines out endlessly with gradually diminishing brightness, as is familiar.

The alien technology seems to be:

1. Confined light accompanying alien/human beings in spacecraft and enveloping them for the purpose of illumination.
2. Confined light projected by alien technology for the purpose of cancelling gravity and enabling transport between UFO and any other place in a line of action. This form of light is apparently produced by the UFO in amplification of the intent of the operators.
3. Confined light in the transporter (elevator) which is apparently in interaction with the conscious intent of the enveloped sentient beings. It is described as being more alive with active sparking and energetic attributes.

Chapter 31

An Extraterrestrial Lesson in Parenting

1995, age 40 years; my son, age 11 years

It was night-time and cold.

S. *We're waiting. We know they're coming, because they've called us out.*

R. *How do they call you?*

S. *"Wake up!" We receive an instruction and both come out of our rooms at the same time ... and we're standing on the concrete outside the house.*

A white light approached, cruising over the boundary trees and paddocks. A circular craft became visible as it slowed and hovered, and a column of yellowish light cascaded close to us. My son and I stepped into it and ascended silently, entering the craft and sitting side-by-side on a bench. After a while a father and his daughter joined us, and I lost track of time until we picked up four more people.

Now we received information from the Grey pilots: we were to be transported between this craft and another! A crew member advised us that we would simply disappear from this craft and reappear on the other, which was apparently close to us at this time. For our protection they would put us in an altered state of awareness for the transfer, and I assumed they were concerned we would not understand the science behind it and some of us might panic. Spontaneously, I held my son's hand, feeling somewhat embarrassed by the fact he was eleven and I was forty, and yet I needed that reassurance.

We all stood close together, confined within a low circular metal area, and a couple of us asked if the procedure was safe. The crew member responded cryptically, "Consider how we transport you all the time." They induced a relaxed state in us.

R. *What happens next?*

S. *I feel a bit dizzy, and then ... black!* [Long pause] *I'm lying on a shelf-bed!*

I assume the transfer was virtually instantaneous and still in an altered state, we must have been taken somewhere to recover. My son and I were now lying on two shelf-beds extending from adjacent walls in a small cubicle with an archway, but no door. It was quiet, warm and dimly lit.

A boy's voice broke the silence, crying and confused, while his mother tried to console him and assure him he was safe. The noise roused my son and he began tossing and turning as he regained full consciousness. Other people were now stirring, with sighs and faint murmurs coming from nearby cubicles.

Three Greys arrived and asked us to assemble in the hallway, and our children accompanied one of them away down a corridor, while we adults were taken to a separate room. A senior Grey was to address us about how humans communicate and interrelate with each other. Naturally this caused some facetious thoughts to pass amongst us at the thought of a Grey telling *us* about human communications.

He entered the room, activated a large screen and officiously asked us to focus on it. Immediately and much to our surprise, some of us viewed ourselves on the screen performing everyday tasks. That really captured our attention!

> *S. How on earth did they do that? We're seeing pictures of inside our homes, and we're all saying to ourselves, "Oh my goodness, there's me! Oh! That's him over there!"*

Although at this stage we did not know how the Greys had obtained this video-like footage, it began to dawn on us what their intention was in showing it to us: rather embarrassing shock tactics.

Each clip showed one of us relating to our children (those who had come onboard with us) and then their responses or reactions. The Grey now moved into streams of hyper-communication, quick-time. This was a lecture about how to parent these particular children, the selected "fourth intellect" children, and it was confronting to recognise some of the mistakes we inadvertently make in our interactions with them as parents.

The senior Grey proceeded to analyse human parental communication and behavioural patterns within families, examining the psychological and sociological impact of these patterns, but from the Greys' perspective. Their children receive a markedly different and broader upbringing in many ways, with input from numerous members of their society or community, as opposed to a smaller nuclear family group, or wider familial extended family as we have.

Moving on, he examined our intellectual, creative, and emotional relationships with these children, with an example of interactions involving each adult in the room and their respective child alternating on the screen to illustrate his points. He offered each of us a brief individual analysis of what we are doing well in our child's upbringing and education, and where we could make positive changes; suggestions on how and why we need to improve our parenting of these intellectually and psychically competent children. Specific parenting techniques will help to establish positive values, patterns of thinking and modes of behaviour. The understandings gained in this session would enhance our children's lives and our input into them. Much of the lecture mirrored and reinforced our own ethical human morals and values, and he emphasised how these children could achieve wider societal influences in their future adult lives with well-developed positive attitudes.

Each parent was also given a run-down of any patterns or traits that are impacting undesirably on their child, and the Grey offered me an insight: I must trust my son's wisdom and discernment, even at this young age.

But he even knew details about my own childhood. He mentioned how because of lack of parental interest in my academic abilities, I had constantly driven myself to reach ever-higher self-imposed standards, but took little pleasure from these achievements. He stated the Greys had taught me alternative modes of coping as a child, hoping I would subconsciously carry these skills over into my day-to-day life. However my parents' attitudes had sometimes overwhelmed this "other" influence. He did not want any of us to perpetuate negative family patterns that might impact on these children.

Although his manner was officious, I sensed no hint of disappointment or superiority towards us, no feeling that any of us were failing as parents. We understood the loving intent behind his manner. He emphasised their desire for us to be better parents because these children are important to them as well, and to their agenda of upgrading our civilisation. Consequently it is vital the Greys have a measure of input into their day-to-day upbringing. He highlighted that an "important change or phase" was about to take place with these children and requested their instrucions be carried out. We felt an underlying expectation from him that we would do it.

S. But this is the first time they've placed this on us. It's not even an expectation, it's definitive. He says, now is the time for the next stage of development with these children, and this is your role in it.

We were all keen to cooperate, but there was more to it than merely improving our parenting skills; the Greys wanted us to understand the level of "extraterrestrial" in these children. Each parent is not only helping the child to be a fully-functioning human, but also to utilise and exhibit their abilities in an entirely human way. The Greys do not want the children's perceptions and intelligence to be seen by other humans as threatening or unusual, but rather as something to be valued and respected. Their extraterrestrial component is greater than what we parents have, and we must understand what that means, how they function, and how our relationship with them must always take this into account. Our bond with the children will be lasting; whatever we do with them will touch them deeply, be it positive or negative, so we must be aware of this.

Some in the group expressed concern that this care may be interpreted by siblings as preferential, but the Grey reminded us their siblings were hand-picked volunteer souls who would also thrive and benefit from our parenting, and whose natures would be accepting of any difference in parenting style (I described in Chapter 12 how I met the soul of my second son and was told by the Grandfather that it would learn to relate to its brother's soul before entering this life).

He perceived our minds were full of questions and began responding to everyone. Open discussion is desirable as it gives them the opportunity to relate to us individually as well as collectively.

The discussion led to other aspects of relationships and he unexpectedly commented there would be those amongst us who would not continue in their relationship with their spouses, due to decisions made before entering this life. This was a bit of a shock to some in the group and I could sense people around me wondering, "Will it be me? Is that going to happen in my relationship?" He reassured them by saying these outcomes must unfold over time. He would not discuss individual cases, but stated those whose relationships faltered would learn significantly from this and it would ultimately be beneficial for their children. However, the prior warning lingered in our minds (my marriage ended the following year).

Now nearing the end of the discussion, the Grey's energetic demeanour changed. His thought-streams softened from officious, to gracious and appreciative of our input and cooperation. He stated they value our parenting, but must place expectations on us to achieve positive future outcomes for our children. He conveyed the concept of *our children* as all encompassing, us and them.

S. *We're all feeling the impact of his energy field reaching right across the room. The mind is powerful, but the energy field is what conveys the emotion.*

Everybody felt the solemnity of the discussions and the work to be done at home, the details of which would filter into our daily lives.

Upon returning to our cubicles, we found the children were already there and we soon received instruction to congregate in the transfer area. This time the Greys told us they would transfer us to the delivery craft in small groups so we could watch the procedure if we wished. Some had no desire to witness the process and so they became the first group called up, and then to simply vanish.

Nobody was perturbed by this, possibly because of the relaxed state induced by the humming noise, a quietening of the nervous system required for the transfer. [60]

My next recollection was of my son and I being lowered in a column of light, and watching the wind outside the beam whipping the trees. My vision or perception seemed different, possibly a consequence of elevated awareness, because small plants near my front door were vividly fluorescent and glowing in a multitude of colours in the nightlight, as if viewed in the ultraviolet light spectrum.

Discussion

Once again, the overriding theme of this experience centred around our children and the importance of specific methods of child-rearing conducive to their needs, and the Greys' influence on their psyche. It further illustrates the Greys' attention to detail where these particular children are concerned.

This was the first time I had any recollection of being transferred between craft in this way, and the instantaneous procedure was carried out without ill-effects.

---

[60] When it became time for Suzy and son to be teleported back to home, the soothing hum was again heard. The hum might have more purpose than just to lull; it might be aligning and phasing up the natural conscious electrical systems of the humans present, as a prelude to the actual teleportation process.

The Greys considered it necessary to place us in a relaxed state for the procedure using a characteristic humming sound, which I believe can vary in wavelength. The effect of a soft hum is relaxation, and therefore receptiveness to the Greys' instructions, or reduced anxiety in some instances. Louder hums induce sleepiness. Excessively loud hums or buzzes induce temporary paralysis and/or a temporary switched off state. It feels as if every cell in your body is vibrating, and the hum or buzz is no longer just heard, it is felt. Extremely loud, fast rasping hums/buzzes are unpleasant, even painful to the nervous system and hearing, quickly resulting in unconsciousness (as described in Chapter 1). [61]

In Chapter 17, I described how a Grey doctor reminded me I had an implant in my eye, which enabled them to see what I see. In this experience I discovered one of the uses of the implant is to allow the Greys to observe and analyse interactions between parent and child.

Significantly, this session took place when the group my son is in was nearing puberty, a time when marked physical, emotional and behavioural changes take place, and many children challenge parental influence – what the Grey accurately referred to as "the next stage of development, an important change and phase for these children", and our role in it.

---

61 A soothing (lulling) hum is sometimes perceived with a specific frequency. A frequency of 60 Hz is very close to a harmonic of the human beta frequency, and I can imagine that it was experienced as a deliberate appeal to our nervous system to give the experience of calm, but it might instead be an offshoot or a side effect of the equipment aboard the craft that is, in some circumstances, enhancing the human and perhaps the alien nervous system (through its relationship to the human brain's beta rhythm).

Chapter 32

Surgery in an Alien Hospital

1996, age 41 years; my son, age 12 years

My son and a small Grey child held each of my hands, enthusiastically pulling me through a doorway. I had been ill and weakness prevented me from sharing their zest. The door behind us slid silently closed with an air-tight seal, and another in front of us opened a split second later revealing a large room.

It was cool in here, with lines of white square tubs standing in evenly spaced rows along the room, containing a variety of unfamiliar plants. The tubs did not contain soil, but I could see a network of clear tubes feeding liquid into them. Wires formed separate square grids supporting each plant, holding them in place in the shallow liquid.

Two tall Greys with elongated skulls busily tended the plants and they began communicating with the Grey child, as if we were expected. One of them approached us and explained the controlled environment in which I surmised the plants were growing hydroponically, or similar. The plants had varying needs, requiring a complex system accommodating these differences and creating individual environments or micro-climates around each plant. On the ceiling above and the floor below each tub were square objects resembling lights, but there was some kind of "field" operating between them, creating exclusive growing conditions. Therefore for example, a plant accustomed to a tropical climate could grow alongside an alpine plant, but as these potted plants were unfamiliar to me, there could have been any number of other conditions required by them. I did not find out whether they were grown for food, or were species from our planet or elsewhere.

After wandering around the room for a couple of minutes we headed off through a similar set of doors on the opposite side of the room and emerged in a corridor on our way to the "hospital wing". I recalled having been in this part of the craft before and we peered into side rooms along the way.

A Grey wearing a white garment stood near the end of the corridor – and he had his arms folded! I considered this unusually human-like and I could not recall ever seeing a Grey use this familiar human mannerism. I perceived he had intentionally struck this mimicking pose as a humorous gesture, as if to say he had been standing there impatiently waiting for us. He was a different mixture of species from the Greys in the plant room, with a bulbous head and noticeable protuberances at the back above the base of the skull. The pose he had struck, plus his head shape and white coat, created a comic image. He ushered us into a small room containing a pedestal bed attached to the wall.

My son had become more animated now and kept up a telepathic chatter with the Grey child about scientific and mathematical topics he must have learned onboard. The child had been instructed to bring me here for a healing session following other activities, and my son had been allowed to accompany me having completed his own tasks. The Grey asked me to lie down on the bed, elevate my awareness and try to mentally increase my energy field. This only served to highlight the lung and bronchial problems I had been experiencing, making it difficult to reach the level I would normally attain here. I had been ill for several months and they wished to check on this condition and carry out repair work.

I felt especially warm towards this entity following his attempt at humour and I examined his appearance as I lay there. His eyes were intense, not negatively so, but just because of their appearance. Another Grey entered the room now, one of the long-skulled taller species, and my son and I recognised him as one we had met before in this medical area. The two children kept up their conversation, but now considerably restrained, demonstrating my son had learned their skill of minimising the intensity of his telepathic communications without ceasing them.

The two Greys moved a large disc-shaped piece of apparatus suspended on an extension arm, over the bed and activated it. Immediately, this phenomenal scanning technology created a clearly defined circle focused on my torso, encompassing everything from collar-bone to mid-thigh. I raised my head to get a better look inside my body. There within the circle was my skeleton! Everything else: organs, tissue, muscles etc, within that circle had become invisible, while the extremities of my body and nightclothes outside of the circle were as normal. One of the entities touched a screen and this adjustment enabled them to see only my organs now. There I was, raised on my elbows and forearms, watching my organs pumping and twitching. Various further adjustments revealed tissue, muscles, ligaments and tendons, the vascular system, and so on. My son thought it was hilarious to view his mother this way.

The Grey who had greeted us in the corridor now formally introduced himself by an exchange of energy, and stated his concerns. I had been suffering from a lung infection, coughing constantly, weak and bedridden much of the time with high temperatures. I'd begun to fear that I might die and worried constantly about what would happen to my sons if I did. The two Greys would analyse the problem, take necessary steps to bring relief, offer advice and assist me to work on self-healing, however they would not entirely fix the problem.

The tall familiar entity began describing aspects of their healing regimes. They do not look only at the physical condition or symptoms, but particularly where humans are concerned, they also look at underlying emotional causes. These can also make us ill, making our body vulnerable and weak so that viruses and parasites can enter our systems causing infection and damage. He acknowledged many humans are already aware of and use this knowledge, and they wished to examine this aspect of healing with me. I told them I felt as if something was eating away my lungs, but they had already begun adjusting their technology to view my lungs, bronchial tubes, throat, and nasal passages.

In the meantime, my son and the Grey child had fetched a small bench to stand on so they could have a better view of the proceedings. The two Greys did not mind at all and commented it was good that my son could watch and learn, and his presence was comforting for me. My son's telepathy with the child ceased now and he watched wide-eyed as they examined the internal workings of my chest and throat.

Suddenly I noticed something strange occurring as I looked at the Grey doctor, and I had never seen anything like this before.

> *S. He has some kind of special ability. One of his eyes is changing colour like a spectrum and he says he's able to see things even beyond what this amazing technology is exposing. Light is coming out of his eye like a laser!*

I felt unnerved, but he reassured me it was his particular skill. He intended to use specific energy projected from his eye to carefully work within my nasal passages, and suggested I close my eyes if I needed to. I was aware of movement, like something wriggling inside the back of my nose, and when it stopped I opened my eyes again, and his eye had returned to normal. He said he had worked on the nasal passages because the problem originated from there, rather than the lungs. He warned me I would not immediately benefit from the effects of their work because toxins needed to be expelled from the body. He now passed the healing session over to the other entity, the "counsellor".

This Grey asked my son and the child to leave the room and wait outside in the corridor. Moving around the side of the bed, he placed one of his hands on my arm and discussed how humans tend to hold emotions in their bodies. He drew images of me as a child from my memories and placed them in my conscious mind, illustrating how actual physical damage was caused within my body through psychological abuse directed towards me by others. I was able to see how I had reacted emotionally at the time. He then drew images into my mind of the physical damage that had evolved over the years as a result of those emotions becoming lodged and locked in my body.

S. I feel like I don't want to accept that! He says, "This is exactly what you are doing! You keep on going, looking after everyone else, but you're not seeing what you are doing to yourself, or what has been happening to you."

The counsellor again read my memory banks, discovering the anger I had felt after my nose was broken during a sports game when I was twelve years old. From that time on I loathed looking at my nose in the mirror, perceiving it as ugly. He pointed out that the actual physical break itself was repaired, but the emotional effect – the anger focused on it – was not, and so it created a weak and vulnerable spot in the body. Other parts of my body had been affected by negative emotional memories, which they could see highlighted by their technology, associated with accidents and injury. The results of their energy-based healing session would filter through to the physical body over time.

He stated the problem with humans is that we feel ashamed to "own" some emotions, or to admit an emotion may be affecting us physically, when in actual fact it's just a part of our human make-up that we don't completely understand yet. Their species could eliminate much illness and suffering on our planet, and could teach us how to use the power of the mind to heal, combined with advanced technology. He noted we are beginning to work these procedures and technologies out for ourselves, with some input from them.

For some time, I had been worrying about looking after my children on my own while coping with chronic illness. The counsellor assured me someone would take care of us, they would ensure this, and I was not to be concerned about it. The doctor projected an information capsule into my mind to assist me. It contained a thought process common to the Greys, which I could draw on to assist and uplift me during difficult times; a little bit of their species that I would take away with me.

I got down from the table and the two colleagues stood as they so often do, still, hands at their sides, faces expressionless, but their minds enfolded me with tender feelings. We moved out into the corridor and my son and the child rushed over to greet us.

S. ... *and I'm seeing something! A likeness in the intensity of the energy coming from his eyes! The Grey says, "Yes, your son is somewhat set apart from you in that his genetic mix is more complicated." I don't know much about genetics, but I know I'm being told my son has similar genes and traits to the doctor.*

The child led us back along the corridor. I turned to look behind at the two adults, aware my son was still streaming communications to them, and they responded with deep affection for him. He raised his hand to wave to them as a child would do, and for a second time I saw the Grey doctor respond uncharacteristically by also raising his hand in farewell.

We passed through a doorway and into a wide exit foyer leading out of the healing area of the craft. Here, large circles around a metre in diameter were embedded in the floor, with different coloured soft lights shining out of them creating a beautiful atmosphere. These were no ordinary lights; they emitted some kind of frequency so that when you stood on them, you experienced a soothing sense of inner and outer warmth and relaxation. Every circle had a slightly different energetic feel or output, so you could move from spot to spot experiencing the difference. The three of us made a game of it, standing on a circle, swapping around, hopping from one to another, feeling the sense of well-being diffusing through our bodies.

The Grey child left us in a room to await departure. The light was dimmer here and my son soon went to sleep with his head on my shoulder.

Discussion

The Grey doctor performed a kind of laser surgery using an intense focused beam of coloured energy. I have since heard a corroborative anecdotal account from an experiencer who states she was taught healing procedures by extraterrestrials using the energy from one of her eyes as a kind of laser eye-beam.

At the time of this contact in 1996, I had been ill and my GP diagnosed me with a virulent form of bacteria resulting in A-typical pneumonia. All antibiotics prescribed so far had failed, as the bacteria simply mutated and over-ran my immune system and I came close to death. A clairvoyant friend came up with an approximation of the name of an antibiotic, which my doctor recognised and prescribed, and I began a slow recovery. Who knows, the Greys may have played a part in the discovery of the appropriate antibiotic as well.

The issue of the Greys not being able to completely heal or fix a problem because of prior soul agreements has come up before. Do we learn from suffering? I certainly learnt from suffering this illness and coming close to death. It made me analyse what and who was really important in my life, and my children and I finally began to thrive and achieve together as a close-knit solo-parent family.

The hospital wing onboard craft was developed for use with humans, and the large soothing circles embedded at the exit point would be a welcome addition to any earthly hospital foyer or dentist's clinic for those arriving feeling nervous or afraid.

The Greys teach that energy influences all life. Our increasing understanding of energy will no doubt create new pathways to both physical and emotional self-healing.

I believe energy medicine will be the basis of our future medicine. There are ample indications emerging in our current cutting-edge research and development of medical technology, that our future healthcare will align with the Greys' and will use phenomenal energy, sound, and light to heal, along with human kindness.

Chapter 33

Into The Mist

1997, age 42 years

Two friends had accompanied me to a function in another city around one and a half hours drive from where we lived. I will refer to them as "Mike" and "Kim". Later, we headed home at around 11.30 pm in Kim's racy two-door car. It was raining heavily, with strong wind blowing the rain almost horizontally at the windscreen.

We drove south on the main highway, eventually taking a turn-off from where the road crossed low rolling countryside towards the ranges, which we would cross over on our journey home. Soon after the turn-off, Kim passed a slow-moving truck and raced around a curve towards a long straight, leaving the truck and a line of cars well behind us.

Suddenly, I registered a distinct "wired up" feeling throughout my entire body, a heightening of senses I have often experienced prior to contact. I briefly looked out the side window at the dark sky and thought, *"They're here."*

We noticed muted red and blue lights flashing further on at a crossroad a kilometre or so ahead of us, and assumed it must be a police car attending an accident caused by the slippery conditions. I looked behind us and saw no sign of the truck and line of cars rounding the bend as yet. Kim began to slow down as we approached the crossroad.

An odd-looking mound of bright white mist sat just beyond the intersection, hanging over the highway like a pile of snow, extending the full width of the road. Wisps of fog gathered increasingly all around our car, as if drawing us in. The flashing red and blue lights illuminated the mist from within, but there was no sign of any people or vehicles. A strong wind was blowing and yet incongruously, despite this, the mist remained compact and stationary across our path. This was the second sign that indicated to me all was not as it may seem.

Kim halted the car and lowered her window a bit and as if on cue, a dark figure emerged from the mist. I undid my seatbelt, leaning forward between the seats, intently watching the figure approaching from the right-hand side of the road. It was wearing a dark hooded jacket, but without any fluorescent safety stripe or insignia, such as a police officer would have on his jacket, and no torch either. Mike and Kim no doubt thought this was just a routine police roadblock, but I was privately wondering what was going to happen next.

The figure moved up to within four metres or so of Kim's window, a dark silhouette just out of range of our headlights with its back to the misty light, and we heard a distinctly monotone tinny-sounding male voice say clearly despite the windy conditions, "There's been a slip. Proceed slowly."

I instantly exclaimed to the others, "But there can't be a slip! There are no hills just here! We're on the plains!"

The figure repeated, "Proceed forward slowly."

Kim shut the window and silently put the car into gear, edging it forward. My last recollection was of the rain beating noisily on the car roof, and I suddenly felt inexplicably relaxed and sleepy. From that point on, I can recall nothing more of what occurred next at the intersection.

I explored this incident through a regression conducted in 2007.

A split second after Kim began driving towards the mist both she and Mike suddenly became still and silent, as if asleep. I was now in some other kind of altered state, a dulled consciousness, but still aware of what was going on around me. The engine failed and the headlights went out. The car rose slowly until it was floating about a metre above the road, gliding effortlessly forward, straight past the figure standing on the side of the road and into the mist. I could not tell whether he turned and followed the car, whether he was floating, or if he was even a real figure.

Suddenly, an extremely bright, narrow beam of light shot through the left rear window and hit me in the middle of the forehead, penetrating my mind and causing a tingling sensation throughout my body like a mild electric shock, relaxing me further.

Concealed within the mist was a brightly-lit metallic sphere less than half the width of the road in diameter. I was intrigued and vaguely wondered how our car would fit inside it! The sphere stood on a tripod with red and blue lights flashing underneath it, and the exterior of the object was formed by geometric panels creating a honeycombed or interlocking effect. Now the mist began to drift away in the direction we had come from, while the car hovered beside the sphere.

> *S. We're going up! Whoever's in the sphere has "locked" something onto the car. It's like an attraction from a magnet, but the car's not touching the sphere. It's just moving up in the air beside it!*

I peered out the windows, feeling totally unconcerned as we ascended higher and swept away over farmland. Looking down towards the crossroads, I noticed the stark white mist neatly disappearing into a spot, like an invisible funnel or hole in the air. The headlights of the truck and cars were finally coming along the road now, as if they had somehow been held back while this rendezvous occurred.

We ascended above the bank of rainclouds, the lights of a small township twinkling through gaps in the clouds to the southwest of the crossroads. Kim and Mike were now slumped forward, hanging relaxed on their seat belts. After a short time I realised we were moving up underneath a dark object that blocked out a large section of starry sky. The underside of the huge craft was outlined and dimly lit by "flat" circular lights (rather than radiant ones) which revealed the shape of the craft: pointed at one end, with sloping sides forming an isosceles triangle, with the backend slightly curved like a boomerang.

The sphere headed towards a large circular opening at the rear of the craft and manoeuvred us into what I assume from past experiences was some kind of energy beam – not a shaft of light, but a visible beam of shimmering coloured energy that now "attached" to the car, drawing it upwards into the craft. The sphere unlocked itself from our car and descended again into the night, and we rose through the opening into glaringly white surroundings, the car moving forward and lowering onto the floor in a hangar area.

My mind now quickly reconnected to the fact I was in familiar surroundings! Three tall Greys waited nearby and one of them immediately opened the car door and released Mike's seat belt. He began communicating, greeting me with familiarity and explaining they wished me to accompany them, however they were not expecting a two-door car and I was in the back seat. He effortlessly levitated Mike's body, floating him out of the car using the power of his mind, straightening Mike out and lying him down on the floor on his back so

I could get out. Kim remained slumped on her seatbelt and leaving my two friends behind, they led me into the craft's interior.

I suddenly sensed a profound feeling of closeness and affection enveloping me. Somebody was reaching out to me telepathically and I recognised it was my lifelong friend and companion, RJ. He had already entered my mind, his consciousness registering all that had taken place in my life since we last had contact, as we hadn't seen each other for some time.

We entered the room where RJ was waiting and after greeting me, he outlined the purpose of this visit: to prepare for a phase in my life where I would need to be able to ascertain people's hidden agendas, and any attempts to adversely influence me. They wished to equip me with a deeper understanding of the power of intent, be it positive or negative. I was entering a crucial phase where my work in the UFO field would increase, and coupled with this were the inevitable pit-falls of human nature, and counter-productive situations created by others that I would face in my private life.

To begin, he wished to further instruct me on energies relating to both living organisms and inanimate objects, and illustrate the effects of thought and the power of positive and negative intent on them.

We began by examining the frequencies of plants. RJ activated the computer and the screen became alive with spiralling colour and movement, images illustrating how certain influences such as chemicals, toxins, or changes in weather and basic requirements can affect the energy fields of plants. Humans are already generally aware of these effects.

We viewed images of trees and plants, demonstrating how natural forces such as sun, rain or wind, can alter the energy fields. The emissions were stunningly beautiful and RJ emphasised how these energetic frequencies are vitally contributing to the atmosphere we live in every day. But he also showed how unpleasant circumstances, even certain noises, and in particular human thoughts, can alter the energy field of plants. Moving on, we examined disturbing images of these negative effects on many other living creatures on our planet, resulting in disease, deformity, and demise.

RJ now illustrated the impact of human-initiated negative circumstances, thought, or intent on *inanimate* objects, and the effect on my emotions again, was immediate and distressing.

R. *What is he showing you Suzy?*

S. *Oh! He's showing me a multitude of things or objects that we humans endow with terribly damaging negative energy through our thoughts and the power of negative intent.*

We viewed images of guns, bullets, trucks, military tanks; a vast range of weapons of warfare. But the images were not limited to these. He showed me the machines that make the weaponry, containers they are packed in, the vehicles, aircraft and ships that carry them, and even the installations or bases where they are stored – a worldwide military and industrial set-up carrying the energy of negative intent, even before any of the equipment is put to destructive use against our fellow humans.

RJ slowed and enhanced images of bombs and bullets passing through the air, making visible the dramatically changed energetic vibration of the air around them. He said this dreadful negative "broth" was affecting millions of people all around the planet, a negative power our species does not fully or even adequately comprehend, originating from the human mind and intent.

Conversely, RJ described how the power of the mind is also capable of transmuting negative energy to positive, and how collective positive intent can influence the mass negative. He stressed I would need to apply this knowledge in my future life and warned me there will be those who are, as we would say, "wolves in sheep's clothing", who I will come across, and who may seek to affect or influence me negatively. It will be important to recognise them by their energetic emanation and know how to combat this negativity; to develop the ability to predict and anticipate other's actions, to ascertain what they are thinking, and why, and whether people are trustworthy or not.

He spoke of a "huge deception", by humans, upon humans that will be revealed in the years to come, thus underlining the importance of developing protective abilities. However immediately following this revelation, he suppressed and "locked" the actual details of this massive deception in my mind, as a form of protection for me. If I was to recall this part of the discussion it may alter my future activities, endanger me, or draw me away from my agreed tasks, but at the appropriate time in the future, I will recognise these events as they occur. Nevertheless, the residue of this discussion would engender watchfulness on my part. RJ stated that they could intervene, but to do so would be an action not mutually agreed upon with the UGB, and it would alter mankind's opportunities for positive spiritual evolution through raised mass consciousness, instigated by societal upheaval, from which the eventual exposure of this deception will emerge.

RJ described how all things are energetically interconnected on our planet, and we have limited understanding of how vital the animal kingdom is to our existence. The source of the planet's energetic equilibrium is the energetic vitality of all living things, and this is essential to our well-being. Much of that vitality originates from the plant kingdom, contributing to our atmosphere and the air we breathe. But in terms of emotions, the animal kingdom is absolutely vital. Animals emanate complex emotional energies in a way that humans have yet to discover and understand, and these contribute to the energetic and synergistic "soup" we all live in. Destruction of forests globally is causing loss of habitat and the demise of many animal species, and thus, a reduction in the complex energy systems vital to our survival.

He explained the Greys can control their ability to see energy, switching this ability on and off at will, activating the mind and power of intent in ways currently unknown to us. We examined and practiced the ability to "observe" energy, not only with the physical eye, but with the entire sensory system of the body "seeing" it in unison, and how to transmute it, further building on skills I have learnt since childhood.

Finally, at his request eight Greys joined us in the room and RJ asked them to direct differing energies towards me, and I had to identify the intent of each stream of energy, and which Grey it was coming from. He made it clear I will use these skills in the future and the ability will unfold naturally as the circumstances arise. The session ended there with a moment of farewell between us.

Once back in the hangar I noticed one of the tall Greys standing over Mike, gesturing towards his body on the hangar floor.

S. Suddenly the air is full of emotion! There is an overwhelming feeling of kindness coming from them, almost a child-like feeling of concern. I can liken it to the sound of beautiful singing!

Attention to detail is important to the Greys and they had placed Mike in a recovery position. At one stage during the session it crossed my mind that Mike should not lie on his back because of health problems, and the entities had registered my concern and acted on it.

I climbed back into the car, but I really didn't want to leave. One of the entities levitated Mike again, suspending him in mid-air in a prone position as he arranged Mike's limbs, reassembling him into a sitting position in mid-air and floating him back into the front seat.

The car lifted, suspended over the exit/entry point, and we begin a long descent in the beam.

S. We're coming down slowly about 30 metres above the ground and now there's a mist forming around us ... the motor has started up! It's as if all is as it was, but we're quite a few kilometres further on than we were when they took us up. Mike and Kim are "coming to". Kim says, "Where the hell are we? I can't see a bloody thing!" And suddenly – whoosh! We're out of the mist! It's absolutely clear, and there are lights below! We are momentarily confused ... I realise something has happened but the other two are unaware of anything.

Discussion

Suzy:

I first spoke about this experience in 2008, at a UFO Research meeting, in Sydney, Australia.

I will refer to my last conscious memory before the contact occurred at the crossroads as the *natural melding point*, where a whole slice of time and memories seem to be "forgotten" and the last conscious memory melds neatly with the next conscious memory following the event. Therefore my memory of the car entering mist on the plains blends with the memory of emerging from mist beyond the summit of the ranges, albeit twenty six kilometres further on from the crossroad. Because it was already late at night we did not think to look at our watches and were unaware of a time discrepancy.

Alternatively, sometimes in these contacts there may be what I refer to as an *incongruous melding point*, such as I have described in Chapter 1, where the experience began in late afternoon sunlight and ended in darkness, with obvious missing time, all of which was incongruous and did not make sense.

Kim and Mike were unaware of anything happening, and even the fact we suddenly emerged from thick mist into clear conditions had a convenient meteorological explanation too. Often there is a distinct change in weather conditions at the summit of the ranges. Wave cloud banks up against the hills on one side, and you cross over the summit into the other region, from rain or mist in one district, to clear weather in the other, and sometimes vice versa. This factor added to the natural feeling of emerging from mist, but there was still a moment of confusion over the city lights we could see.

During this experience I received instruction on aspects of energy associated with positive or negative intent. RJ explained the individualised nature of this instruction by the fact I was entering a crucial phase in life when I would need to recognise concealed negative intent disguised as something positive.

His statement that my work in the UFO field would increase, along with difficulties in life, was correct. I spoke at my first international UFO conference that year in 1997, and founded the UFOCUS NZ Research Network in 2000. As described in Chapter 8, I was negatively influenced by "agents" at the Laughlin conference in 1999, and I described how the woman seemed to exert mind-control influence over me, so it seems I did not utilise this new-found skill on that occasion! However, this could explain why the strange (hybrid?) male later ended up in the rental company car with us, restoring my confidence and equilibrium.

During this contact RJ showed me fields of energy around inanimate objects, a concept which was not unfamiliar to me given that I have experience in psychometry (the ability to pick up information about an object's history through the energy field surrounding it). However the extent to which these energies can affect the whole of mankind was a sobering discovery. It casts new light on the expression "cause and effect". In my mind, RJ's lesson also validates psychometry, a so-called "paranormal skill" based on attached energy, which mainstream science does not accept – as yet.

An aspect of this experience I did not include in the account, so as not to distract the reader, is a humorous moment I shared with RJ as I left. He was amused by the fact I was wearing a long, calf-length woollen coat with knee-high boots, when previously he has only ever seen me in nightclothes. My response was to make fun of his short stature, as I now towered over him in my high-heeled black leather boots. I have always found humour an integral part of relationships with the Greys.

Sightings of large black triangular craft have been reported worldwide for many years, and New Zealand has had its share of them, as described on the UFOCUS NZ website. It is entirely possible some of these may be secret military aircraft however others such as the craft I was on are clearly extraterrestrial in origin.

Dr. Schild:

Before the contact and when on the road, Suzy describes suddenly having a "wired up" feeling throughout her body, commonly reported by abductees/experiencers. I have assumed that this experience or feeling is probably induced by an implant at the base of the brain stem in the back of the neck.

I assume the implant is a kind of resonator which becomes activated by a signal projected over a large land area by the Greys to locate the human immediately before arranging the pick-up. Because it causes a reaction throughout her body, it must activate the nervous system's electrical activity. However because it becomes activated even when experiencers/abductees are in Faraday-cage-like automobiles and ships, the activation signal is likely to be not electro-magnetic waves like light or radio, but rather like consciousness heliacal waves.

It is interesting that Suzy mentions seeing the truck and line of cars approaching the crossroad location as her car is floating away, guided by the UFO/craft. She mentions that something seems to have slowed their progress. I think that in fact the experience of time has been accelerated for Suzy and those transporting her, and that the occupants of the truck and following cars noticed and experienced nothing.

Elsewhere in the book, Suzy recounts being in rooms aboard craft and seeing the walls of the room expand and change their form and shape. I suspect that just as the Greys can warp space, they can warp time, and the roadside experience being described here is an example of warping (expanding) time. Recall that in the Relativity theory, space and time are independent but coupled dimensions. The process by which the Greys use consciousness to warp space would logically allow them to warp time.

When Suzy described being shown images of plants and their energy fields, she described the computer screen becoming alive with spiralling colour and movement. Such spiralling or heliacal patterns seem to be an important aspect of life force energy. Others have already noticed this; Wilhelm Reich, for example, noticed and drew spiralling waves and their 2-D projection as a cycloid figure.

The main point of the contact was for Suzy to learn about the nature of evil and negative energy. What she describes is consistent with the dyadic property of the universe, which is understood within the quantum hologram (QH) formulation through its dyadic principle.

Dr. Edgar Mitchell, in his book, *The Way of the Explorer*, describes how for every attribute of the universe, there is a dyadic opposite attribute. In other words, for there to be good, there must be evil, and for there to be happy there must be sad. These attributes are expressed as holographic 3-D wave/phase patterns and such patterns can have positive or negative amplitude. Thus it is easy to understand our universe as having been made from nothing as quantum information, and the QH for all attributes are in positive-negative balance, which is why the universe has dyadic opposites of all attributes.

In this experience, Suzy was shown the dyadic opposite of life-affirming energies, and taught to recognise the difference between the experience of two dyadic opposites, good and evil.

PART THREE

CHANGES

"Coming events cast their shadows before."

Johann Wolfgang von Goethe

Chapter 34

A Dire Warning: Chaos on our Planet

In February, 2010, I retained memory of attending a somewhat disturbing meeting with hundreds of other people in an underground facility. We conducted a regression exactly one year later to further investigate the sketchy details.

2010, February, age 55 years

Preparations to address large groups of humans: coming Earth changes, and global political and civil upheaval

The underground tunnel resembled a long wormhole which seemed to go on and on, sloping uphill into the distance. It looked as if it had been drilled out of rock, or perhaps it had been drilled out of earth and the walls had been coated or lined. The surface was surprisingly smooth, with rounded floor, sides and ceiling, much of it painted a pale cream colour. The tunnel was brightly lit with regularly spaced oval lights high on the curved walls.

To the left of me, the tunnel widened into a line of docking bays where larger craft were arriving from above ground and moving into position, while others glided away. Scores of people were alighting from them, crowding into the corridor and milling around looking at each other. On the opposite side of the tunnel were curved archways, each with sliding metal doors that met in the middle. Two Greys and a tall Mantis entity emerged from one of these doorways and immediately caught the attention of the congregating groups of humans. This particular Mantis's eyes were captivating to look at and I was not the only person trying to catch a clearer glimpse of him through the crowd.

A human male dressed in navy overalls strode down the tunnel slope on the other side of this area, and although he had aged and his hair had greyed, I recognised him as the young male who had addressed a group of us about disclosure some years ago. He communicated adeptly with the Greys as he approached, before asking us to move closer together as there were more craft due to arrive.

More people poured out of these craft and there were now several hundred of us grouped in this area, quietly conversing with each other both verbally and telepathically. The two Greys and the Mantis overrode our conversations, instructing us all to begin raising our awareness, rather like mentally and energetically shifting up a gear until our bodies felt filled with light.

The male asked us to follow him and the mass of people began moving silently up the slope towards a right-hand curve in the tunnel. Eventually he stopped outside a set of open doors and gestured that we should go through, now entering a huge hollowed-out cavern painted cream and brightly lit like the tunnel. Hundreds of seats were layered up in grandstands, complete with individual sloping desktops you could lean on.

It took some time for everybody to move in and ascend into the rows of seats, politely shuffling along and sitting down. The two Greys and the Mantis entered the room last of all and stood to one side. Although it appeared the human would conduct this meeting, from previous experiences I guessed these entities would actually be the planners or facilitators of the event. Undoubtedly I was not the only person present feeling anticipation tinged with a good measure of curiosity about what might be expected of us on this occasion. The atmosphere was electric.

While waiting for proceedings to begin I was able to observe the three entities near the door. The Mantis was also surveying the mass of humans seated before him, and I tried to get a good look at his extraordinary eyes without appearing to stare at him. His eyes were positioned more towards the sides of his head and were oval, tapering at the outer edge. The entire eye was black, but with a long bright blue vertical slit, and although I had seen other genetic mixtures of this species, his eyes were different again.

I perceived the human's thought processes were akin to the Greys' and he now stood in the centre of a low platform down in front of us, with a large screen behind him. We all received a message from him that images would appear in quick time, with rapid telepathy.

Images began flashing on the screen, initially, one every few seconds or so. However as our concentration was established and maintained, this then increased to one image roughly every second and then several images each second. There was no time to blink.

S. *We are registering them all* (but) *we cannot dwell on any particular one because of the terrific speed. It makes my eyes*

jerk and water. Oh! They are tragic images! Tragic images!
[crying and deeply disturbed by the images]

(At this point in the regression recording, I ceased speaking altogether and my entire body shook as if in a state of sudden shock. According to the regression therapist, I hyperventilated and my teeth hammered together loudly for a full two and a half minutes, as I relived the intensity of hundreds of futuristic images.)

They depicted shocking natural disasters on our planet, extremes of weather, internal and inter-nation wars and chaos in societies, all involving massive loss of life and suffering – a stream of tragedy, sending a bolt of terror through us all. Everyone was shaken, but our eyes remained fixed and riveted to the screen with tears streaming down our faces, as all within the space of a couple of minutes we were given a dire insight, a warning of events to come on our planet.

Then equally as quickly, the atmosphere switched as the images ended.

S. *Um, we are calming down now. He has cleared it away.*

R. *Who has cleared it away?*

S. *That's why this particular Mantis entity is here. He's got some extraordinary ability and I know it's coming from him.*

The entity sent out a telepathic blanket of calm that descended over us all, instantaneously soothing our jangled emotions with his mind as the shock dissipated, and we felt composed again. The understanding of what we had seen was still in our minds, but because of his influence, we could now think about the implications calmly and clinically and put emotions aside.

The human explained the futuristic images of earth changes, wars and societal upheaval were events that *will* occur, however the timing, intensity and duration may vary according to mankind's decisions in the interim. In other words, our mass consciousness and actions play a part in creating our collective future. Tragic events sometimes promote growth and change.

He went on to say that as people who have been trained by the Greys, we were now being asked to take on a different role, that of tutoring for them. This was conveyed as a request but at the same time, there was a subtle element of requiring us to do this. We understood it was not a threat or imposition, but rather an expectation of commitment, and having seen tragic future portends affecting our civilisation, our very consciences required us to cooperate. This group of several hundred people was one of many being activated by the

Greys' (and it seems, associated humans), and each person would soon address large groups of humans.

He gave a brief introduction on what was required of us and that it concerned "survival of large numbers of people" through leadership and logic, as an alternative to relying on humanitarian aid. He commented many nations have the capacity to help our fellow humans in times of adversity (through such groups as Civil Defence, Red Cross, and many other groups set up to aid mankind) however, this was not going to be sufficient to cope with coming events. These humanitarian groups are often hindered by financial constraints, requiring huge sums of money in order to transport food and necessary supplies across great distances. Complex political, military, social, religious and cultural barriers often prevent these groups from reaching those in need, and difficult protocols must be overcome in both emergency and long-term humanitarian aid situations.

Structures are needed that can bypass these problems, a network of people to provide leadership and other vital forms of survival assistance, people or groups who are trusted within their communities. But he also mentioned the importance of intuition, being able to tap into common or shared thought structures or processes, aspects we have been trained in.

We were all astonished by his next statement, that the Greys have put a great deal of time into using specific consciousness-technology to "sweep" or scan whole cities, communities, towns, and villages to detect specific energetic frequencies emitted by people. They are able to determine which people have the intellectual, emotional and intuitive capacity to fulfil significant roles in the future within their communities.

He prepared to step aside, informing us the Mantis entity would give us instructions, sets of protocols and a lecture outline, which he would put into our subconscious minds in the form of what I refer to as "thought-seeds" – information packages of a different kind that are not limited in their content, but can be added to, adapted, or interpreted by the user. They would also give separate information packages to us, which we could pass on to others. The human stated they intended to bring us here again soon to lecture to groups of humans. The Greys would not dictate how we should convey this information to our audiences, but they would provide a basic structure in the thought seed. They trusted that we each had the knowledge and understanding to be able to enhance, add to and enrich their information with our own experience and advice. In fact it was vital that humans should facilitate these meetings and there would be minimal extraterrestrial presence.

The visiting groups of people will be brought onboard in an altered mind-state and they will not consciously remember the experience however, the information they receive will be triggered and emerge at a time of crisis. We must communicate verbally to the humans rather than telepathically as they will not be receptive to that (presumably each of us will lecture to groups according to our spoken language). He added we can insert information packages into people's minds as deemed necessary.

Now everyone fidgeted in their seats as the Mantis entity stepped forward, all of us a little over-awed by his presence. Without hesitation, he began another energetic overlay, a protective process to further relax us following the traumatic images we had viewed. He reached into our minds, calming the deeper effects of shock. Once we were completely relaxed, he inserted the various packets of suggested information, thought-seeds, into the subconscious. This process was completed within a short time and I soon felt my body coming back to normal. I sensed his role was expansive and he carried a weight of responsibility requiring a clinical approach to issues. The two Greys appeared to have maintained a support role, although it is possible they had some input in the procedure which we were not aware of. The process was soon completed and the three entities moved back to one side.

We all began moving down out of the grandstand and while we shuffled out into the corridor, the human telepathically provided us with some background information. He revealed the Greys and groups they are working with have "insider knowledge" of impending turmoil because some of "their own people" are working on the planet amongst us, and they provide information. However the Greys and associates are not only watching what is happening on the surface of the planet, they are also monitoring the planet itself: tectonic plates, its magnetic field, and everything physical that makes our planet what it is. They have been planning and preparing in anticipation of these events for a long time.

Natural catastrophic events have occurred since the beginning of time on this planet, but along with further earth changes, there will be a rapid exponential rise in other events, resulting in massive changes within cultures and countries. This has been going on at a relatively slow pace for some years, but will speed up. Over-population in some areas of our planet means these changes have disastrous potential for loss of life, and the Greys and associates are attempting to pre-empt certain situations by putting vast preparatory measures in place to minimise this: to assist us to help ourselves. These lectures are part of that process.

As we moved towards the docking bays, the human continued his stream of information, telling us that tonight's lecture was just the first of many such visits and there would be a second one coming up soon. The information packages will open up and basically at the click of our fingers, we will be able to execute and deliver these lectures, on our own.

Discussion

As described in other chapters, the Greys and associates are able to produce futuristic images, perhaps indicating an ability to manipulate time, or access future time periods.

This regression was conducted in New Zealand while the therapist was staying in my home for a week in February 2011, a year after the contact experience. Having completed the regression, we briefly discussed the information that had emerged, before deciding to take a break and drive into the city for lunch.

On our return home at around 2 pm, we learnt that a powerful earthquake registering 6.3 on the Richter scale had just hit the South Island city of Christchurch, New Zealand, and the surrounding area, causing severe damage and loss of life. It seemed more than coincidental to have investigated this particular meeting regarding impending earth changes, earlier that morning, a sobering and poignant confirmation of my initial memories of such events a year earlier. We watched the breaking news on television as soon as we arrived home and were shocked at the widespread scenes of destruction in our South Island city.

Sadly, more tragic news eventuated two and a half weeks later when an earthquake measuring 9 on the Richter scale occurred off the coast of Japan, creating a massive tsunami which hit the east coast of Japan on Friday 11 March, 2011 (NZ time). The resulting series of tsunami waves caused unprecedented destruction and loss of life along parts of the eastern coast of Japan and precipitated the partial meltdown of the Fukushima nuclear reactor plant.

The growing ferocity of natural disasters and the effects of climate change and severe weather have continued to occur globally as "super-storm" becomes a new terminology and a deadly reality.

Political and civil upheaval has occurred across the Middle East (the Arab Spring) and Northern Africa, with political regimes and/or dictators deposed or challenged.

Major civil unrest and natural disasters have since occurred in countries where poverty and lack of resources have exacerbated the suffering, and where aid agencies have struggled to provide even basic assistance. Limited medical aid and preventative services have now contributed to the spread of the deadly Ebola virus disease through four countries in Africa (2014).

For weeks after this meeting in an underground facility my mind turned often to the magnitude of the shocking, mind-numbing images of coming earth changes, wars, societal disintegration and chaos, which I had observed.

Chapter 35

Thought-seeds and Soul-lights

2010, March, age 55 years (one month later)
Appealing to potential leaders

R. Where are you?

S. On a craft. It's very big though ... like a town.

I had joined around thirty people and we were divided into small groups, each assigned to a Grey. Our escort took us to a room where he gave us minimal instructions, as we had been partially prepared for this occasion a month earlier and now we knew exactly why we were here – to lecture.

I entered an auditorium where a couple of hundred people sat waiting quietly, coughing and shifting in their seats. They had been transported onboard semi-cognisant, their awareness limited to their bodies ticking over, yawning or sneezing if they needed to. This shallow receptive state allowed an awareness of being "somewhere", but closed off to any deeper thoughts about where and why. I knew they were all respected and active people in their communities, brought here for this reason.

As I stepped onto a low platform at the front I registered their reactions, as if they were casually thinking, *oh look, there's someone who's going to talk to us.* Only then did I realise the enormity of the task.

I introduced myself verbally and without any preparatory thoughts on my part, the outline of one of the thought-seeds implanted in my mind a month earlier began to unfold. Information just rolled off my tongue and at the same time as I was speaking, I was also listening intently to myself! After a little while I realised I could add a bit here and there just as the Greys had previously suggested, anecdotal snippets and pieces of personal experience.

The lecture unfolding from my subconscious, through my conscious mind, was about relating to people: mediation, being a positive influence on others, relating to different kinds of personalities, and approaching people in the right way in order to gain their trust and cooperation under adverse or emergency situations. I discussed coping mechanisms and methods of encouraging distressed people to calm down and listen by using clear instructions and discipline, assisting people suffering from severe shock, and helping people to think and act logically in these situations and engage with others in need. I had little or no experience of some of these situations myself, but the information just kept rolling forth and I felt quite comfortable about conveying it to the group with my own input.

I began to blend these interpersonal issues with the idea of potential natural disasters and other dangerous situations that may occur in their countries or communities. Although they were in a relatively confined state of awareness, they were able to participate, offer input or ask questions of the rest of the group, and draw on their expertise and experience within their communities. We covered a lot of ground bringing certain issues to their awareness, such as the importance of preparatory measures and organisational procedures in their communities, and readiness for potential emergency situations they had not really considered before. It had become a relaxed talk rather than a formal lecture now, promoting plain common sense, appealing to their own sense of logic and practicality in dealing with difficulties in life, not making it too deep or gloomy, but conversational. A final task was to transfer one of the thought-seeds the Mantis entity had provided at the previous meeting, from within my own mind, into their collective subconscious minds.

S. *It relates to an awakening that will happen for them should something* (disastrous on a major scale) *occur in their lives, in their communities, and they will know what to do ... like a programme switching on.*

As the session ended, a woman at the back of the auditorium slipped out of her relaxed state and cried out as she realised she was in unfamiliar surroundings, and suddenly I sensed a "rushing wind of thought" coming from behind a wall on my left. The woman instantly reverted to a relaxed state and I realised the group was being monitored by the Greys, who did not wish to show themselves, but who wanted to ensure nobody came to any harm.

My thoughts were interrupted by instructions from the Greys, now asking me to direct everyone to file out of the auditorium to a reception area, where they would be met by human-looking hybrids. Once again, care was taken not to frighten any of the humans brought onboard.

S. *I'm telling them to follow* (the hybrids) *and I feel like my instructions are almost hypnotic. When I say certain words to them about leaving, it's as if at that point they start shutting down.*

Appealing to departing souls, and sceptics

R. *Is there anything more that happens after the people are taken out?*

S. *Yes, I haven't finished yet. There's another session.*

I returned to the small room with other members of my group and the Grey instructor explained we had a further session to complete this evening. He indicated it would be distinctly different from the first and our input into this lecture and the specific way we conveyed material, was crucial. When we entered our individual auditoriums again we would understand why this was so, but he was not going to tell us more at this point as he preferred our reactions to be spontaneous and he wanted to observe our responses to the situation. We were all curious about this.

Upon entering the auditorium I was confronted by an unexpected, but familiar sight. There were no people! Instead, over two hundred soul-lights in a myriad of luminous colours hung in the air, an incredibly beautiful sight that momentarily took my breath away. This was the "distinct difference".

Immediately, a simple statement dropped into my mind from the Grey instructor nearby: *we are moving to a higher and more complex level of the overall programme now, with this second lecture to souls.*

He informed me there were actually two different groups of souls in the room and communication would be telepathic this time. First I needed to close off one group from my telepathy, while I addressed the other.

Now waves of more tragic images, sounds and emotions washed over me. Sadly, I realised the first group of souls were those of people who would soon face natural disasters, war and violence in their countries of origin, and who would lose their lives in these events. I needed to be delicate in the way I approached them.

Unfolding from my mind, I conveyed information about these future events on our planet and many of the souls reciprocated, poignantly indicating they were already aware on a soul level that their lifespan would end soon, because in this soul state they had a universal awareness of the future. If I can put it this way, by comparison, the humans I lectured to earlier in the evening did not have this capacity because they were using their human minds rather than a wider soul-consciousness.

These souls had full awareness of the life they were leading, but this super-awareness was overlaying it, enabling them to discuss their coming departure from this life calmly and rationally. They knew they had agreed to this destiny prior to entering this life, and perhaps they had achieved their desired spiritual goals and learning in their lifespan leading to this point. Now it was time to offer these souls opportunities to continue their spiritual evolution by assisting mankind through other avenues.

Three options were open to them: 1) the Greys were offering them the opportunity to prepare for a future life on Earth in a changed political, cultural, and environmental climate. Acceptance of this option meant the souls would not need to return to the Field of Consciousness, but instead, they could return to the Greys for a time of preparation, 2) their souls/spirits could remain in the spirit realms and work with the UGB to guide and assist both people on Earth, and souls departing from Earth, during and after the approaching time of turmoil, or 3) their souls could return to the Source Field to await another life opportunity elsewhere.

Discussion and consideration ensued, and the thought-seeds I placed in their subconscious minds containing the choices offered, would emerge again in their soul-consciousness at the moment of their passing.

S. I thank them all sincerely. The opportunity must remain their independent choice when the time comes.

I now closed this group off in preparation for addressing the other. The second group of souls was that of people who hold specialist positions: medical staff, scientists, engineers, rescue workers, and the like. Information opened in my mind for me to work with, and I discovered to my surprise that they were also all true sceptics!

It was ironic that in their day-to-day lives these particular individuals may consider such subjects as intuition, UFOs, aliens, telepathy, or psychic abilities to be flaky, or the premise of New Age thinking. They had been hardened sceptics all their lives.

But by using the "sweeping" capabilities described in the previous chapter, the Greys had identified them as potentially receptive, with latent intuitive abilities. They held positions of authority or effectiveness in their careers and all had the skills and capacity to make significant positive differences in the lives of many people during such events as natural disasters or war.

The Greys had appealed to each one's universal soul-consciousness to attend this lecture. It was essential they visit onboard craft in their receptive soul state rather than their physical human body and sceptical psyche.

I conveyed information to them containing the same kinds of details I had discussed with the previous group about foreseeable tragic events on our planet. We discussed whether they would accept a thought-seed containing constructive information and guidance, basically a "short-cut" to their consciousness, the core of their being, which would open in their minds at a time of great need.

Their sceptical personality traits dictate that they analyse and rationalise new information when decision-making. These are valid traits, but it sometimes means they ignore gut feelings or spontaneity, or even data that does not fit their framework of logic. By accepting an information capsule of this kind, they will experience intuition and pre-cognition at a time of crisis, which may not "fit" their actual circumstances at the time, or their sceptical mind-set, however the human mind will not override the information capsule and instead of discarding it, they will act on it by making important decisions. These souls would survive chaotic events to save, assist and lead people.

Without exception, the soul-lights conveyed their acceptance of the information capsules, and their understanding of the magnitude of their individual roles in future events.

R. And is there anything else?

S. No, I'm going back down the corridor now. There is just a feeling of "warning", a prior knowledge of preparedness for difficult times ahead.

Discussion

We were told these lectures will take place onboard craft again and again with the two distinct groups: humans who will assist humans to survive and help each other; and humans who may lose their lives, but who can become volunteer souls contributing to a better future world for mankind by fast-tracking their reincarnation into a future life on Earth, or by assisting others while remaining in a soul state.

When I addressed the first group of souls (those who understood they were unlikely to survive future events), I could feel their sorrows and regrets, and their thoughts of families and friends they would be leaving behind, but also the anticipation of moving on in their spiritual journey. Even though these souls understood the continuing cycle of life and demise of the physical form, I also sensed their present consciousness coming through, as the human being leading a valued life with loved ones.

I was surprised the second lecture involved communicating with sceptics, but it illustrates how intervention and change can take place by addressing the universal soul-consciousness, which is unclouded by such factors as human conditioning, pre-conceptions, or lack of relevant data.

In summary, the Greys and associates are able to, 1) identify people/souls as potential volunteers, 2) at the soul level of consciousness, request they attend these meetings onboard craft, and 3) through discussion and agreement, recruit and educate people/souls to lead future lives on Earth to upgrade our civilisation.

Through this process, mass consciousness can be influenced positively by accessing the individual's soul consciousness rather than the human awareness. A massive positive shift in humanity's awareness can result from this intervention.

However some researchers and authors claim the Greys are "stealing" or "capturing" souls and are somehow cloning them as part of a negative agenda to take control of our planet and species. I have never seen any evidence of this with the particular Grey species I have had contact with. Every meeting between Greys and souls that I have witnessed has involved agreements, and seeking permission and cooperation.

1990 and 2010 were not the only times the Greys spoke to me about how they are part of a plan of action with our UGB, involving "calling" or recruiting souls to come to the assistance of our planet and civilisation at a crucial time in our existence. I recall when I was in my twenties (in the 1970s) a group of Greys showed me our planet rotating on a screen. With magnification, I saw great beams of light or energy emanating from distinct shapes like volcanoes, until I realised they were raised structures, perhaps pyramids or ancient towers. The beams of light/energy broadened as they shone out into space and I gained the impression this was some kind of signal sent out into the universe as a call for help. Perhaps they used these images symbolically by way of explanation, and as I watched, the images zoomed out again to show the rotating planet, only this time the entire surface was covered with an intricate matrix of interconnecting lines of white light. The Greys explained this had a two-fold meaning: 1) the ultimate desired outcome of interconnectedness and unity of mankind as a result of a massive influx of souls, each one a part of an overall plan to raise mass consciousness, and similarly 2) on a more personal level, the need for me to make connections with like-minded, trustworthy people with integrity.

Over recent years in particular, I have followed news emerging about significant natural disasters happening throughout the world. Although some scientists state the actual number of natural disasters occurring has not increased much over many years, it is the severity and intensity of these events that has increased.

These alien species, along with cooperation from humans groups, have initiated vast preparatory measures to assist us to help each other.

Chapter 36

The Three Waves: Willing Souls Drawn to Lives on our Planet

1990, age 35

Back in 1990, I was given significant information by the Greys relating to what they referred to as the "Three Waves", an influx of volunteer souls incarnating over a wide time frame with the aim of assisting our planet in its evolution. The information was comprehensive and specific. However, this same information was also intimated to me by the Greys in 1962 at the age of eight, when the Grey instructing me embedded vast information in my subconscious mind about my future son, and the group of specialised children he would belong to.

I first publicly revealed information about the Three Waves Agenda when I spoke at the 2nd International Scientific and Metaphysical Symposium, in Sydney, Australia, in June 2007. Since that time, a handful of other researchers and regression therapists have discussed or published similar concepts.

Many souls born on the planet have long forgotten their spiritual origins and reasons for being here, and our UGB broadcast a Universal call for assistance. As outlined in Chapter 9, Soul Origin, in order to implement an agenda of up-grading and assisting a planet on a retrograde spiritual path, agreements were initially sought between our UGB and volunteer souls, various alien species including the Greys, humans (souls) already living on the planet, and other entities inhabiting our planet's atmosphere and energy field that belong to this planet as we do.

We might assume the agenda is just about the human race and the physical planet, but it is not. We are part of the bunch, bonded to others, and what affects one sector of the galaxy, affects all, and we cannot be left behind in the expansion and evolution of the universe. The concept of the Three Waves of volunteer souls was initiated and certain programmes were formulated.

This chapter outlines the Three Waves information as conveyed to me, although some of the terminology used is my own as it best conveys the sense of what I was told. The Greys imparted this information to me in order to: 1) help me understand my own position and that of my son, both in their programmes and within the greater structure of this planetary assistance, and 2) to pass this information on at the right time in order to help other experiencers and people who feel they are part of *something,* but do not know what it is. It catapulted me into finally writing this book.

In examining this agenda of assistance, I can see endless associations have been formed with souls involved in the Three Waves. It is vast and incredibly clever, involving multi-layered complex programmes. The whole agenda is measured, detailed and structured. The Three Waves are interwoven, interdependent, and there is no hit and miss. It needs to be complex because anything simpler could be circumvented or compromised by human ignorance, arrogance, or naivety.

The First Wave

The First Wave is comprised of two distinct groups of volunteer souls incarnating here over a long time span, one earlier, the *innovators,* and one much later, the *enlighteners*. Their motto could be "challenging the norm".

Some of them may never have lived a life on planet Earth before and so their soul-source may have acquired technological, environmental and spiritual understandings on other planets or existences in our universe, in other lives. However they have all felt the "tingle" I described in Chapter 9, a call to enter a new life, this time as a human, volunteering to play an important part in assisting our planet to evolve out of our stagnant state. In general, those incarnating in this First Wave do so, not so much for personal learning, but for significant contributions to mankind through the introduction of new ideas and the manifestation of psychic/intuitive/kinaesthetic skills.

The innovators make up the smaller part of this group, trailblazers who have faced difficulties because their ideas and perspectives challenged the norm. They began to incarnate as early as just before and after the turn of the 20th century. By the 1930s through to around the 1960s, many of them had become inventors, critical thinkers, and scientists, involved in the advancement of industry and technology, as well as sociological trends. Many were involved in esoteric subjects and early spiritualist and mediumship movements, sometimes resulting in leadership or oracle status with large followings. Others were involved in early "flying saucer" research.

The second and larger part of this First Wave, the enlighteners, agreed to be born on this planet much later around the 1980s-90s onwards (thus crossing over with the emergence of the 2nd and 3rd Waves). Many enlighteners are now in early adulthood, while others are still children, or yet to be born. They have come to be known variously as the *Star Kids, Indigos, Crystal Children, or New Humans.*

In part, enlighteners have come here to accustom us to kinaesthetic and metaphysical skills that are beyond the present every-day capability of most humans. Many have deep spiritual understandings and recall past lives from an early age – often as extraterrestrials – which they are open about. Enlighteners are quite natural, or even sometimes overt about their abilities. They may be futuristic thinkers, emanate a sense of "free spirit" and positive energy, and generally do not fit into existing education systems because they think outside-the-box. Many become involved in environmental, healing and spiritual pursuits, and art and music.

Sensitive and intuitive, the enlighteners will alter our perceptions about many previously taboo metaphysical topics, and open our minds to the psychic potential they exhibit. This has been carefully choreographed by the UGB and extraterrestrials to occur at the time when significant numbers of the Second Wave are revealing their crucial personal information on UFOs and contact experiences.

The enlighteners will also pave the way for the emergence of the Third Wave group, with even more extraordinary abilities to reveal.

The Second Wave

An apt catch-phrase for the Second Wave would be, "an unrelenting sense of purpose and commitment" in their lives. The Second Wave is also comprised of two groups: the *pioneers* and the *communicators*. People in this group generally began incarnating around the 1940s through to the 1960s. Significantly, they encompass most people in the three distinct groups involved in contact: contactees, abductees, and experiencers.

More so than the other two Waves, many Second Wavers feel out of place and different, as if they do not quite fit anywhere, even sometimes feeling they do not belong in their own families. Having arrived here on Earth, many do not like their surroundings and would prefer to go back to the peace of the Source, and they struggle with the difficult (but strengthening) lives they have found themselves in (but agreed to), and the attitudes of many of the humans around them. They often describe feeling as if there is something they need to do in this life, but they do not know what it is! This can lead to feelings of frustration and lack of fulfilment, but this may quickly pass once their destined tasks in life unfold before them. However those who have arrived with an inherent understanding of what it is they need to accomplish in this life, feel a strong commitment to its completion.

Many in this wave have the hardest task of all three waves in terms of public exposure: that of introducing mankind to the idea, through public personal testimony, that we are not alone and in fact share our universe with other sentient beings that have already made contact with humans. Some may face criticism, scepticism and scrutiny. Many will have experienced contact right throughout their lives and some will have retained memories of this, while others have yet to uncover them.

The pioneers began their work early, many of them being involved in the contactee movement, which engendered huge interest and popularity worldwide, telling of positive contacts. Much of this interaction was reported to be with gentle human-like cosmic visitors whose teachings, along with those of the spiritual innovators of the First Wave, helped give form to New Age philosophies. The idea of peaceful human-like visitors was easy to accept for many, but although some pioneers still experienced ridicule and scrutiny, they made vital preliminary steps towards opening the way for the emergence of the communicators.

This second group, the communicators, includes many abductees and experiencers, who each in their own way have promoted the reality of an extraterrestrial presence and have advanced it further into the global psyche. Many communicators are now aged in their 50s-70s, with a wealth of life experience behind them. Abductees in this group began talking about their experiences as far back as the 1970s (some earlier) and many suffered at the hands of the media, even so, their sometimes negative or traumatic accounts were valuable in once again focusing public attention on the potential of life in the universe.

Around the 1990s more communicators came forward as the experiencer group evolved. Having come to terms with their contact experiences, they spoke of positive and transformative accounts of contact with non-human entities. This synchronised neatly with the emergence of the First Wave enlighteners (Star Kids etc), who reinforced and exhibited many of the detailed descriptions experiencers provided pertaining to telepathy and psychic skills in communication with these entities.

From around the 1970s through to the present day many communicators have written books, appeared in documentaries, formed UFO groups and contact support organisations, and have spoken publicly about their contact experiences. I believe many more will come forward in the years to come until a critical mass is reached and their accounts are more readily accepted. *As presented in this book, their information of alien technology and communication will begin to blend with, and be corroborated by new understandings and discoveries about consciousness, physics and other areas of science.*

The Second Wave includes people from all walks of life, including scientists and members of the military.

It is worth mentioning here that some Second Wave people experience broken marriages, their first marriage having served a genetic purpose in producing specific off-spring. Sometimes a marriage break-up occurs when the Second Waver realises their true path in life, and they seek to make changes to facilitate this, that are not accepted or understood by their spouse. A second marriage is often with a person who supports their endeavours and is like-minded.

But most significantly, among the communicators is a smaller group of people who have come into this life with dual souls and are the parents of the Third Wave humans. This *dual soul connection* facilitates a proliferation of humans, extending into the Third Wave, who have an enhanced awareness, with extraterrestrial support and guidance, *a group that is central to a positive agenda for humanity.*

The Third Wave

The Third Wave consists of the offspring of these specific members of the Second Wave. I have called the Third Wave *the implementers*, because they will be responsible for implementing sweeping positive changes in our world – change from within. Thousands of Third Wave humans have been born on the planet since around the 1980s/1990s onwards. *Like their parents, they all have dual souls.*

All of the Third Wave children are the end result of selection within four generations of families that have been genetically identified and tracked by the Greys, and are referred to by them as end-point children. The term "end-point" does not indicate there will be no generations of children beyond this point, but as previously mentioned, the familial component comes into play here and it simply means these souls incarnated into the fourth generation of these genetic lines.

A specialised group within the Third Wave, referred to by the Greys as *Fourth Intellect children* (most now young adults) were selected as babies because they exhibited the attributes of desirable genes, early advanced psychic capabilities and an aptitude to relate easily to any extraterrestrial species they were exposed to. As with their parents, Third Wave children were involved in preparatory meetings prior to incarnation, with the UGB and various species. They have participated in multi-levelled programmes administered by the Greys, and have been trained to use much of the Greys' own advanced technology with natural ease and competence.

The Greys have sometimes referred to the Third Wave as "*the concealed ones*" because they must remain dormant for some time while they are raised and sent out into the world by their parents. Most of them do not recall their extensive relationships with extraterrestrials and they likely will not, until certain events take place on the planet or in their lives. It is desirable for these young people to lead normal lives while they achieve highly in their education systems and chosen professions. There are other reasons for concealment relating to protection and safety for this group, as the Greys do not want the group to move too fast or become visible yet.

However, in the same way that I experienced intuitive abilities as a child and learnt to keep that hidden, so must these children. They will exhibit these abilities from birth but they will not express them overtly, but rather will instinctively prefer to utilise the skills imperceptibly.

When the Third Wave begins to develop full memory of contact they will need their parents' guidance to assimilate this information into their lives. By then, many of their parents will have progressed to having considerable memory of their own contacts. Some Third Wavers may initially have difficulty in assimilating the fact they have had a lifetime of contact, however the Fourth Intellect group will likely accept this quickly and easily. The Third Wave awakening will happen slowly in the lead-up to them gaining positions of positive authority and influence in their chosen careers.

Third Wavers will grow up with strong positive values, equipped with wisdom beyond their years. Throughout their lives they will naturally exhibit qualities which most humans recognise and aspire to: kindness, humility, wisdom, warmth, intelligence, integrity. This is not to say that many other humans do not display these same qualities because of course they do, but in the future, when these good human qualities are combined with high psychic abilities and full memory of what they have been taught by the extraterrestrials throughout their life, the Third Wave will present a powerful positive human force.

They will not to feel the need to publicise these memories, but rather they will quietly use them to good effect. The Greys' aim is that the implementers will just be seen by other humans as highly educated capable people with integrity who will rise to prominence, yet humans with unusual insights and skills. Their positions of authority in a wide range of professions will enable them to make sweeping positive changes in our world and they will use this power with wisdom and compassion. Abuse of power will be unthinkable because it will not be in their nature, and their leadership and example will be widely accepted.

All of this will be timed to a period when humanity will be in chaos, grasping for hope. They have been trained to overcome negativity and volatile chaotic resistance, and will gain the support of the masses that will see them simply as exceptionally good leaders.

The UGB, the Greys and other species treasure these humans, considering them like their own. They hold great hope for our future under the guidance and intelligence of this group, and feel confidence and surety in their eventual success in bringing about positive change globally.

The *Fourth Intellect group* is more specialised, and will be involved in leading the way to our future relationships with extraterrestrial civilisations. They and/or their offspring (who will share their genes and abilities) may eventually become the bridging species of our future, communicating openly between humans and extraterrestrials. They are the first of the *future humans*.

Chapter 37

Implementing Change from Within: Future Humans

Summary: A World in Transition

I do not think anybody can deny that our world has reached a critical stage. Climate change, over-population, environmental and ecological problems, natural disasters on a global scale, wars, disease, terrorism, and societal upheaval are creating unprecedented damage to all life forms and the planet itself. Religious, cultural and ethnic differences have festered, and periodic clashes are ever-imminent.

Despite phenomenal technological advances in only a few decades, it seems we have not matched this progress spiritually and do not always use technology with integrity. Technological and scientific breakthroughs that could assist humankind are sometimes utilised negatively, with an emphasis on power and accumulating wealth.

From my understanding, the UGB, the Greys and associated species foresaw the need for massive changes to take place to divert us from creating our own annihilation. To facilitate crucial changes in the midst of predicted global upheaval, they formulated the *Three Waves Agenda* to assist us to help ourselves. Constructive transitions must unfold subtly and discreetly from within humanity, rather than from without. Positive, progressive change from within was considered to be more desirable than humans perceiving a sudden "alien" presence as a threat.

However in this time of exposure and confusion, we might ask how long this positive transformation might take. On one occasion the Greys provided me with an analogy to explain the timeline of their agenda:

Imagine you are about to get on a train to complete a journey which has a starting point (the station you leave from) and an endpoint (the final destination.) The train may not be running on time and so you are not able to determine the exact time you will arrive at the destination. It may depend on how many stops the train makes (steps required in the agenda), how many people board the train at each stop (coordination of groups, species, or individuals involved in it), or whether the train breaks down and has to be repaired (glitches in the implementation of the agenda). The thing to remember is that *you will eventually reach the destination.* Patience is necessary.

Like a steady influence at a deep level, the Third Wave humans in particular will affect people's mindsets with their intelligence and knowledge, introducing far-reaching changes in many areas, but especially in worldwide policy and decision-making, based on integrity. This has the potential to alter people's lives for the better and lift global consciousness, creating a step-up for mankind right across the board. The Third Wave "mind" has an inherent ability to cut through vast amounts of extraneous detail to examine the core issues constructively.

Some of this change will be made by stealth (in a positive sense) because very few people will know who or what the Third Wave really are, or the combined human and extraterrestrial educations upon which they will base their knowledge. Their influence will keep unfolding into the future as younger Third Wavers reach maturity, with their mid-thirties to mid-fifties being the optimal time for them to have reached positions of effectiveness in their chosen careers. A measure of concealment is necessary because during this time, which may continue for years to come, close examination will arise of anything that threatens institutions and belief systems that currently provide a measure of stability in many people's lives, or alternatively, which may cause dissension and disruption. The possibility of an alien presence, perhaps depicted as an "alien threat", may be seen to fall into both categories. Hence the necessity for the Third Wave humans to remain in the background until the timing is right on the planet for them to shine.

A period of time may follow when certain negatively powerful sectors of society will realise their dominance is at last being stripped from them, and that the common people understand things they didn't understand before. If this covert power-base aggressively fights back, it will be members of the Second Wave who will come to the fore at that time to meet any challenges in regard to UFO and extraterrestrial issues, with their wealth of contact experiences and information.

Each of the Three Waves is a vital part in the whole agenda and dependent upon each other like the cogs in a wheel, in preparation for the evolution of humanity. The Three Waves agenda is designed to move us on into a future of evolving values and spiritual awareness, increasing peace and eventually, intergalactic relationships – if we are collectively willing.

Some readers may question why the UGB chose a Grey species (among others) to implement these programmes. From my understanding, they were selected for their attention to detail and planning, consciousness/mind capabilities, genetics, their technology (which appears to have already developed further along a similar path to our own), and in particular, their experience in working with souls – soul-enhancement, soul-insertion, and dual souls. However other species are contributing to this long-term plan as well, but in effect, humans are interfacing mainly with the Greys and mixed species in these programmes. They have stated they are aware their intentions may initially be misunderstood by many.

The Greys are seeking further volunteer souls from within humanity itself, those whose life-spans are near to completion. They will facilitate a short-cut for these souls, and under their guidance, these souls will prepare to return quickly to new lives on our planet or perhaps even another planet in the future, arriving in their new lives with elevated spiritual and environmental awareness. They, along with the Fourth Intellect group and their children, will be the future humans. Ultimately the Three Waves are the introductory process towards this end, with the Third Wave initiating this world transition.

But for now, at this critical convergence of events in human history, unpredictable game-changers are shaping our current and near-future lives (the stations stops and hold-ups along the train journey), such as risks of a severe pandemic or a nuclear attack, civil and religious wars, political conflict and terrorism. Add to this dramatic climate change and the intensification of existing weather patterns, along with the likelihood of increased demands for water, food and energy. The Third Wave policymakers and implementers will need to understand The Big Picture, and how to be proactive at a high level within a destructive environment. Our civilisation may first come close to rock-bottom, before the skills of the Third Wave can come into effect.

But the progressive activation of millions of people comprising the Three Waves also has the potential to create an unprecedented expansion of awareness around the globe, eventually leading us to new levels of understanding pertaining to our planet and everything it contains.

In the world of our future, mankind will need to adopt policies of global cooperation, effective conflict resolution, sharing, and supporting more vulnerable countries. I believe the positive future trends will be that individual self-responsibility, constructive empowerment and spirituality will accelerate globally, and there will be the reduction of poverty and disease, with new types of conscious technology and communication methods. Advanced technology will be used to clean up the environment and provide new kinds of healthcare and sustenance. Trillions of dollars previously spent on warfare can be channelled into transforming our planet. It is my hope we will start thinking cooperatively as a species, rather than as fractured groups and individuals. But for now, whether such a vision happens in our near or our distant future, or at all, is up to each of us.

The UGB and our cosmic neighbours cannot force us to change or impose conditions on us without being seen as an invading alien force. Perhaps they can only induce and trigger us into greater self-responsibility. That is acceptable in Universal Law and the Three Waves play an integral part in this process.

A powerful longing is stirring in people: a desire for change.

We are not alone. We have never been alone. Look up at the sky on a brilliant starry night and ask yourself, how could we be?

Without a doubt, a commitment to positive transformation is building momentum on our planet, and beyond, and it is up to each of us to make the choice to become a part of it, and eventually, take our place in a wider cosmic community, in a universe teeming with life.

Suzy Hansen

"What greater purpose for our lives could there be?"

Dr. Rudy Schild.

A Scientist's Epilogue

An Alternative Reality

In many ways, the experiences of Suzy Hansen represent glimpses of our future. We human beings are indicated to live in a much greater universal community of civilisations. We have evolved knowing of ourselves only, but we now confront the fact that we are not alone. In speculating about others, what perspective do we gain of ourselves?

In our civilisation today, astronomy has made us aware that effectively all stars shepherd a family of planets because the parent planet bodies were made early in the history of the Universe. To form a star, they coagulated together to gravitationally bring the star mass to the centre, and shed their hydrogen to fuel the new star. The Earth was ten times heavier, but lost its hydrogen envelope to the forming sun, which left behind a metal-rich core that we call home. This is how the earth came to have its iron core surmounted by oceans of water.

Since this process would have been typical, we are free to speculate how it played out for most other stars. The planetary swarm around each star would have spawned solar systems with one key property that favours the emergence of life: water.

I think of our sun's planetary system as follows. The planets discovered are in orbits fixed by the sun's mass, and the sun is a typical star in its basic properties of mass and rotation, and the planets are arrayed at a large range of distances, with some like Mercury being too close and therefore too hot for water to exist. Venus is more distant but still too hot, while Earth is just right for water and life to emerge and thrive.

Mars is presently too cold, but in the past had a denser atmosphere and held water at its surface, while Jupiter and all the rest are too distant to support liquid water.

Insofar as our solar system is typical, probably most stars host a range of planetary bodies with temperatures ranging from too hot to too cold, with one just right and potentially hosting life as we know it. So when I sit outdoors under the dark clear skies at the observatory, I think about the seven thousand stars I can see as hosting many life-bearing planets.

To me, the processes that brought life to our Earth worked for them too.

This was once an article of faith in my life, but is today confirmed by the experiences of Suzy Hansen. Whereas my life has been dominated by study of the physical workings of the Universe, Suzy's life has been devoted to a program of education about the nature of life beyond our planet's confining atmosphere, because life in the larger universe seeks to envelope us as soon as we are prepared to accept responsibility for its needs, which are our own future needs.

Such needs must be both physical and mental. Today our terrestrial civilisation is coming to understand that the preservation of our physical environment is one of the most vital needs of our thriving life. This awareness has been brought home by our brave astronauts, who speak of the transformative experience of seeing our seemingly vast ocean of atmosphere as but a pale tenuous blue line surrounding our rocky home base. This is all that is left of the large cloud of gases once present, but now fuelling the sun.

Our mental and emotional needs are being equally challenged. Over past eons of time, we have apparently been subjects of study by off-planet civilisations also spawned by our vast Universe. Just as we study our animal kingdom to learn about ourselves, it seems other planetary civilisations evidently have been studying us, leaving behind modest, but hardly overt traces of their visits and agendas. The television series, *Ancient Aliens*, has collected up large residual bodies of evidence of such visitations. And just as we have learned to adopt and modify medicines from our plant and animal kingdoms, to aid our growth and development, so we must also allow that off-planet visitors have done likewise throughout the history of their visitations.

But something profound has happened in the course of events. The dropping and testing of nuclear weapons in anger and fear has broadcast to the universe a message of sickness in our terrestrial civilisation, to which our universe has responded with a program of help. The profound message of Suzy Hansen is that the wider universe has initiated a program of genetic and social manipulation to assist us in our development. This has included spawning new generations of humans able to cope with knowledge of off-planet civilisations, and to accept responsibility for participation in a wider community of living entities and perhaps even a living Universe.

While Suzy Hansen describes the program of beneficent off-Planet visitors to upgrade our civilisation to prepare it for the monumental challenge of joining a wider community, I am also aware that within our human medical community there exist practitioners who have taken a Hippocratic oath and who nevertheless have demonstrated the ability to be motivated by greed and competition, not necessarily to the betterment of the human condition. As above, so below. In our human civilisation we have documented a wide range of visiting spacecraft and living beings, and we must assume that there are some who are not primarily focused on our human betterment. Nevertheless, in my appreciation of the Universe as having a purpose and design for life to emerge and thrive, so I believe that the benevolent forces guiding our wider participation in civilisation for its betterment will prevail.

As I have followed the writings of Suzy Hansen and contemplated the care with which the agenda of benevolent evolution is being developed around us, I have come to understand the magnitude of the challenge. Our civilisation must confront challenges to its social structure and sciences that are reminiscent of our emergence from the Dark Ages to the age of enlightenment. In what follows I shall attempt to address some challenges to science.

This is necessary because the science challenge has contributed to our doubts about alien visitations. It is well understood, following Einstein, that no particles can exceed the speed of light. At the speed of light, minimum transit time to the nearest star is four years, and as we speak of visits from multiple off-planet civilisations we are necessarily speaking of minimum flight durations of hundreds of years.

This consideration is not well-founded. It assumes that their spacecraft are as clumsy as our own, meaning that the transport is in solid-body spacecraft like our own.

And fundamental to the standard thinking of light-limited speed, is the assumption that nothing can travel faster than light. But transport of quantum information describing the state of matter, at more than 10,000 times the speed of light, has been demonstrated by Szalard and others, which conceptually opens the door to instantaneous transport through the universe as information, not solid body objects made of particles. I say this knowing that the Einstein General Theory of Relativity links gravity and quantum theory, and it is an assumption of our physics that gravity propagates at the speed of light, and the theory of gravitational waves requires this. At the same time, many years of searching with sensitive instruments for the gravitational wave signature of the nearest binary neutron star, or pulsar, have significantly produced no detection, leading us to favour Einstein's "spooky action at a distance," and instantaneous propagation of quantum information. Thus transport would require a craft that can scan the quantum information of itself plus its occupants, and propagate that information to the place of its choosing.

A second attribute of the universe is called "empathy" within the university crowd, which avoids acknowledging how frequently ordinary people experience pre-cognition, telepathic communication, Near-Death-Experiences (NDEs), remote viewing, past life experiences, etc. The university-brain research community manages to bumble along and dismiss all such phenomena as purely psychological and originating within the brain.

An alternative approach has been to look to string theory for alternative paths through the universe borne on tiny hidden dimensions. The first attempts at this were the Kaluza-Klein theories of the 1920's era, wherein a 5th dimension was invoked. But this did not seem to produce a relativistic quantum field theory, and in the past two decades an elaborate string theory has been devised. Its ultimate development introduced 12-and even 13-dimensional spaces, and it was claimed that strings could explain all anomalous phenomena.

The problem with this approach is that such theories are so broad that they do not allow any limits on possibilities, and so they can claim to explain anything and everything, but they were so unlimited that they did not in any way limit possibilities and could not make any predictions that could be tested by astronomical observations or laboratory experiments.

My alternative approach is to adopt a kind of alternative to string theory by going back to the fundamental concept of quantum mechanics that, associated with every point in space is a 3-dimensional wave that describes all information about the mass in the universe. This caused many to wonder, what is the medium that is waving? … and many researchers began anew the discussion of ether.

My alternative is to view the Einstein 4-dimensional space of [X, Y, Z, T] co-ordinates as complex numbers, with real and imaginary components. Such a 4-dimensional space would be called a Stein manifold, with the real dimensions describing physical reality, and the imaginary components describing existence reality. The relationship between the two attributes of space is given in the theory of complex numbers as Parseval's theorem.

Then the physical reality in our universe is described as the Einstein General Theory of Relativity as always, and the Strong Principal of Equivalence aspect of the theory is automatically described by the mathematics of imaginary numbers. This is seen in the covariant line element ds = sqrt{dt^2 – (dx^2+ dy^2 + dz^2)} which remains real for all time-like spatial coordinate transformations, and becomes imaginary for all space-like relativistic coordinate transformations.

This view of the Universe easily includes the Edgar Mitchell description of the quantum hologram describing all information in the universe, so the quantum hologram can include consciousness as a waveform that mixes with the physical reality of our everyday lives as described by the Einstein theory, but notice that now consciousness, like gravity, becomes an aspect of the curvature of space and propagates throughout the Universe instantaneously (spooky action at a distance).

With these remarks the technical lecture is over, and we can discuss qualitatively the nature of consciousness as revealed by the brain research community.

Some results from brain research

Three important developments from brain research fuel a new understanding of the nature of consciousness and the brain.

The first is the discovery of the mirror neuron system within the brain. Originating with Rizolitti in Parma, Italy, a networking of neurons within the brain can resonate with the quantum hologram and establish electrical currents in brain wave patterns that carry the patterns of the waves the brain is receiving. This is the resonance process that Edgar Mitchell called Phase Conjugate Adaptive Resonance. The enabling micro-tubular structures within the brain were described by Sir Roger Penrose and Stuart Hammeroff. The mirror neuron network allows the brain to interact with the universal quantum hologram and both receive and transmit information through it.

The second is the discovery from functional magnetic resonance imaging (fMRI) that all humans sharing any particular state of information or emotion develop the same 3-dimensional brain wave pattern. Researchers Gazzola and colleagues were able to show that all 15 of the human subjects tested while experiencing the same emotion from viewing identical images on a TV screen developed the same brain wave patterns. Very significantly, the brain wave pattern in the left side of the brain was the mirror image of the pattern observed in the right side.

The third is the discovery by Dean Radin that the brain is able, with concentration, to affect a physical system, in this case a laser interferometer. This proves that brain emissions are real and measurable, and can underlie the brain-to-brain interactions experienced by some in telepathy, remote viewing, precognition, and all other psychic phenomena.

All of this understanding of the brain's functioning in resonance with the universe and the existence of a universal field of quantum information has been confirmed in the extraordinary experience of brain researcher Dr. Eben Alexander, who lay brain-dead in a coma for a week but when revived told an elaborate description of his experience of ecstatic travelling through the universe, experiencing oneness with all people and things and even with the Creator, and with the purpose of the universe itself. To many, Dr. Alexander and his description of the interaction of his soul with the wider universe demonstrates that the key aspects of consciousness lie in the existence of a greater reality, and also a soul reflecting the human experience of self.

Throughout Suzy Hansen's writings we find references to amazing abilities of aliens and advanced humans to communicate telepathically in numerous unknown ways. Communications with alien (Grey) beings were ordinarily telepathic, and Suzy often speaks of the aliens "searching her mind to find the word or concept that describes the information." She also mentions that when she is with other humans who do not share any human language they find it easiest to communicate telepathically. And she mentions that young humans encountered aboard craft are able to do so.

All of these aspects are easily understood within the framework of the quantum hologram description of waveforms related to all concepts, such that instead of associating a sound wave pattern as in any human language, in telepathy the practitioners have learned to associate a 3 (4 including time) dimensional waveform in the brain's resonance with the universe. Similarly, Suzy describes recognising individual human and alien Grey beings by their energetic emanations. The fundamental process involved in all cases is the brain's resonance with the universal quantum wave to create internal brain electrical patterns that the brain recognises as the standing wave patterns in the mirror neuron system associated with the particular informational or emotional content. This process Edgar Mitchell calls Phase Conjugate Adaptive Resonance, and the mathematician calls 4-dimensional correlation.

In this way we also understand the other tricks of telepathy described by Suzy which arise, because associated with the universal quantum wave, lies the quantum waveform describing each of us sentient beings. Thus Suzy describes that advanced super-intelligent aliens have been observed to telepathically connect to several humans with different instructions and information simultaneously, and also tune into the thoughts of several people in their presence simultaneously. The fact that Suzy experienced transmission of information and entire images in "quick time" suggests that our human clock regulating the beta rhythm registration of conscious activity can be sped up in some circumstances.

The Light

Suzy frequently mentions a strange light often seen in alien contact phenomena. In its simplest form, she notices that the illumination is different from ordinary light in that it does not spread from every illuminated source. Thus she mentions being aboard craft in which light from an illuminated room does not spread beyond the room's open entryway. And she mentions walking along corridors surrounded by a 3-dimensional bubble of light that does not seem to spread and illuminate their surroundings. She describes her experience as being in a bubble of light that surrounds and accompanies her.

Similarly it is frequently mentioned that the UFO spacecraft creates powerful illumination of an entire valley, revealing fine detail in the veining of leaves on trees there. And a powerful bright beam joins a spacecraft to an automobile being levitated. Also, the tractor beam that levitates humans is observed to envelop the levitating human, but the beam closes, or ends, just below the specimen/person being levitated.

It is not clear if the light is entirely a by-product of the anti-gravity process involved, since the beam surrounding persons and beings aboard the spacecraft seem to be created for the purpose of efficient illumination. However given that strong light is often observed during abductions/contacts that are closed off to involuntary bystanders, it appears that in at least some circumstances the strong light is an unintended side effect of gravity manipulation.

It is thus probably not a coincidence that the light is effectively 3 dimensional, meaning that it "fits into a box of finite size," whereas ordinary electromagnetic radiation shines to infinity with diminishing intensity. Our ordinary light is described by two dimensions, the direction of the ray and the direction of its polarisation. The UFO light, in contrast, is created and described by the 3-dimensional quantum waves that also describe mass in the quantum description of matter. Because the General Theory of Relativity describes how the quantum waves describing mass and gravity are related, it is unsurprising that the related light would have a 3-dimensional description. However, at present no quantum field theory of gravity including a theoretical framework for light emission is presently available. Because consciousness as spiralling quantum waves are involved in the operation of the spacecraft, the associated light may only occur when consciousness is being amplified, just as ordinary light is always created in the presence of electrical currents.

The Sounds

The topic of sound comes up in Suzy's descriptions in 3 contexts. She describes a quiet humming sound in situations where there is a need to calm and quiet humans. And she describes the alien Grey vocal sound, rarely heard because all communication is telepathic; this she describes as "crystalline".

Perhaps the most interesting sound is the alien Grey music, which she heard at the "disco parlour" during the recreational spiritual dance (Chapter 26, *A Glimpse of Cosmic Culture)*. This she described as not dominated by our human Western patterns of melody expressed in octaves, combined with third and fifth harmonics. Nevertheless she described it as indescribably beautiful, especially in combination with visual spiralling energy waveforms.

I suspect that this onboard musical/visual ecstatic experience is based upon profound spiralling waves of consciousness. Since it is understood that the spacecraft is under thought control, it is likely that amplification of thought waves of spiralling form is a principal attribute of the machine (craft), which is often described as being semi-alive. This is also implied by the fact that individuals in the dance were observed to merge with the energy field within the "disco theatre", and produce luminous spiralling wave forms in place of the solid bodies of the individuals present. These intermingled and danced in communal ecstatic experience, accompanied by sounds described as an unfamiliar form of music.

It is unsurprising that the sound accompanying the experience would significantly depart from human music, which is dominated by rhythmic patterns and tonalities found in nature, and re-organised by instruments and voice to produce a sense of appreciation related to our human fondness of nature. But our music is essentially one-dimensional, being primarily dominated by frequency, and with directional quality only of secondary importance. The sound experienced in the onboard "disco" is more likely intended to resonate with consciousness, and to have therefore a profoundly 3-dimensional character as describes the spiralling consciousness waveform. As such it would not be dominated by octaves and harmonics, but rather have a fractal quality covering a broad frequency band, and its power is thereby in the ecstatic resonance with mental waveforms.

The Spacecraft

Two generic kinds of spacecraft are described in this book, which is about a (human) lifetime of experience of contact with extraterrestrials. A small pickup type with a crew of one or two does the local pick-up and return deliveries, whereas a huge mother ship high above the terrestrial atmosphere is the host ship for the long duration missions of its permanent crew, and contains many specialised rooms for experiments and instruction, as well as crew quarters. In addition a number of undersea and underground bases are used similarly, and are equipped with similar technologies. Suzy describes many types of spacecraft seen in the hangar of the mother ship, probably indicating that a variety of alien species are involved with the interactions with humans. This accounts for the wide variety of spacecraft forms encountered in our internet photographs and descriptions of extra-terrestrial sightings and interaction.

Particularly interesting is Suzy's description of operating one of the small pick-up craft. In one mode of control, she was instructed to place her hand in a moulded pad that received her intentions (thought-instructions), and caused spacecraft motion. In a second mode, she operated a small lever that guided the craft, much like the "stick" of an old generation of aircraft.

Of particular interest is her description of compensation for an instability of the spacecraft propulsion and anti-gravity function. She mentions encountering and compensating for the spacecraft's "falling leaf" manoeuvre, also seen by other experiencers. As the pick-up spacecraft slowly descends, it is observed to rock from side to side.

In my understanding, the pickup spacecraft achieves anti-gravity by amplifying consciousness in the quantum hologram wave, which is spiral in form. I picture this waveform as having a coil shape, with the energetic focus advancing along the coil shape with a time period of approximately a second. Such wave forms have been described within the quantum research community as heli-waves. Evidently the spacecraft has difficulty manipulating gravity in its interaction with the field of such waves, and the operation of the spacecraft is somehow an intermediation of the human operator and universal consciousness.

The Alien Quantum Technology

Throughout these descriptions of the amazing technologies described by Suzy Hansen we see the operation of quantum effects not yet adequately understood in our terrestrial human scientific and technological base. Although many instances of telepathic human experience are persistently reported by responsible leaders, such phenomena are not systematically investigated and researched. Instead the university community dismissively mentions "empathy" as problems within human experience and fails to research them, largely because they are not easily amenable to repeatable and reliable research. Which university has departments researching remote viewing, past life experiences, out-of-body experiences, samadi, alien abductions/contact, and UFO sightings? Are such topics investigated with public funding? Is it not obvious that within these areas of investigation are important solutions to our civilisation's energy and medical problems?

In my view, the needed technologies are intimately involved in quantum effects that are in most cases related to consciousness. Our human experiences of the telepathic communication, the strange light and music, and the spacecraft transport phenomena are described within a framework of 4-dimensional (3 space and 1 time) quantum waves which are already adequately described within the framework of the relativity and quantum theories.

Suzy Hansen is to be understood as one of the heroines of our civilisation. Her life has been devoted to advancing our civilisation by mastering unknown technologies, and facing doubt and demeaning with her confidence and personal judgment. Her example of courage and determination inspire us to look beyond mundane daily lives to a future of intimate contact with a Universe dominated by deeper involvement, profound understanding, and growth. May our own individual pursuits be inspired by her telling of this boundless potential for participation in a greater civilisation of our future.

Dr. Rudy Schild
Emeritus Astrophysicist
Harvard-Smithsonian Centre for Astrophysics
Cambridge, USA

Resources

Alexander, Dr. Eben, *Proof of Heaven*, Simon & Schuster, 2012
Cambridge Declaration on Consciousness, authored by Philip Low, edited by Panksep, J., Reiss, D., Edelman, D., Van Swinderen, B., Low, P., and Koch, C. (Francis Crick Memorial Conference on Consciousness in Human and non-Human Animals, Cambridge, UK, 2012), source: Nexus Magazine, Vol. 20, No1, 2013
Carlsberg, Kim, Beyond *My Wildest Dreams – diary of a UFO abductee*, Bear & Company Publishing, 1995
Cathie, Bruce, *Harmonic 33,* A.H. and A.W. Reed, 1968
Coleman, Peter F., *A Unified Theory of Ball Lightning and unexplained Atmospheric Lights*, Canterbury Physics and Astronomy Research
Gisborne Aerial Phenomena Research Group newsletter, *Saucerscan*, 4Feb, 1978
G*isborne Herald* newspaper, January 26, 1978, "Valley was lit up by beam from object", (and various other stated references from Gisborne Herald)
Hashimoto, Isao, A time-lapse map of every nuclear explosion since 1945: https://www.youtube.com/watch?v=LLCF7vPanrY
Hopkins, Budd, *Missing Time*, Richard Marek Publishers, 1981
Hynek. J. Allen, *The UFO Experience: A Scientific Inquiry,* Henry Regnery Co, 1972
Jacobs, Dr. David, *Secret Life – Firsthand Accounts of UFO Abductions*, Simon and Schuster, 1992
Leir, Dr. Roger, *The Aliens and the Scalpel*, The Book Tree, 2005
Maccabee, Dr. Bruce, *The Fantastic Flight of JAL1628*, brumac.8k.com
Mitchell, Dr. Edgar, *The Way of the Explorer*, New Page Books, revised 2008
Mitchell, Dr. Edgar, and Staretz, Robert, *The Quantum Hologram and the Nature of Consciousness,* Journal of Cosmology, Volume 14, April-June 2011, section XII. http://journalofcosmology.com/Consciousness149.html
Newald, Alec*, Coevolution*, Nexus Magazine Ltd, 1997
Randles, Jenny, *Abduction*, Guild Publishing, 1988
Salas, Robert, *Unidentified – The UFO Phenomenon*, 2013
Doctors control their own brains' pain response to better treat patients, The University of Chicago News Office, www.-news.uchicago.edu/releases/07/070927.decety.shtml
Wilde, Sherry, author of *The Forgotten Promise, Rejoining our Cosmic Family,* quote from speech synopsis, 2014

Index

Page numbers followed by *n* indicate footnotes.

V

W

Y

Author's Bio

Suzanne had a career in school teaching/education, and in counselling.

Following a lifetime interest in UFOs, in 2000, she founded the UFO Focus New Zealand Research Network (UFOCUS NZ), a nationwide organisation that investigates UFO sightings and provides support for those experiencing alien contact. Suzanne has been involved in UFO research for forty two years, and she lectures internationally at conferences about New Zealand UFO sightings and her own alien contact and interaction experiences. She also speaks publicly on spiritual and metaphysical topics.

As Director of UFOCUS NZ, she lobbied the New Zealand Chief of Defence Forces during 2009-10, for the release of the NZ Ministry of Defence UFO files, which occurred in 2010 and 2011.

Suzanne's focus for the last decade has been on encouraging members of the scientific community to participate in examining the wealth of science-related detail contained in accounts of human interaction with extraterrestrial species, as well as aspects of UFO sighting investigation data.

She believes one of the major issues facing mankind in the future will be open contact with other civilisations in the Universe. In the meantime, there is much to be learnt from humans who have already made this tremendous leap in consciousness, and who have witnessed the vast array of potential benefits available to mankind and our environment through such associations.

Suzanne runs a support organisation for those experiencing contact with non-human species and intelligences.

www.communicatorlink.com

Scientist's Bio

Dr. Rudy Schild is a career astronomer at the Harvard-Smithsonian Centre for Astrophysics, and Editor-in-Chief of the Journal of Cosmology. From this position, he is aware of the latest developments in the frontiers of knowledge of the nature and history of our Universe. Dr. Schild's own observational studies of Black Hole (MECO) structure and microlensing studies of distant quasars have shown that the ordinary matter of the universe remains dark because of its collapse into a vast network of planets formed in the early history of the universe. From these primordial gas structures star formation came at the end of a chain of hierarchical accumulation and build-up, so that it is almost certain that all stars have a full solar system of planets, comets, and asteroids, as potential abodes of life. Thus it seems inevitable that life exists throughout the Universe.

Because our own solar system is quite young, other civilisations must have emerged and become much more advanced than our own. Thus it is unscientific to fail to explore all possibilities that such life is aware of our mankind, and is even concerned for our well-being, having faced extinction dangers of its own.

Thus Dr. Schild has explored the accounts of individuals who describe their alien contact, both to learn more of the nature and purpose of the Universe, and to jump-start mankind's deeper understanding of the physical laws and the advanced technologies described. This exploration leads to deeper understanding of the nature and purpose of life, with ultimate understanding of the Creator and of the Creation.

The box-shaped Craft

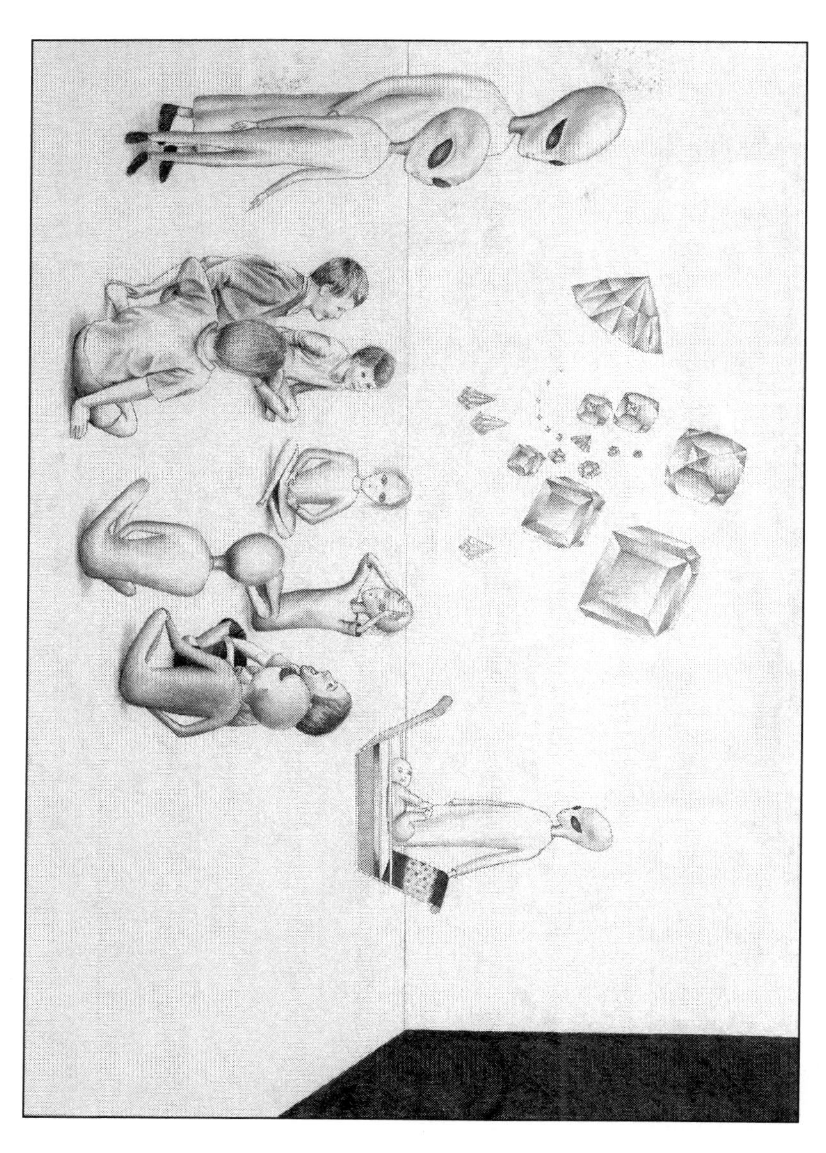

Kids having Fun: creating Crystalline Holograms

Made in the USA
Middletown, DE
01 December 2017